Applied Linguistics and Language Study

General Editor: C.N. Candlin

Learning to Write: First Language/ Second Language

Selected papers from the 1979 CCTE Conference, Ottawa, Canada

Edited by

Aviva Freedman,
Ian Pringle and
Janice Yalden

Longman

London and New York

Longman Group Limited
Longman House, Burnt Mill, Harlow,
Essex CM20 2JE, England
and Associated Companies throughout the world

Published in the United States of America by
Longman Inc., New York

First published 1983
Second impression 1984

ISBN 0 582 55371 7

BRITISH LIBRARY CATALOGUING IN PUBLICATION DATA
Learning to write: first language/second language.
— (Applied linguistics and language study)
1. English language — Writing — Congresses
I. Freedman, Aviva   II. Pringle, Ian
III. Yalden, Janice   IV. Series
808'.042   PE1408

LIBRARY OF CONGRESS CATALOGING IN PUBLICATION DATA

CCTE Conference (12th: 1979: Ottawa, Ont.) Learning to write.
(Applied linguistics and language study)
Bibliography: p.
Includes index.
1. English language — Rhetoric — Study and teaching —
Addresses, essays, lectures. 2. English language —
Study and teaching — Foreign students — Addresses, essays,
lectures. I. Freedman, Aviva. II. Pringle, Ian.
III. Yalden, Janice. IV. Canadian Council of Teachers
of English.   V. Title.   VI. Series.
PE1404.C36   1979   808'.042'07   82-13981

Set in 10/12pt Times New Roman
Printed in Hong Kong
by Commonwealth Printing Press Ltd

The Contributors

James Britton
Institute of Education, University of London

Carl Bereiter
Ontario Institute for Studies in Education

Marlene Scardamalia
York University

H.G. Widdowson
Institute of Education, University of London

Donald H. Graves
University of New Hampshire

Andrew Wilkinson
University of East Anglia

Daniel R. Kirby and Kenneth J. Kantor
University of Georgia

Lee Odell
Rensselaer Polytechnic Institute, Troy, New York

James L. Kinneavy
The University of Texas at Austin

Robert B. Kaplan
University of Southern California

Patrick T. Kameen
University of Louisville

Stephen P. Witte
The University of Texas at Austin

Bruce Bennett
The University of Western Australia, Perth

Nancy Martin
University of Surrey

John Dixon
Bretton Hall College of Higher Education, Wakefield

James R. Squire
Ginn and Company

W. Ross Winterowd
University of Southern California

Keith Johnson
Centre for Applied Language Studies, University of Reading

Ann Raimes
Hunter College, City University of New York

Acknowledgements

We are grateful to the following for permission to reproduce copyright material:

Canadian Council of Teachers of English for 'Shaping at the point of utterance' by James Britton and 'A pluralistic synthesis of four contemporary models for teaching composition' by James L. Kinneavy from *Reinventing the Rhetorical Tradition* edited by A. Freedman and I. Pringle, Conway, Arkansas, L & S Books 1980; Hutchinson Publishing Group for extracts from *English and Examinations* by F. Stevens; Teachers of English to Speakers of Other Languages for 'Syntactic skill and ESL writing quality' by Patrick Kameen from *On TESOL '79*.

Contents

Preface

This newest addition to the *Applied Linguistics and Language Study* series has for me, and I suspect, for its Editors, an ulterior objective than merely presenting a rich account of current research and practice from various centres in different parts of the world. That objective is to look beyond Writing itself, as if some unitary skill, to the connections that can be made between our knowledge of the world and ways of representing that knowledge, so to speak 'on record', to its connections with other skills, its bases in socio-psychological abilities which pertain in general to our human capacity to communicate, to its place in the process of what Halliday refers to as 'learning how to mean'. Once we identify this ulterior objective, then we should find it as natural that an examination of the product and process of writing leads us into psycholinguistic, sociolinguistic, linguistic and pedagogic concerns which override simple distinctions between first and second-language learning, thus justifying the title of the volume.

Skilfully, however, the Editors (as accomplished writers) have overlain this objective with three valuable, and complementary, patterns of organization within the volume. First, readers obtain a review of major themes in Writing research and pedagogy. This is in part achieved by the papers themselves, and in part by the valuable introductions the Editors offer to each of the four Parts. Second, we are continually presented with a characteristic applied linguistic interplay of research and practice, each affecting the other, in a mutual and interactive manner. Third, the issues of 'Writing as Product versus Writing as Process', or 'The Teaching of Writing Skills versus the Development of Writing Abilities' or 'The Use of Writing for Learning and Knowing' are not merely issues affecting Writing alone but language learning and teaching as a whole, and one might add, the entire process of education. Like any good piece of writing, then, this volume allows us, the readers, to make our own meanings mediated through the contributors' text. In this journey, we are, however, guided and helped by the careful construction of the book and the signposts provided by the Editors. We move from a consideration of 'Writing as Product' to 'Writing as Process', from there in Part Two to discussion of the development of Writing abilities, and then in Part Three to an examination of the distinctions to be drawn between text and discourse. The final section, Part Four, which deals with pedagogic reflections of what has been thus far proposed, and which also puts forward its own challenges to Writing research, is in this way both prepared for and well-grounded.

In stressing at the outset of this Preface that the Editors had (or so I think) other things in mind than merely an account of what a conference of specialists thought Writing was, it would be unfair not to underline and identify what I take to be their own definition. They see writing as an *interaction* between a number of necessary contributors in the process of recording our personal meanings and intentions, and those of others with whom we associate. These contributors we can cite as *encoders, decoders, texts, contexts* and *tasks*. In any piece of writing *all* are present, all have significant parts to play. Their necessary presence does not, of course, imply that every analyst of writing, every teacher of writing to first or second-language learners, will accord each of them the same importance, either generally, or on any given occasion. Some will want to focus on the encoder, the writer himself or herself, eavesdropped in the process, others will want to examine the reactions of the reader, the decoder, making sense and imagining the standpoint of the writer on a given issue of interest. Still another, teacher or researcher, will want to examine the text as a kind of meeting-ground between the discourse and meaning-making processes of encoder and decoder, taking a look at the evidence, as it were, and how it is laid out. Others, rightly seeing writing as bound up with social and interpersonal objectives, done even in a study with some consciousness of the world, will want to stress the context in which the writing is done, and in particular the rights and obligations held by the writer or incumbent upon him or her. Finally, there will be those who focus their attention upon the variability of writing tasks, from shopping lists to *belles lettres*, and the burden each task places upon the writer. Just as these different contributors can be separately identified and focussed, so they each provide an entry point into the understanding of what the process of writing and learning to write entails. They are points of departure for teaching and research. Significantly, however, they cannot for long be treated in isolation from each other. Each compels consideration of the others, despite their individual preferred method of treatment and their different properties. Writing thus implies contact and negotiation among the contributors in its process of creation. As encoders constantly take decoders into account, so they do task and context, and, above all, the text, as their resources to hand. In the same way, tasks offer encoders strict constraints, as do contexts. For second-language learners, and for many first-language learners, text offers the sharpest control and the keenest limitation. From this interaction it is possible, as the Editors suggest, to motivate a pedagogy. One which will see it as necessary for writers, not merely researchers and teachers, to be judging where they stand in relation to these contributors, formulating what and how to write, in the light of their purposes and their resources. Writing is thus a negotiative and exploratory act requiring great judgement.

A characteristic of this volume, and indeed of the conference from which it originates, is the new directions for teaching and research in Writing to which it gives rise. Let me use this Preface to identify some of these, among many possible candidates.

1. If context is a central contributor we need, *inter alia*, to consider its effect on the selection of appropriate text. Where writers are writing not in their first language, we need to evaluate what effect the culture associated with that language has on their choice of text in the second language.

2. We need to investigate similarities and differences in processing strategies in the activities of reading and writing. In what ways are they reciprocal?

3. To what extent is second-language writing a writing or a language problem?

4. To what extent, in our pedagogy, can we make writers aware of the nature of the writing process and its contributors?

5. How can we characterize the mutual influences of first-language writing and second-language writing? Are second-language writers only deficient in terms of text?

6. How can we evaluate alternative modes of presentation of information in speech and writing, for their clarity, their effectiveness?

7. What arguments could be advanced for involving special purpose learners in reading and writing 'expressive' texts?

8. What evidence for learning strategies can we derive from examining learners' communication strategies in writing, both in their first language and in a second language?
9. If writing is as much 'rhetoric' as it is 'composition', how can we assess the rhetorical appropriateness of the composition?
10. In evaluating the development of writing among students, what links can we make between their texts and their cognitive development?

Many other questions will suggest themselves to readers concerned with writing as a difficult process; they will find in this volume a great deal of insight and suggestion for practical teaching and research.

Christopher N. Candlin   *Lancaster*
General Editor   *October 1981*

Introduction

Despite rumours that literacy is becoming less important than it used to be, learning to write in English, whether it is one's first language, or a second or third, continues to be a major educational undertaking throughout the world. Learning to write in English, however, can mean many things. To consider only English as a first language, at one extreme learning to write means acquiring one aspect of minimal literacy: the ability to write *something*, even if that ability is called on only to jot down shopping lists. This ability is comparable to an ability to read which does not extend much beyond the laborious deciphering of street signs and tabloid headlines. At the other extreme it is the ability to produce major creative works of literature or long research studies.

Attitudes towards learning to write cover a comparable span. Sometimes learning to write is regarded as the acquiring of basic skills on which other, later, and probably more important skills can be built, and without which further education may be largely impossible. It is commonly assumed that learning to write in this sense is fairly easy, something that should be got out of the way fairly early in the educational process. Yet it is clear enough from the more or less perpetual outcry at the writing abilities of students who have completed their education, or have completed a lower level than that at which one happens to teach, that some students somehow have still not learned to write, even as late as the end of their elementary education, or their secondary education, or even their post-secondary or post-graduate education. In Chapter 2 in this book, Bereiter and Scardamalia suggest why this should be so: they describe writing a long essay as 'probably the most complex constructive act that most human beings are ever expected to perform' — a view which is clearly near the other end of the spectrum of attitudes.

In the second-language context, the difficulties involved in learning to write are compounded; for, to all the difficulties in learning to write one's own language at a level beyond that of minimal literacy are added all the further complexities inherent in trying to master a second language. It is no longer only a matter of trying to master a different medium and learning how to handle its special exigencies; it is also a matter of learning how to express oneself appropriately in a different language and in a different culture. So numerous are the new variables which may be added when learning to write in English becomes learning to write in English *as a second language* that conceivably it will never be possible to devise a complete taxonomy even for descriptive purposes.

In their different ways, the papers in this book are all concerned with exploring the gulf between, on the one hand, easy assumptions that learning to write is a basic skill which is easily acquired and ought to be acquired early, and on the other hand the considerable difficulty which Bereiter and Scardamalia, and many other experts, perceive in the task of writing (a level of complexity which popular dissatisfaction with student writing abilities certainly attests to, even if it does not explain), and the still greater complexity probably involved in learning to write in English as a second language.

In general there are four areas of concern. Logically, the first of these is the properties of the finished work of linguistic production, the piece of writing. What are its properties? What is it exactly that our students are supposed to produce when they write? The second concern is then the process through which such a piece of writing comes into existence. When we ask our students to write, what is it in reality that we ask them to do? Thirdly, assuming that we know what kinds of processes they are supposed to go through, how do they acquire the relevant complex of skills and mental abilities? What aspects of linguistic and cognitive development are called into play as students' writing abilities grow over time in response to the various demands that are made on them in the course of their education? The last area of concern is pedagogical. What do teachers need to know in order to help their students acquire the ability to write? What kinds of programmes foster the development of writing abilities?

The field of research represented by these papers is in a sense a reflection of one of the oldest areas of academic study: the field of rhetoric. In the last fifteen years or so, that field has gone through one of the intense periods of upheaval which sometimes overtake an academic discipline, leaving it fundamentally and permanently changed. Because the focus of attention in this re-vitalized field has been above all a focus on the writing process, and especially the process of writing English as a first language, it is in that area that one can see most clearly what the study of writing has come to be in recent years. Consequently we have made that section of this book, the first section, Part One. The second section, Part Two, then looks at the development of writing abilities, and more particularly the various research studies which have attempted to devise some way of describing and measuring development. Part Three is concerned with certain properties of the finished piece of writing. Finally, Part Four explores some of the implications of the kinds of research described in the previous sections for the work of practising teachers who have the responsibility of teaching English as either a first or a second language. It should be stressed, however, that none of the papers is limited in its concerns to the topic of the section in which we have placed it: in all sections there is a great deal of overlapping and cross referencing to the papers in other sections.

These papers have been selected from among those delivered at the international conference 'Learning to Write', the twelfth annual conference of the Canadian Council of Teachers of English, held at Carleton University in Ottawa, Canada, in May 1979. One aim of this conference was to share the different areas of expertise of those working in first-language and second-language approaches to writing. For, as the papers collected here demonstrate very clearly, there are enormous differences between the two fields. Yet they share a number of common concerns, and it is reasonable to suppose that those working in one field should benefit from the work going on in the other. In one sense, indeed, learning to write in the first language may be rather like learning a second language. Stephen D. Krashen, for one, has described 'the acquisition of planned discourse' as learning 'written English as a second dialect' (Krashen 1978). Some of the implications of this notion are explored by W. Ross Winterowd in his paper in this volume. Moreover, much of the standard research into one aspect of the development of writing abilities, namely the studies of the effectiveness of teaching grammar as a means of improving writing ability, suggests that what Krashen has also recently suggested in relation to the acquisition of second languages may also apply to the acquisition of writing abilities even in the first-language context. Briefly, Krashen proposes a distinction between learning, which is what takes place in response to structured teaching and is what is tapped by most kinds of testing, and acquisition, which takes place in response to needs and is tapped as the need arises for real communication; secondly, he proposes that what is learnt does not normally relate at all to what is acquired except insofar as the former can be invoked as a monitor to check what has been produced through acquired abilities (Krashen 1981). This proposal is only speculation: a great deal more research will be needed before we can accept such a hypothesis. Yet it is not only a very tempting and plausible hypothesis; it also points to what is certainly a fact: that learning to write in the first language is a special kind of extension of normal language acquisition, perhaps to an even greater extent than the acquisition of a second language is; and that the kind of instruction traditionally offered to help students learn how to write may have little or no relationship to their acquisition of writing abilities.

The conference at which these papers were first presented provided a forum for their delivery. It also generated a great deal of discussion among those who attended. No book can do more than report the sense of excitement on the campus of Carleton University as writing specialists from five continents gathered to exchange theories, research insights and pedagogical techniques. What a book can offer is both a collection of some of the most important of the papers, and a more synoptic view of the ideas generated as a result of their presentation. We know that this book does the first of these things. We hope that it does the second as well.

Aviva Freedman   *Department of Linguistics*
Ian Pringle   *Carleton University*
Janice Yalden   *Ottawa, Canada*

Part One
The writing process: three orientations

The study of writing has about it the aura and excitement of a discipline in its early stages of growth, yet interest in writing is, in fact, not new. There is, first of all, the long-standing tradition of conventional 'composition' teaching, which in one sense has fathered this new field of inquiry, but which bears little similarity to its progeny. A more congenial ancestry, however, can be found in a much older tradition — the centuries-long tradition of 'rhetoric'.

Even before Aristotle, theorists and teachers were interested in analysing the process of producing discourse as well as its products in order, initially, to formulate a set of rules that might guide those learning the art. With Aristotle, this analysis was raised to a theoretical and philosophic level: the province of rhetoric was defined (as the area of contingent human affairs); its mode of reasoning was described (probabilistic judgements rather than the pure logic of mathematics or science); and the various parts of the rhetorical process were analysed, as was the interaction between speaker and audience. The study of rhetoric was clearly established as a scientific discipline, and the history of the classical period, in both Greece and Rome, shows that the art of rhetoric and the study of that art continued to seize the imagination of the most prominent thinkers of the time, reflecting both the significance of the art in practical affairs and the central role accorded the discipline by scholars and students.

During the middle ages and Renaissance, rhetoric continued to capture the interest of the best minds and to maintain its central position within the school system. In fact, its scope broadened to include not only the art of persuading but also the art of communicating in general, and increasingly written discourse became part of its sphere.

Gradually, however, its position was eroded. A significant blow was struck when Petrus Ramus, in his attempt to rationalize the school curriculum, appropriated what had been considered the first part of the rhetorical process — 'invention' — for the study of logic or thinking. Until then, the rhetorical process had been conceived to include not only the organization of ideas and their expression in the best possible words but also the discovery of those ideas — a broad conception of the process which the contemporary discipline of writing has restored. Ramus' truncation and the subsequent narrowing of attention by rhetoricians to aspects of style ultimately led to the limited conception of the process associated with the term 'composition'. The decline of the discipline was slow, but by the nineteenth century rhetoric had become composition, and by the twentieth century, the discipline was, in E.P.J. Corbett's words, 'moribund, if not door-nail dead' (1967, p. 171).

This is not to say, however, that writing was not studied in the schools; for in the meantime, as suggested above, there had arisen that very limited tradition of composition teaching which is so familiar to all of us in first *and* second-language situations, with its emphasis on 'correct usage, correct grammar, and correct spelling', and its focus on 'the topic sentence, the various methods of developing the paragraph . . . and the holy trinity of unity, coherence, and emphasis' (Corbett 1965, p. 626).

Richard Young (1978) calls this tradition 'current-traditional rhetoric' and he argues that its practitioners' emphases and pedagogic techniques were all determined by certain tacit but shared assumptions concerning the nature of the composing process. Chief among these was the Romantic conviction that the creative aspects of the process are mysterious, inscrutable, and hence unteachable. What can be taught and discussed are the lesser matters of style, organization, and usage.

In the 1960's, those involved with the teaching of writing became increasingly dissatisfied with the current-traditional paradigm and began searching elsewhere for new pedagogic techniques and ultimately for a new explanation of the process. They turned both to the classical tradition of rhetoric as well as to such contemporary disciplines as linguistics, psycholinguistics, speech-act theory, cognitive psychology, sociolinguistics, and educational theory, in an attempt to come to a new understanding or at least to formulate appropriate questions for, and methods of, inquiry. And thus, the new discipline of writing has emerged over the past fifteen to twenty years, a discipline which can increasingly be characterized by its own sets of assumptions, its own preoccupations and characteristic strategies.

The first-language articles in this volume indicate some of the common interests and underlying assumptions which bind the new discipline. (For further analysis of the new paradigm, see Young 1978; Emig 1980; Freedman and Pringle 1980; Carroll 1980). First and understandably, there is an attempt to redefine its roots, a search for a more hospitable ancestry than 'current-traditional rhetoric'. Commonly, as suggested above, contemporary rhetoricians point to the classical tradition as their appropriate heritage (see, for example, Bilsky 1956; Weaver 1967; Hughes and Duhamel 1962; and especially Corbett 1965), and many classical insights have been borrowed from antiquity and re-interpreted for use in contemporary contexts; for example, the division of the rhetorical process into five parts, with a focus especially on the first, invention; the three different kinds of appeal — an appeal based on the moral character of the speaker, an appeal based on logic, and one based on the audience's emotions; and the effect in general of audience and the importance of context or occasion.

Besides the classical tradition, however, the new discipline derives much of its vigour from a very different source — from an extraordinary synthesis of many of the pervasive notions of twentieth century thought. In her important essay, Janet Emig (1980) identifies many of the figures of what she calls the 'tacit tradition', whose ideas have formed the unacknowledged matrix from which much current work on writing draws its vitality. Specifically, these include Thomas Kuhn, George Kelly, John Dewey, Michael Polanyi, Susanne Langer, Jean Piaget, Lev Vygotsky, A.R. Luria, and Eric Lenneberg.

This continuing attempt to find its roots, to locate an appropriate heritage, has been characteristic of the new discipline. Having rebelled so defiantly against the tradition into which it was born, it seems to feel a need to define its intellectual context by locating a more hospitable tradition.

Another characteristic emphasis of the new rhetoric, one that reflects its radical departure from 'current-traditional rhetoric', can best be understood within the framework of the so-called communication triangle described by Kinneavy in Chapter 8. This model of discourse posits four elements in every communicative situation: the encoder or speaker or writer; the decoder or audience; the message or text; and the reality to which it refers.

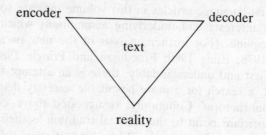

As Abrams (1953) has pointed out in his analysis of literary critical approaches and Kinneavy (1971) in his discussion of discourse production, an analyst or producer of text may emphasize any one of the four different elements and further any of the many possible interrelationships. Widdowson, for reasons discussed below, insists on the primacy of the writer-audience relationship. Conventional composition teaching focussed on the message, the product, the written composition, analysing style, organizational patterns, rules of usage. The new rhetoric, in contrast, has consciously and deliberately shifted its focus to the encoder or writer, investigating especially the process of writing itself and the development of writing abilities within that encoder. (In second-language studies, these abilities may be relatively narrowly defined, but the focus is nevertheless very similar.) Thus many current thinkers have turned to the field of creativity theory for general insights into the creative process which might also cast light on composing. The four-stage model of the process described by Helmholtz (1903) and Wallas (1926) has been modified variously by contemporary rhetoricians (for example, Young, Becker, and Pike 1970; and Winterowd 1980), and considerable attention has been devoted to theoretic and pedagogic speculation about the first stage, the preparation, and especially to the kind of heuristic strategies that might be successfully employed by writers. Some have recommended contemporary versions of the Aristotelian topics (Wallace 1975), others have modified Burke's pentad (Irmscher 1976), and Young, Becker, and Pike (1970) have developed a model based on tagmemic linguistics.

In addition to borrowing from research done in the field of creativity theory, however, those involved in the study of writing have developed an indigenous tradition of research on composing. With her seminal study, *The Composing Processes of Twelfth*

Graders (1971), Janet Emig was the first to attempt to investigate the writing process scientifically and systematically. Basing her analysis on tape-recorded pre and post-writing interviews as well as on transcribed composing-aloud sessions, Emig focussed on eight twelfth-grade students engaged in several distinct writing tasks. More recently, Sondra Perl (1979) has refined this methodology in order to explore the composing behaviours of unskilled college freshmen, while Flower and Hayes have been accumulating a massive library of what they call 'composing-aloud protocols', that is transcripts of writing sessions where subjects are asked to record every thought that comes to mind during the writing process. On the basis of a painstaking analysis of the transcripts of both professional and apprentice writers, Flower and Hayes have developed a powerful model of the conscious processes involved in writing.

At the same time, researchers such as Pianko (1979) and Matsuhashi (1979) have employed a different methodology: they have videotaped their subjects while they write, without any requirement that they compose aloud. After each session, they review the tapes with the writers, probing for information concerning what went on in their heads at crucial points. Characteristic behavioural sequences have thus been identified, and pauses have been measured and correlated with grammatical and rhetorical units to glean other kinds of insight into the nature of the composing process. Jones (1980a, b) has initiated the study of the writing processes of ESL students using the same techniques.

This characteristic focussing on the composing process is represented in this volume by the essays of Britton (Chapter 1) and of Bereiter and Scardamalia (Chapter 2). Each of the two essays goes beyond reporting on research, although both emerge out of large-scale projects investigating writing and its development. Beyond such research, however, Britton's work comes out of long observation of children and discussions with teachers eliciting their observations; he draws as well on that rich intellectual context defined by Janet Emig as the 'tacit tradition', and in his work Britton exemplifies the wedding of abstraction with experience, the continuous interplay between intellectual generalizations and the rich texture of reality that he and the school of British educationists he is part of declare to be essential for real knowledge of the world.

Bereiter and Scardamalia, in contrast, are cognitive psychologists whose speculations in the essay included in this volume are based primarily on the results of a large-scale, long-term research project involving a great number of carefully conducted, specifically designed experiments with children in the elementary and secondary years. The subjects of these experiments were sometimes involved in conventional writing tasks, but more frequently performed carefully constructed tasks designed to reveal the kinds of cognitive strategies they had available to bring to the writing task at particular points of their development. For example, instead of being assigned a topic for a short story, pupils were asked to write a story that would conclude as follows: *And so, after considering the reasons for it and the reasons against it, the duke decided to rent his castle to the vampires after all, in spite of the rumour he had heard.* In another typical experiment, pupils were asked to write on an argumentative topic and, when they announced they were finished, were simply asked to write more — again and again. Such an assignment revealed that even after the children felt they had completed the task, they still had more to say on that topic and, though it seems bizarre, were quite happy to be asked to do so. Bereiter and Scardamalia have used such experiments to reveal the kinds of cognitive strategies children need to acquire in order to learn to write. The theorizing about the nature of the composing process presented in the Bereiter and Scardamalia essay in this volume is based on the findings of many experiments of this kind.

Although at first reading the language (and certainly the terminology) and approach of the Bereiter and Scardamalia essay seem radically different from that of the Britton essay, and although the starting-point and certain of the implications of their arguments are clearly different, if not diametrically opposed, beneath the differences we can perceive some of the common factors that bind the discipline. Both essays reveal a distrust of much that takes place in conventional composition classrooms and that is presented in traditional texts. Both focus their attention, as we have said, on the person composing rather than the composed product, and both place an extraordinarily high value on what this process can do for the writer especially in his relations to reality, his world-view.

Some of the differences between the essays, however, are worth dwelling on as they suggest different paths within the discipline. Britton bases his discussion on what he sees as the potential similarities between speaking and writing, arguing that we should be able to transfer the spontaneous inventiveness of speech to writing. 'Successful writers adapt that inventiveness [from spontaneous speech] and continue to rely on it rather than switching to some different mode of operating'. Bereiter and Scardamalia, in contrast, point to the fundamental differences between conversation and composition and argue that much of the difficulty involved in learning to write derives from the fact that in order to write we must learn a whole new set of cognitive strategies that are not called for in the production of oral language.

What appears to be a more fundamental opposition, however, turns out to be more apparent than real. Bereiter and Scardamalia make a distinction between two kinds of composing: the low road and the high road. At first glance, the low-road writing seems remarkably similar to the 'shaping at the point of utterance' that Britton advocates. Certainly, what Bereiter and Scardamalia say about the 'running jump strategy', sounds reminiscent of Britton's Newcastle boy's introspective comments. 'The running jump strategy . . . consists of rapidly rereading the text produced so far and using the acquired momentum, as it were, to launch themselves into the next sentence'. The Newcastle boy explains his process thus: 'It just comes into your head, it's not like thinking, it's just there. When you get stuck you just read it through and the next bit is there, it just comes to you'.

A closer analysis, however, reveals that what Britton is advocating is not what Bereiter and Scardamalia call 'knowledge-telling', the simple emptying of one of our memory file holders. Britton describes shaping at the point of utterance thus:

> shaping at the point of utterance involves . . . drawing upon interpreted experience, the results of our moment by moment shaping of the data of the senses and the continued further assimilation of that material in search of coherence and pattern; and secondly seems to involve by some means getting behind this to a more direct apperception of the felt quality of 'experience' in some instance or instances; by which means the act of writing becomes itself a contemplative act revealing further coherence and fresh pattern.

And he quotes at length Perl and Egendorf (1979), who talk about the writer's continual shuttling back and forth between the non-verbal sense of what they want to say and the words on the page. Bereiter and Scardamalia describe children on the high road as those 'who start to think about what they are writing down on paper as having relations to various other things in their minds. Most importantly, they may begin to see that there is a relationship, and not necessarily an identity, between what they write and what they mean. . . . Writing becomes a task of representing meaning rather than of transcribing language'. In other words what Britton describes as 'shaping at the point of utterance' is the 'high-road writing' that Bereiter and Scardamalia praise; what the latter refer to as the 'low road' is not dealt with by Britton except perhaps as the mere fluency he alludes to that teachers distrust.

Although the fundamental conception of writing then is similar, the emphases in the two essays differ: Bereiter and Scardamalia insist on the difficulty of the task and imply a kind of conscious awareness and manipulation of the constraints of the task that is absent in Britton's description of the process. In this way, Bereiter and Scardamalia evoke and indeed invoke Flower and Hayes, whose work on the composing process involves an analysis of composing-aloud protocols and necessarily, consequently, of the conscious processes involved in the process. Britton, in contrast, allies himself with pedagogical theorists such as Murray and Elbow, who distrust excessive consciousness and preplanning, who insist that the writing itself is a discovery process whose flow must not be impeded by our all too active monitors and editorial censors.

Despite such differences in emphasis, what is striking about the two strands in the discipline are the fundamental similarities revealed in their preoccupations and assumptions, especially in the extraordinarily high value attributed to the act of writing at its best. Writing is not simply a way of communicating what is known, but, in Emig's formulation, is itself a 'mode of knowing'. As Bereiter and Scardamalia argue, 'writing becomes for many people the organizing force in their mental development'. And this is the thrust of the educational movement begun in Britain and now spreading rapidly across North America — 'language across the curriculum'. The central argument of its early proponents — Douglas Barnes, Harold Rosen, James Britton — is that real learning in any discipline is only accomplished when we can talk or write about the concepts of that discipline in our own language; parroting back stretches of memorized passages does not constitute what Barnes calls 'action knowledge', knowledge that is so assimilated within our mental map that we can act on it. We construct our representations of the world through language and assimilate new concepts within that representation (in the process adjusting that representation accordingly) by the productive use

of language, through talk or writing, especially relaxed exploratory talk and 'expressive' writing, that is writing whose aim is to
express one's thinking rather than to communicate a message to
some other. Bereiter and Scardamalia would argue that writing
is, in fact, even more effective than talk. 'Although a powerful
generator of thought and knowledge, conversation's outputs are
social products, negotiated meanings. We do not truly own our
thoughts or experiences until we have negotiated them with
ourselves and for this writing is the prime medium'.

For Britton and the British educationists, writing is valuable
not only because it helps us to acquire school knowledge but
more significantly because it allows us to come to terms with our
lives: Britton (1980) calls this 'learning 2'. Through talk or writing
we are able to tell our own stories, to make or perceive the meanings and patterns which allow us to rise above the anonymity and
consequent feeling of helplessness that might otherwise be our
lot.

This high evaluation of the potential scope and power of writing is fundamental to the new paradigm in first-language writing
study. Writing is seen ultimately as the great humanizing force; it
is not the practical, mundane, communicative advantages of writing that are celebrated but rather its power to give form and
significance to our lives.

Such an emphasis is not apparent in the second-language papers. Widdowson (Chapter 3), for example, writes: 'I will begin by
stating the obvious. Writing is a communicative activity'. First-
language rhetoricians do not start from, and certainly would not
base their arguments on, such a premise. In fact, Britton at least
would argue that a great deal of writing is not communicative primarily; that communication is only one of three possible aims.
The other two he characterizes in his taxonomy as 'expressive'
and 'poetic', and there is no question that what he calls 'transactional' is seen as, if not less important, at least less interesting.
And certainly he argues that the communicative intent is secondary; what must precede a desire to communicate is a grasp of
what is to be communicated; transactional writing must succeed
expressive, which is the matrix.

Consequently, Britton and Widdowson come to radically
opposed perceptions of the composing process. And, given the
pre-eminence of Britton's stature in the first-language field (if
there is a scholar who represents it archetypally, he is Britton)
and the wide currency of Widdowson's views in ESL, their differ-

ences point up the pervasive differences between the approach to writing in the two fields. Whereas Widdowson sees the process as an internalized negotiation between writer and reader, Britton argues that concern for a reader, what Perl and Egendorf call 'projective structuring' must be secondary (at least in time); what is anterior is 'retrospective structuring', the shuttling back and forth between one's preverbal sense of what one wants to say and the words on the page. In fact, premature concern with audience is what characterizes the processes of 'unskilled writers'.

The contrast between Britton's and Widdowson's perceptions of the process of writing is, of course, due in the first place to the different functions that writing in another language generally has in the individual's life, compared to the important role writing in his own language can have in shaping his grasp of the world around him. In addition, the functional-notional or communicative approaches to second-language teaching, which are becoming increasingly current, require that teaching be directed fairly narrowly toward the learner's language needs in some future or 'target' situation. While this is a requirement which it is clearly very difficult, if not impossible, to meet in preparing second-language teaching programmes for the young, it is a reasonable objective in doing so for adults — young and not so young. And in teaching English as a second language, programmes for adults represent a very important proportion of the teaching which goes on. It is possible to argue — and often is argued within the communicative approach — that adult second-language learners do not have enough time left in their lifetimes to travel the same long road that they did when they set out to learn how to deal with reality through their first language. If this is so, then Britton's 'expressive' and 'poetic' aims, while still very desirable ones, are manifestly less central to their future second-language requirements than is the 'transactional' aim. That this is in fact the case in most second-language situations outside the traditionally oriented classroom can easily be confirmed if one examines typical statements of objectives set out for language examinations given in the workplace. In fact, the suggestion of many researchers is that all second-language tests should be redesigned to measure what the learner can 'do' through the language (Carroll 1980; Morrow 1979; Canale and Swain 1980, etc.). It is thus assumed that the other two will be largely reserved for first-language instruction, and for the very small numbers of individuals who are willing and able to benefit from a more general language teaching programme.

Widdowson's contribution to this volume represents a considerable corpus of work in all of which he examines the non-linguistic or non-formal aspects of language and provides a perspective that had been lacking on the difficulties that the learner confronts when he tries to write in another language. Particularly if language is considered from the standpoint of purposeful communicative activity, it must involve much more than knowledge of linguistic rules alone, and must represent something more than 'composition' only. Widdowson discusses another kind of knowledge required in addition to that of formal rules: that of 'the world of fact and of social convention'. For the second-language learner, this world may be in many respects very different from the one he already knows. Hence the relationship between the two types of knowledge becomes a focus for Widdowson's discussion. Pointing out the need for interlocutors to share the second kind of knowledge in order for communication to take place easily and comfortably, he refers repeatedly to the notion of 'negotiation' in communication, and contrasts it with that of unequivocal precision. He then applies this argument to second-language teaching, especially of writing, and relates the teaching of writing to the present controversy over which of the dual goals of fluency and appropriateness to the social context on the one hand, and linguistic accuracy on the other, should take precedence in our second-language teaching programmes.

Widdowson's treatment of written discourse as 'an interactive process of negotiation' and his explanation of how, in his view of the act of composing, the character of the information conveyed is influenced by the interactive nature of the writing process sheds a good deal of light on the problems surrounding the treatment of writing in second-language programmes. It also reveals what numerous difficulties lie in the path of the writer in his attempts to achieve communication with his invisible audience and how he must strive to create 'textual patterns' which he expects his readers to interpret, despite his physical absence while they are engaged in reading his production.

The pedagogical implications are very considerable, and are bound up with the view of learners' language needs referred to above. The student, Widdowson writes, 'should know who he is addressing and why'. Past insistence on production of writing samples is seen as being merely insistence on exercises in linguistic forms and rules of usage, and does nothing to help the student learn to write for some purpose. In teaching writing to those who are already literate in another language, and especially to adults, Widdowson accepts the fact that in general the learner is expected to know a good deal about the nature of the task. He does not accept that the best — indeed the only — approach to helping him exploit that knowledge is through large doses of 'grammar'. For that leaves knowledge of the discourse process unactivated, and Widdowson insists that we need to create a methodology which will activate it. The ideas expressed in his paper are having a far-reaching effect on teaching writing in English as a second language, for he distinguishes clearly between the difficulties of the writer working in a second-language from those of an individual working in his own. They are an invigorating contribution to the discussion of developing writing skills in any second-language situation, and are becoming the basis for a much more comprehensive approach to the problem.

1 Shaping at the point of utterance*

James Britton

The two words, 'spontaneity' and 'invention' as we ordinarily use them must surely have something in common: an element of surprise, not only for those who encounter and respond to the act or expression, but also for those who originate it. I want to suggest here that rhetoricians, in their current concern for successive drafts and revision processes in composing, may be underestimating the importance of 'shaping at the point of utterance', or the value of spontaneous inventiveness. It is my claim, in fact, that a better understanding of how a writer shapes at the point of utterance might make a major contribution to our understanding of invention in rhetoric.

In all normal speech we do, almost of necessity, shape as we utter. Syntactically, we launch into a sentence and hope somehow to reach closure. We had a Director at the Institute of Education where I once worked who was a very powerful speaker, but also a great 'um'-er and 'ah'-er. As you listened to him it would go something like this: 'It seems to me, Mr Chairman — ah — in spite of the difficulties Professor X has raised — ah — that what we most need — ah — in the present circumstances — ah — and — ah — at this moment in time — ah — is some way to bring to a conclusion this intolerably long sentence.' Listening, we could tell precisely at what point he foresaw his total structure, the point at which he 'took it on the run'.

What is not so easily demonstrated is that the shaping as we speak applies not only to syntactic but also to semantic choices. When we start to speak, we push the boat out and trust it will come to shore somewhere — not *anywhere*, which would be tantamount to losing our way — but somewhere that constitutes a stage on a purposeful journey. To embark on a conversational

* *Reprinted from* Reinventing the Rhetorical Tradition, *ed. Aviva Freedman and Ian Pringle. Conway, Arkansas: L & S Books, for the C.C.T.E., 1980.*

utterance is to take on a certain responsibility, to stake a claim that calls for justification: and perhaps it is the social pressure on the speaker to justify his claim that gives talk an edge over silent brooding as a problem-solving procedure. Heinrich von Kleist, the early nineteenth-century German writer, puts this point boldly in an essay he called, 'On the Gradual Fabrication of Thought While Speaking':[1]

> Whenever you seek to know something and cannot find it out by meditation, I would advise you to talk it over with the first person you meet. He need not be especially brilliant, and I do not suggest that you *question* him, no: *tell* him about it ... Often, while at my desk working, I search for the best approach to some involved problem. I usually stare into my lamp, the point of optimum brightness, while striving with utmost concentration to enlighten myself ... And the remarkable thing is that if I talk about it with my sister, who is working in the same room, I suddenly realize things which hours of brooding had perhaps been unable to yield ... Because I do start with some sort of dark notion remotely related to what I am looking for, my mind, if it has set out boldly enough, and being pressed to complete what it has begun, shapes that muddled area into a form of new-minted clarity, even while my talking progresses.

As teachers, we are likely to have similar evidence from much nearer home: how often have we had a student come to us with his problem, and in the course of verbalizing what that problem is reach a solution with no help from us?

Then what about writing? First it must be said that students of invention in writing cannot afford to rule out of court evidence regarding invention in speech: there must be some carry-over from expression in the one medium to expression in the other. Shaping at the point of utterance is familiar enough in the way young children will spin their yarns to entertain an adult who is willing to provide an audience. (A ten-minute tape-recorded performance by a five-year-old boy winds up: 'So he had ten thousand pounds, so everyone loved him in the world. He buy — he buyed a very fast racing car, he buyed a magic wand, he buyed everything he loved, and that's the end of my story what I told you.' A five-year-old sense of closure!) There is ample evidence that spontaneous invention of this kind survives, and may even appear to profit from, the process of dictating, where parent or teacher writes down what the child composes orally. That it is seriously inhibited by the slowing down of production when the child produces his own written script is undeniable. But it is my argument that successful writers adapt that inventiveness and continue to rely on it rather than switching to some different mode of operating. Once a writer's words appear on the page, I believe they act primarily as a stimulus to *continuing* — to further writing, that is — and not primarily as a stimulus to *re*-writing. Our experiments in writing (Britton *et al*. 1975, p. 35) without being able to see what we had written suggested that the movements of the pen capture the movement of our thinking, and it is a serious obstacle to further composition not to be able to reread, to 'get into the tramlines' again. An eight-year-old Newcastle schoolboy wrote about his own writing processes: 'It just comes into your head, it's not like thinking, it's just there. When you get stuck you just read it through and the next bit is there, it just comes to you.' I think many teachers might regard the outcome of such a process as mere 'fluency', mere verbal facility, and not the sort of writing they want to encourage. It is my argument that highly effective writing may be produced in just that spontaneous manner, and that the best treatment for empty verbalism will rarely be a course of successive draft making.

'It just comes into your head, it's not like thinking': it seems that Barrett Mandel would agree with the eight-year-old, for he calls his recent article on writing, 'Losing One's Mind: Learning to Read, Write and Edit.' I quote his views here because they are in part an attempt to make room for the process of shaping at the point of utterance. He sets out the three steps that occur in his own writing process: '(1) I have an idea about something I want to write; (2) I write whatever I write; (3) I notice what I've written, judge it, and edit it, either a lot or a little' (1978, p. 363). And his claim is that the relationship between (1) and (2) is not one of cause and effect; rather, 'step one *precedes* writing and *establishes a frame of mind in which writing is likely to occur*' (1978, p. 363). 'It is the *act of writing* that produces the discoveries,' he claims, and, by way of explanation, 'words flow from a pen, not from a mind; they appear on the page through the massive co-ordination of a tremendous number of motor processes . . . More accurately, I *become* my pen; my entire organism becomes an extension of this writing implement. Consciousness is focussed in the point of the pen' (1978, p. 365).

So far, so good, but since Mandel goes on to approve of his colleague, Janet Emig's, description of writing as 'a form of cognition' it seems to me a little perverse to propose (by his title, 'Losing One's Mind') a mindless form of cognition. 'Freeing one's mind' would be more appropriate, the freedom being that of ranging across the full spectrum of mental activity from the autistic pole to the reality-adjusted pole, as Peter McKellar (1957, p. 5) has described it. Or, as we might speculatively describe it today, right brain and left brain in intimate collaboration.

I want to associate spontaneous shaping, whether in speech or writing, with the moment by moment interpretative process by which we make sense of what is happening around us; to see each as an instance of the pattern-forming propensity of man's mental processes. Thus, when we come to write, what is delivered to the pen is in part already shaped, stamped with the image of our own ways of perceiving. But the intention to *share,* inherent in spontaneous utterance, sets up a demand for further shaping.

Can we go deeper than this, penetrate beyond the process of drawing upon our own store of interpreted experience? Perl and Egendorf believe we must if we are to provide a full account of writing behaviour. In an article they call 'The Process of Creative Discovery', they speak of a new line of philosophical enquiry, the 'philosophy of experiencing', and quote from the writings of Eugene Gendlin (1962). 'Many thinkers since Kant,' they suggest, 'have claimed that all valid thought and expression are rooted in the wider realm of pre-representational experience, (1979, p. 121). 'Experiencing', or pre-representational experience, 'consists of continuously unfolding orders rather than finished products' (1979, p. 122); in Gendlin's words, it is 'the felt apperceptive mass to which we can inwardly point' (quoted in Perl and Egendorf 1979, p. 122). It is fluid, global, charged with implicit meanings — which we alter when by expressing them we make them explicit. D.W. Harding, psychologist and literary critic, explores a similar distinction in his book, *Experience into Words*: 'The emergence of words or images as part of our total state of being is an obscure process, and their relation to the non-verbal is difficult to specify . . . The words we choose (or accept as the best we can find at the moment) may obliterate or slightly obscure or distort fine features of the non-verbal background of thinking . . . a great deal of speaking and writing involves the effort to be a little more faithful to the non-verbal background of language than an over-ready acceptance of ready-made terms and phrases will permit' (1963, pp. 170–72). Perl and Egendorf comment on that effort as they observe it in their students: 'When closely observed, students appear to write by shuttling back and forth from their sense of what they wanted to say to the words on the page and back to address what is available to them inwardly'

(1979, p. 125). This is in essence the process they call 'retrospective structuring', and its near inevitability might be suggested by comparing writing with carving: the sculptor with chisel in hand must both cut and observe the effect of his cut before going on. But retrospective structuring needs to be accompanied by what the authors call 'projective structuring', shaping the material in such a way that the writer's meaning carries over to the intended reader. It is in this aspect of writing that 'discovery', or shaping at the point of utterance, tends to break down: a mistaken sense of a reader's expectations may obstruct or weaken the 'sense of what they wanted to say' — or in Harding's terms 'obliterate . . . fine features of the non-verbal background of thinking'. Observing unskilled writers, Perl and Egendorf comment: 'What seems particularly unskilled about the way these students write is that *they apply prematurely a set of rigid, critical rules for editing* to their written products' (1979, p. 127). 'Prematurely' might be taken to mean at first draft rather than at second or third, but I think this does less than justice to the authors' meaning. Minor editing — for spelling, for example — is better left, we can agree, to a rereading stage. What is at issue here is a more important point: that too restricted a sense of a reader's expectations may result in 'projective structuring' coming to dominate the shaping at the point of utterance, to the exclusion or severe restriction of the 'retrospective structuring', the search for a meaning that in its expression satisfies the writer.

Such a conclusion would gain general support from a neat little study by Mike Rose, a study he calls 'Rigid Rules, Inflexible Plans and the Stifling of Writing'. A case study of five fluent writers and five with 'writer's block' leads him to conclude that 'the non-blockers operate with fluid, easily modified, even easily discarded rules and plans, that are often expressed with a vagueness that could almost be interpreted as ignorance. There lies the irony. The students that offer the least precise rules and plans have the least trouble composing' (1978, unpublished paper).

What I have suggested, then, is that shaping at the point of utterance involves, first, drawing upon interpreted experience, the results of our moment by moment shaping of the data of the senses and the continued further assimilation of that material in search of coherence and pattern (the fruits of our contemplative moments); and, secondly, seems to involve by some means getting behind this to a more direct apperception of the felt quality of 'experiencing' in some instance or instances; by which means the act of writing becomes itself a contemplative act revealing further coherence and fresh pattern. Its power to do so may depend in part upon the writer's counterpart of the social pressure that listeners exert on a speaker, though in this case, clearly, the writer himself is, in the course of the writing, the channel through which that pressure is applied.

I must now add the much more obvious point that in the initial stages of learning to write a child must draw upon linguistic resources gathered principally through speaking and listening, and apply those resources to the new task of writing. Some children, however, will also be familiar with some forms of the written language derived from stories that have been read to them. A four-year-old, for example, dictated a fairy story of his own composition in which he said, 'The king went sadly home for he had nowhere else to go', a use of 'for' that can hardly have been learned from listening to speech. Thus the early writer shuttles between internalized forms of the written language and his general resources recruited through speech: that he should maintain access to the latter is important if he is to embark on the use of writing to fulfil a range of different purposes. His progress as a writer depends thereafter, to a considerable degree, on his increasing familiarity with forms of the written language, the enlargement of his stock of 'internalized' written forms through reading and *being read to*. (The process of recreating the rhythms of the written language from his own reading must derive from that apprenticeship to an adult's reading.) To put it simply, if rather crudely, I see the developed writing process as one of hearing an inner voice dictating forms of the written language appropriate to the task in hand.

If it is to work this way, we must suppose that there exists some kind of *pre-setting mechanism* which, once set up, continues to affect production throughout a given task. The difficulties many writers feel in 'finding a way in' or in 'finding one's own voice' in a particular piece of writing, as well as the familiar routine of running through what has been written in order to move on, seem to me to supply a little evidence in favour of such a 'pre-setting mechanism'. Beyond that I can offer only hints and nudges. There is, for example, the phenomenon of metric composition. Read aloud a passage in galloping iambics and most listeners are enabled to compose spontaneously in that rhythm; young children's facility in picking up pig-Latin or dog-Latin is probably another example of the same sort of process. And by way of explanation, there is Kenneth Lashley's longstanding notion of a 'determining tendency' in human behaviour: 'The cortex must be regarded as a great network of reverberatory circuits constantly active. A new stimulus, reaching such a system, does not excite an isolated reflex path but must produce widespread changes in the pattern of excitation throughout a whole system of already interacting neurons' (1961, p. 194). Such a determining tendency, he argues, is related to an individual's *intention*. In this and other respects the notion parallels Michael Polanyi's (1969, p. 146) description of focal and subsidiary awareness. Applying that to the writing process, a writer is subsidiarily aware of the words and structures he is employing and focally aware of an emergent meaning, the meaning he intends to formulate and convey. And it is the focal awareness that guides and directs the use made of the means, of which he is subsidiarily aware. In similar fashion, a reader's attention is not focussed upon the printed marks: he attends *from* them to the emerging meaning. To focus on the words would be to inhibit the handling of meaning by writer or reader. 'By concentrating on his fingers', says Polanyi, 'a pianist can paralyse himself; the motions of his fingers no longer bear then on the music performed, they have lost their meaning' (1969, p. 146).

Painting in oils, where one pigment may be used to obliterate another, is a very different process from painting in watercolours, where the initial process must capture immediately as much as possible of the painter's vision. Do modes of discourse differ in production as sharply as that? And does our present concern with pre-planning, successive drafting and revision suggest that in taking oil-painting as our model for writing we may be underestimating the value of 'shaping at the point of utterance' and hence cutting off what might prove the most effective approach to an understanding of rhetorical invention?

Notes

1. I am grateful to Geoffrey Summerfield of York University and Frank Smith of the Ontario Institute for Studies in Education who introduced me to the articles by Heinrich von Kleist and Kenneth Lashley respectively.

2 Does learning to write have to be so difficult?

Carl Bereiter and Marlene Scardamalia

Writing a long essay is probably the most complex constructive act that most human beings are ever expected to perform. Although there are many other acts of equal or greater complexity — such as designing and building buildings, doing experimental research, choreographing a ballet sequence, presenting cases in court, and reorganizing a company — most people aren't expected to do such things. These tasks are reserved for people of special talent and training. But school and society seem to expect that just about everyone should be able to produce a coherent four-thousand-word essay on a topic such as women's participation in sports. The complexity of this task could, however, rival that of the other tasks, which we assign only to the elect.

During the past four years we have been studying how children acquire (to the extent that they do) the ability to handle complexities of prose composition. We suppose it is a fair judgment on the norm of college writing to say that most people never do get very good at expository writing. But, coming to the matter as psychologists, we are mainly impressed that people manage to write as well as they do. Even the most rambling and ill-developed student essay seems, on analysis, to have required the juggling of large amounts of information and the orchestration of a large number of skills ranging from penmanship (rather a marvel of complex coordination itself) on up to some kind of ability to function within the bounds of genre and topic. How is all this accomplished, and how was it learned?

From the beginning of our research we have been struck by the fact that people who discuss learning to write almost invariably equate skill with quality. People who produce equally good writing are judged to be equally skilful, despite the fact that what some do with ease and finesse others do laboriously and haltingly.

Similarly, those who produce bad writing are all judged to be lacking in skill, even though they display the same vast range of differences in facility. In a current euphemism people who produce bad writing are called 'novices', even if they have been writing for years. The confusion is understandable in teachers who have an over-riding concern with quality, but for psychologists setting out to understand writing it seemed important to recognize that skill can take different forms.

Looking at schoolchildren from this point of view, what we saw was not children failing to learn to write. We saw children *succeeding* in learning to write poorly. That is perhaps putting it too dramatically, though not inaccurately. We saw children succeeding at acquiring a skill in composition that would permit them, with increasing economy of effort, to meet the demands of school, university, and adult work. These children did not know — and one must ask what could cause them to care — that the path they were on would at best lead to polished mediocrity and would most likely lead to writing of the kind people point to in lamenting the decline of literacy.

At the same time, however, we saw some children learning to write well. These children were in the same classes as the others, doing the same assignments, getting more-or-less the same attention from their teachers. What made the difference? Talent, most would say. But that is far too circular an explanation to be of use. Effort, others would say. But effort directed how, toward what? To say effort directed toward writing well is to slip again into circularity. In any skill, the direction of effort is much of what is learned. It is part of the skill, not something outside that can be used to explain the skill. To get beyond mere descriptions and circular explanations, we need to go beneath the surface of learning to write and study its dynamics.

In another paper (Bereiter and Scardamalia 1982), we have analysed the problems of learning to write as problems of converting a language production system geared to conversation over to a language production system capable of functioning by itself. Although this sounds like a relatively simple matter, the further one penetrates it with experimental research the more complex and difficult it begins to appear. Simply learning to continue producing language without the prompting that comes from conversational partners turns out to be a formidable achievement. And more formidable achievements lie beyond: learning to search one's own memory instead of having memories triggered by what other people say; planning large units of discourse instead of planning only what will be said next; and learning to function as both sender and receiver — sustaining this dual role out of which grows the ability to revise.

In the preceding paper we were trying to understand the problems of learning to write in their universal aspect — to understand what we all have to go through by virtue of the fact that we learn to speak before we learn to write and arrive at discourse as a form of social interaction. In this paper we want to start considering differences in the paths people take towards literacy.

As soon as we ask the title question of this paper, *Does learning to write have to be so difficult?*, we have to face the fact of individual differences. Learning to write is easier for some people than others and, moreover, it is not necessarily easiest for those who show the most talent! For some people writing gets easier as they get better at it and for others it keeps getting harder. There is nothing paradoxical about this. The task of writing is not fixed but is very much what the writer makes it. People for whom writing keeps getting harder are people who keep reformulating the task into one of increasingly complex demands. Such people are headed for greatness, though of course they may not end up there. They may end up with a chronic case of writer's block instead.

Does learning to write have to be so difficult? Our answer is that it depends on what path the student is following toward competence. There is a high road to writing and for students on that road the answer is, yes, learning to write has to be difficult. Being on the high road means always pursuing goals that are just over the horizon. It can't be anything but difficult. But there is also a low road which leads to competence, although to competence of a different order. For students on the low road learning to write is not necessarily difficult. There can be serious difficulties, but these involve obstacles that can, at least in theory, be reduced. For students on the high road, on the other hand, the difficulties are inherent in the nature of what writing means to them.

Allocation of mental capacity in writing

At a global level, the high road and the low road are easy enough to characterize. The high road is characterized by struggling to master the art of writing in all its complexities. Depending on how the struggle goes, the metaphor of Sisyphus or the metaphor

of the chambered nautilus may apply. The low road is characterized by striving to avoid or minimize the burden of those same
complexities.

We want to propose a deeper analysis, an analysis that will
make it clear, for one thing, why we are talking about two roads
rather than ten roads or ten million. The central idea in this
analysis is allocation of mental capacity.

The idea of limited mental capacity plays a key role in much of
recent theorizing about human cognitive processes.[1] While our
memories can store vast amounts of information, we have the
capacity to handle only relatively small amounts of information at
any moment. Holding a ten-digit telephone number in mind long
enough to dial it can overtax the capacity of a person whose long-
term memory holds the dates of all the major events in European
history. Writers often face a capacity limit problem in planning an
essay. They are aware of a number of different variables that
need to be taken into account and of numerous possible permuta-
tions of the material they intend to include, and they struggle
vainly to hold all those things in mind at once. Finally they are
likely to be forced to make some decisions arbitrarily, simply because they cannot manage to take simultaneous account of all the
elements that they know are relevant to a considered judgment.

Typically, activities require less mental capacity as one becomes
practised at them. For learner drivers, handling an automobile
and attending to traffic so fully absorb their mental capacity that
they have none left over for anything else. Eventually one becomes practised enough that the routine requirements of driving
take very little mental capacity and one is therefore able to con-
verse, listen to the radio, or even, as some prodigies can do,
compose prose by use of a dictating machine.

For children first learning to write, the mechanics of the process clearly take up most of their mental capacity, and they have
little left over to devote to such concerns as content (Scardamalia
1980). When we see some ten-year-olds labouring like engravers
over their handwriting, we marvel that they are able to produce a
sentence that holds together, let alone a sentence that continues a
line of thought from the sentence before. You may get some idea
of what writing must be like for a child by trying to do some original writing with your wrong hand. You are likely to find it difficult to think very much beyond the word you are writing.

In time the mechanics of writing, like those of driving, become
sufficiently practised so that they no longer take much mental

capacity. The process by which this happens is called 'automatization', a term clearly applicable to the lower-level skills of writing. If you decide to write the word 'contrary', its spelling and the way to form its letters in script come automatically, requiring no attention or conscious direction at all. There seems to be a loose sort of progression upward in the writing skills that become automatized. Handwriting starts to become automatic even while children are still having to deliberate on the spelling of many words; at the time when spelling of common words and end punctuation are well automatized, interior punctuation continues to require conscious attention;[2] automatization of syntax proceeds from common to less common forms, with certain complex constructions probably always requiring mental capacity.

As automatization proceeds, the crucial question becomes, what does the student do with surplus mental capacity as it becomes available? One possibility is that mental capacity will not be put to any purposeful use at all. Students may dawdle, daydream, or simply *rest* while they continue to grind out text by largely automatic processes. These would be cases of extremely low motivation. While such cases may be common in school writing instruction, they do *not* represent what we mean by being on the low road. Students in such a state have obviously pulled off to the side of whatever road they might be on.

For students who do apply their leftover mental capacity to the writing activity, there are two main ways they can do it, and these two ways distinguish between the low road and the high road. In the low-road way, mental capacity is applied exclusively to the task at hand. The student tries to do efficiently and well what the task is already understood to require. The emphasis is on streamlining the process, eliminating errors, and achieving a final product that 'does its job' as this job is conceived. There is nothing intrinsically disreputable about this approach. It is how most of us go about acquiring skill at most of the things we do, be it washing dishes, shovelling snow from sidewalks, paying the monthly bills, doing statistical calculations, or finding references in libraries. It is not, however, how we approach those activities that we consider central to our professional or mental lives. For those, if we are truly bent on professional or intellectual excellence, we choose the high road.

The high road: writing as a self-constructed problem

On the high road, mental capacity is continually being channelled into changing the nature of the task. Let us assume that at some early stage in learning to write there is no discernible difference between the low road and the high road. For all children the task is simply to get down on paper, in an acceptable form, the language that comes into their minds. This does not mean that what comes to mind is free association. If there is a topic on which the child already feels some urge toward self-expression and if the child already possesses an appropriate mental scheme (e.g. a story grammar) for shaping discourse on the topic, then the language that comes to mind may lead to quite coherent writing. The point is that the language does 'come to mind'. If it doesn't, as may happen with a difficult or readily exhausted topic, the child will not be able to write. The child doesn't at this stage have the means or capacity to bring language to mind through mental effort. Mental effort, as we have noted, goes instead into producing the written transcription of language. This is the age when we see children dictating to themselves (Simon 1973). We might take self-dictation as a crude indicator of a heavy commitment of mental capacity to transcription. If so, we may conclude that it is around grades 3 or 4 that transcription ceases to hog all the capacity and that, accordingly, children can begin to think about something else at the same time that they are writing down words.

Children on the high road, we believe, start to think about what they are writing down on paper as having relations to various other things in their minds. Most importantly, they may begin to see that there is a relationship, and not necessarily an identity, between what they write and what they mean. Accordingly, they may begin to devote mental effort toward enhancing this relationship. Attending to this relationship does not just become an additional part of the writing task, it in a very important sense reconstitutes the whole task. Writing becomes a task of representing meaning rather than of transcribing language. This immediately makes writing a much more difficult task and sets the writer off on a road that increasingly diverges from the transcription of language come freely to mind.

There are other relationships which, when taken into account, further transform the writing task. There is the relationship between the meaning represented in the writing and the meaning a reader of different bias or background will extract. Cultivating this relationship leads to reconstituting writing as a communication task. There is the relationship between the way one has represented a meaning and other possible ways of representing it in writing. Work on this relationship leads to incorporating conscious attention to style as a part of the writing task. And then there is the relationship between the meaning one has recorded and other possible meanings that might have grown out of a larger context of meaning. To focus on this relationship is to use writing as a way of advancing one's own thinking, and this again transforms the task radically.

In an earlier paper (Bereiter 1980), it was suggested, with much reservation, that there might be an orderly progression from one of these formulations of the writing task to the next. We have not traced individual children longitudinally, but the findings of Donald Graves, who has, would indicate that there are qualitative stage shifts in individual children that form coherent scenarios. We do not see any reason to believe, however, that either the high road or the low road may be described by a fixed sequence of milestones. It is the overall direction of mental activity that distinguishes the two roads.

Individual children on the high road keep incorporating new relational considerations into the writing task and thus keep reconstituting the task at a higher, more complex level. But they do this in their individual ways, and certainly with little help from a curriculum, and so order and emphasis are quite variable. Some adult informants tell us they fastened early onto the idea that writing was learning. Regardless of what the school writing assignment might call for, they incorporated its requirements into the more comprehensive task of doing a piece of writing from which they might learn something interesting or useful. This doesn't mean they ignored or subverted the assignment, but that they enlarged upon it or, more precisely, subsumed it under an assignment of their own creation. Other informants precociously defined the writing task in relation to audience (the teacher, of course). But this meant quickly going beyond the idea that pleasing the teacher consisted merely of writing correctly. They recognized the teacher as a human being capable of being amused, confused, bored, etc. and so they began to incorporate into the writing task a panoply of audience-related considerations. Although eventually all writers who travel the high road must, we suppose, incorporate all the same major dimensions into their constructions of the writing task, differences in detail and emphasis must be enormous. Surely the exuberant variation among writers, all of whom could be judged to be products of the high road, must indicate that for different ones of them writing is a markedly different kind of task in its overall construction. This is only reasonable, given that they have each constructed the task by themselves. It is writers along the low road who tend to be much alike; and this too is reasonable, given that for them the task of writing has been defined externally.

The low road: writing as knowledge telling

What happens to students on the low road, once they begin to have mental resources to spare, not taken up with transcription? We know a great deal more about students on the low road, because there are so many of them. As transcription ceases to be so much of an obstacle, children shift most of their attention to the next big obstacle to fluent writing, content generation. This problem is viewed by them as 'thinking of what to write next', there being at this point no very functional distinction in their minds between an idea and the language in which it is expressed. Students in the middle school years will seize eagerly on any device that will help them think of more to write. We have found this to be true when providing them with sentence openers, word lists (including lists they generate themselves), and cues to types of text elements. Even a format for analysing audience characteristics was taken up by them as a way of generating more content ideas. Undoubtedly students are learning by themselves during these years various strategies for solving the 'next sentence' problem. One frequently noted is the 'running jump' strategy, which consists of rapidly rereading the text produced so far and using the acquired momentum, as it were, to launch themselves into the next sentence.

Overcoming the content-generation problem typically gives rise to a new problem. Having acquired the ability to generate text freely, students tend to ramble. Some low-road writers live happily with this fault, of course, but others are forced, either by teachers or their own awareness, to confront it as a problem. Possibly low-road students come to recognize rambling as a problem because it interferes with one of their top-priority goals, namely, getting the job done. Rambling is, of course, more a symptom than a fault. It shows lack of an overall rhetorical purpose and plan for a composition. But the creation of such a plan, even the creation of a well-elaborated purpose, requires a great investment of mental capacity and, indeed, presupposes that one is on the high road and already well advanced along it. Students on the low road must, accordingly, find more expedient ways to cope with rambling. One handy way is the topic outline (not the sentence outline). Since the topic outline requires considering only what you will write about and not what you will say, it can be produced with only a modest investment of mental effort. Adhering to such an outline will not altogether solve the rambling problem, but it keeps it in bounds and creates an overall impression of planfulness that serves to hide incoherence at deeper levels. Another strategy available to the more fluent of low-road writers is to ramble freely and then cut during revision. Both of these low-road strategies, it may be noted, come highly recommended by school and college composition texts.

Many other problems and obstacles may be encountered along the low road to writing competence. For some students, in fact, the problems can be devastating. Mina Shaughnessy (1977) showed over what a range of problems this is true for students whose spoken dialect deviates greatly from the written standard. Students with perceptual-motor handicaps may also have a very hard time, because they have to keep investing mental capacity in handwriting and spelling long after these functions have become largely automatized in other students. Students hampered by problems of dialect, perceptual-motor handicap, low reading ability, and so on, may in normal curricula have no choice but to take the low road. The high road would simply require more mental capacity than they can afford to spare from coping with the elementary demands of written language production.[3] Our concern in this paper, however, is with students who do have a choice.

Students on the high road and the low road end up dealing with many of the same matters — audience considerations, purpose, organization, coherence, style, etc. The difference is that for students on the low road all these are obstacles to be overcome, to be handled in such a way that they no longer take much time or thought. For students on the high road these are not obstacles but properties of the task, and their aim is not to minimize them but to unify them into a coherent task construction so that they may be dealt with as parts of a whole rather than piecemeal.

We have already mentioned the diversity among people on the

high road. There is diversity among those on the low road too, of course, most of it having to do with how far they are along the road. People who progress far enough along the low road may develop into quite capable writers, since they will have learned how to deal with all the major requirements of writing — readability, interest, organization, etc. However, since the goal of people on the low road is coping, low-road people are likely to settle on certain common optimizing strategies and therefore to write like one another more so than people on the high road.

A common low-road strategy that we see developing in school children is one we call the 'knowledge telling' strategy. Imagine memory to be a filing cabinet. (This is not a very good metaphor for most purposes, but modern theories do attribute some filing-cabinet-like properties to memory and it is just these properties that are significant in the present context.) Executing a writing task then, consists essentially of selecting a file appropriate to the task and telling what is in it. For most narrative and expository writing, the telling can be a simple report, guided by the way items are already organized in the file. Sometimes, as in writing an opinion essay, a special selection criterion must be applied in going through the file. For instance, if you are trying to argue that guns should be banned, you do not indiscriminately report everything that is in your gun knowledge file but instead you go through the file selectively and report items that imply something unfavourable about ownership of guns. Failure to maintain such a selection criterion can lead to this sixth-grade gem of knowledge telling:

> People should not be allowed to have guns because they could be dangerous if they did not know how to use them. But if people know how to use them they could have guns. Guns are sometimes used to kill people or things. Some hunters use them for killing animals. The animals they kill are deer, rabbits, fox, and birds. People should not have guns because some people use them for the wrong purpose. People should not have guns because it does not look right and it is not safe. You usually can't have guns unless you have a license. It is against the law if you don't have a license. If you don't you get charged or get your gun taken away. People use •guns for robbing banks or robbing jewelry stores or even grocery stores. People use guns for defending their selves and for show on their walls. They are mostly used for hunting in woods or on the lake shooting at ducks. Some people use them for shooting at people for being on their property. Some people use them for shooting at targets. But I think it is not safe to have a gun unless you know how to use one.

Holding on to a criterion of relevance to the point one is trying to make will result in a much more coherent composition, like the following one, also from grade 6:

> People who use guns, to hunt animals, should have a license and they should not kill them and leave them. Most people who have guns are very careful with what they are shooting at, but some other people are not. Murders most often happen with guns and I think that the people who use guns to kill other people should have their guns taken away and they should be put in jail. Police always have guns with them, but they are hardly ever use them unless they are in a situation where they have to. Guns sometimes are very necessary, but in this world, we could live without them, so I think that people should not own guns. Help to keep Canada a peaceful country.

Although this composition is quite a step up from the first one, it is still clearly the product of a 'knowledge telling' strategy. It consists basically of a string of items drawn from the file and commented on. Its superiority over the first comes from greater selectivity. In the last sentence, however, we may observe the writer closing her gun knowledge file and taking a larger view of the topic. This is still consistent with the 'knowledge telling' strategy and represents one of the refinements one sees developing around grade 6. It consists, if we may pursue the filing cabinet analogy, in moving up to the level of the filing cabinet instead of the file folder and saying something about one of its major categories — hence, drawing on a knowledge item of greater generality than those used in the body of the composition.

The 'knowledge telling' strategy is extremely efficient compared to its high-road alternatives. Generally, a high-road strategy starts with analysis and elaboration of a rhetorical problem and then draws on knowledge from a variety of files. This knowledge, moreover, is not simply reported but is used in strategic ways to accomplish the rhetorical objective. (See Hayes and Flower 1980; Flower and Hayes 1980.) Although this high-road approach has much greater potential for literary excellence, it is also obviously much more demanding of mental capacity and more susceptible to break-downs. The 'knowledge telling' strategy, on the other hand, is in its primitive form easy enough for beginning writers to handle. Moreover, it lends itself to gradual refinement. Thus, instead of indiscriminate knowledge reporting, the low-road student may add an interest criterion. By reporting only items meeting this criterion, an expository essay of some reader appeal may be produced. By introducing a 'best reasons' criterion, a more persuasive opinion essay may be achieved. With sufficient refinements the low-road strategy can achieve writing comparable to most of what people on the high road can produce.

What is wrong with the low road?

We have tried to make it clear that being on the low road does not mean becoming a bad writer. It means never becoming a superb writer, but one could argue that those who have the makings of superb writers will manage somehow to find the high road themselves. Certainly one could argue against subjecting all students to the rigours of the high road if in the end it only matters to those who will write professionally. We would agree that if one takes a purely pragmatic view of writing, seeing it as nothing more than a communication skill, then the low road is not only acceptable, it might even be preferred.

But we should not get the idea that the low road is a primrose path. Writing is a painful, anxious experience for many people, and most of those people are on the low road. People on the high road have their difficulties, but since the difficulties are largely of their own construction, they tend to feel in charge of them, to experience them as challenges and, when skill increases, as opportunities for gratifying accomplishment. To people on the low road the task of writing is defined externally and problems, also, are experienced as coming at them from outside, unpredictable as to magnitude. If they are not confident of their skill, people on the low road see writing as outside their control, full of menace. The road of 'coping with the task', in other words, does not necessarily lead to comfortable coping.

Our principal objection to the low road, however, is that it keeps writing from having a role in a person's mental life. Low-road writing is used to communicate thoughts and knowledge, but it serves at most a clerical role in the development of thought and knowledge. High-road writing, on the other hand, plays a central role in mental life. Because it is such a massive integrative process and because its dimensions reflect the dimensionality of intellect itself, writing becomes for many people the organizing force in their mental development. Conversation can be a powerful generator of thought and knowledge, but its outputs are social products, negotiated meanings. We do not truly own our thoughts or experience until we have negotiated them with ourselves, and for this writing is the prime medium. We will go so far as to say that people who know only the low road of writing do not have a mental life in the same sense that people on the high road do. As we have argued elsewhere at length, (Bereiter and Scardamalia, in press), the development of such a mental life, in which mental effort is continually directed toward the construction of meanings, is the primary responsibility of modern education.

How can students be shifted to the high road?

Most students — it is just a guess, but we would say over 90 per cent — are on the low road to writing competence. Writing instruction, understandably enough, is geared to them. Teachers play into and support the 'knowledge telling' strategy, striving through suggestions, criticisms, and examples, to get students to refine the strategy. Through pre-writing activities, conferences, and through encouraging procedures of topic outlining and free-writing, they help students avoid the mental burden of considering several aspects of the writing task simultaneously. Proposals for reform seldom have anything to do with getting students off the low road. They have to do either with accelerating progress along it or with enhancing the meaningfulness of the experience. Clearly, it will not be easy to produce any major change in this situation. Any substantial changes at all are likely to be sporadic.

One of the few lines of reform that seems to be aimed at getting children heading onto the high road is found in the work of Donald Graves, primarily in his use of 'conferencing', (see, for example, Graves 1973, 1979 and especially Graves forthcoming). As we see Graves's conferencing approach, it involves the teacher as an active, though limited collaborator in the composing process. The teacher's collaboration does not extend to supplying content or language, but it does extend to conceptualizing the writing task at a higher and more integrative level than the child has done and helping the child to operate in light of that conceptualization. It also seems that some of the negotiation which, in the high-road writer, goes on between writer and text, goes on here between child, teacher, and text. Thus the child is at least exposed to, and may actually participate in, the sort of problem reformulation that is the mark of high-road mental activity. It remains to be established experimentally how readily children will transfer this cooperative mental activity into activity that they carry out independently. The progression from do-it-with-help to do-it-alone is a time-honoured one in pedagogy, but when it is applied to purely mental activity it is sure to take considerable sensitivity on the part of the teacher.

While we are prepared to believe that Graves's approach *can* work to get at least some children headed on to the high road, we doubt if very many teachers can be found to make it work in this way. Besides requiring sensitive individual instruction that is hard for even very talented teachers to achieve in the one-to-many classroom situation, it has an additional requirement that immediately eliminates the great bulk of elementary school teachers. The requirement is that teachers be on the high road themselves (and note that this is different from merely saying that they should be good writers). Somehow, if there is to be a change that gets much beyond the each-one-teach-one level, we must find ways to foster movement onto the high road that do not require teachers who are already there themselves.

Notes

1. See, for instance, Case (1974) and Simon (1972).
2. We would even go so far as to conjecture that, in setting off material with commas, placement of the first comma becomes automatized before placement of the second, which accounts for the frequent omission of the latter by people who know perfectly well that the commas should be there.
3. There may be at least partly effective ways around this barrier, such as through expressive verse (Kohl 1967).

3 New starts and different kinds of failure

H.G. Widdowson

In my experience writing is usually an irksome activity and an ordeal to be avoided whenever possible. It seems to require an expense of effort disproportionate to the actual result. Fortunately for my self-esteem, this experience is a common one. Most of us seem to have difficulty in getting our thoughts down on paper. Certainly T.S. Eliot did, whose poem *East Coker* provides me with my title:

> . . . every attempt
> Is a wholly new start and a different kind of failure.
> Because one has only learnt to get the better of words
> For the thing one no longer has to say, or the way in which
> One is no longer disposed to say it.

Of course, Eliot was referring to the writing of poetry. But one does not have to be a poet biting the truant pen to suffer the agonies of written composition. To be sure, if one is simply dropping a line to relatives or writing a letter in conformity with established routines there is much less of a problem. This affords us a clue to the difficulty, which I will return to a little later. For the moment let us note that getting the better of words in writing is commonly a very hard struggle. And I am thinking now of words which are in one's own language. The struggle is all the greater when they are not.

Why should writing present such difficulties? And what exactly *are* these difficulties? They are clearly not linguistic in any straightforward sense since they are not solved by the acquisition of linguistic competence. What I want to do in this paper is to consider possible answers to these questions and so to define the objectives that the teaching of writing should aim to achieve.

I will begin by stating the obvious. Writing is a communicative activity and so is carried out in accordance with certain general principles which underlie the use of language in communication. We may move towards a specification of what these might be by considering what happens when language is put to communicative use in spoken interaction.

A is conversing with B. The conversation involves the engagement of two kinds of knowledge: knowledge of linguistic rules and knowledge of the world of fact and social convention. To the extent that such knowledge is shared, the interaction will proceed satisfactorily. If there is a lack of shared *linguistic* knowledge there will be an increasing reliance placed on shared *world* knowledge, and the reverse. If A does not know B's language, communication is clearly going to be a difficult business. Not impossible though. It is surprising what can be achieved if the interlocutors share a knowledge and view of the world and are motivated by common or congruent interests and intentions.

Thus pidgin languages arise to facilitate and extend contacts and collaboration already established without a common language. They do not spring immediately into being. And as lovers know, there can be communion without overt communication and then no words are needed. So it is that John Donne and his mistress achieve understanding by silence:

> Our soules, (which to advance their state,
> Were gone out,) hung 'twixt her, and mee,
> And whil'st our soules negotiate there,
> Wee like sepulchrall statues lay;
> All day, the same our postures were,
> And wee said nothing, all the day.
>
> (*The Extasie*)

Unfortunately, we cannot entirely rely on the congruence of the world view and the negotiation of souls (although, as we shall see, negotiation of a different kind does have a central role to play). We must grant that a lack of a shared language is normally a serious impediment to communication, while noting, nevertheless, that a shared language is not a necessary condition of interaction. A common language by no means guarantees mutual understanding. It provides the means whereby a context of shared world knowledge and social convention can be created. But such a creation of context is not always easy to accomplish. If A and B share the same knowledge of linguistic rules, they have the possibility of establishing a common frame of reference, but they will need to work at it and failure is frequent.

The point I am trying to make (and in the attempt illustrating the difficulty I am trying to explain) is that communication is a matter of transferring information of various kinds from the context of A's world knowledge to that of B and that linguistic rules *facilitate* the transference. They are a means to an end not an end in themselves. It is not enough to have a knowledge of linguistic rules: one also needs a knowledge of how to use them. Consider a simple example of what Schegloff (1972) refers to as 'formulating place'. Suppose that in the course of a conversation, A asks B:

Where do *you* live?

What is B likely to reply? We cannot say, of course, because we have no information about the frame of reference that has been set up between them. We know what the sentence means, but we do not know what the speaker means. The utterance may occur in the context of a discussion on the relative advantages of urban and rural life, for example, and in this case B will interpret it as referring to a type of locality and perhaps reply:

I live in the country.

A different reply, like:

I live in Townsend Road

would relate to a different frame of reference (cf. Van Dijk 1977, Chapter 5). It would be informative but not relevant. On the other hand, if A and B have established that they live in the same town and B is making reference to where *his* house is, then a reply like:

I live in Townsend Road

would be relevant. It might not, however, be sufficiently informative. In that case, A and B might have to build up a frame of reference which makes it so. For example:

A: Where do *you* live?
B: Townsend Road.
A: Where's that?
B: Off Charles' Street.
A: Near the cemetery?
B: That's it.
A: I know.

Alternatively, B might himself take the initiative in frame making:

A: Where do *you* live?
B: Townsend Road.
A: Where's that?
B: Do you know where the cemetery is?

A: Yes.

B: Do you know Charles' Street?

A: Yes.

B: Well Townsend Road is just off that.

A: Right.

What A and B are doing here is using linguistic rules to negotiate an effective transfer of information, to achieve a convergence of knowledge. Notice that the negotiation ends not when the meaning of the expression is precisely specified but when the interlocutors are satisfied that they know enough to serve their purposes. This is a crucial point. In communication we are not concerned with what an expression means but with what the producer of the expression means by using it, and the receiver will only negotiate that meaning to the extent that he needs to: once he feels satisfied that for the purposes of the interaction there is sufficient convergence of knowledge then he will close the negotiation. This means that communication is always relative to purpose. It is never precise but is always only approximate.

An attempt to achieve precision beyond communicative requirements will in fact tend to disrupt the interaction. In Garfinkel (1972) there is a demonstration of this. Garfinkel instructed students to 'engage an acquaintance or a friend in an ordinary conversation and, without indicating that what the experimenter was asking was in any way unusual, to insist that the person clarify the sense of his commonplace remarks'. The following is one of the results:

> On Friday night my husband and I were watching television. My husband remarked that he was tired. I asked, 'How are you tired? Physically, mentally, or just bored?'
>
> S(ubject)   I don't know, I guess physically, mainly.
>
> E(xperimenter)   You mean your muscles ache or your bones?
>
> S)   I guess so. Don't be so technical.
>
> (*After more watching*)
>
> S)   All these old movies have the same kind of old iron bedstead in them.
>
> E)   What do you mean? Do you mean all old movies, or some of them, or just the ones you have seen?
>
> S)   What's the matter with you? You know what I mean.
>
> E)   I wish you would be more specific.
>
> S)   You know what I mean! Drop dead!
>
> (Garfinkel 1972, p. 7)

But this, you may say, is an example of ordinary casual conversation, commonplace talk, where there is of course no premium on precision. What about kinds of communication like that of scientific exposition which require a more exact conveyance of information? Even in these cases, exactitude is only relative to particular communicative requirements and much must be left unspecified. And here I can cite the philosopher Karl Popper in my support:

> ... the idea of a precise language, or of precision in language, seems to be altogether misconceived. . . . *The quest for precision is analogous to the quest for certainty*, and both should be abandoned.
>
> I do not suggest, of course, that an increase in the precision of, say, a prediction, or even a formulation, may not sometimes be highly desirable. What I do suggest is that *it is always undesirable to make an effort to increase precision for its own sake — especially linguistic precision — since this usually leads to loss of clarity*, and to be a waste of time and effort on preliminaries which often turn out to be useless, because they are bypassed by the real advance of the subject: *one should never try to be more precise than the problem situation demands*.
>
> (Popper 1976, p. 24 — emphasis as in the original)

It is in fact, self-defeating to strive for precision in language use beyond the requirements of the communicative occasion: a point which, as language teachers, we do not always bear in mind.

I am suggesting then that communication by means of language involves the use of linguistic rules to negotiate the transfer of information and so to extend an already existing area of shared knowledge of fact and convention. The success of the transfer is to be measured by reference to the extent that it satisfies the recipient's requirements for the information. Meaning, in this view, is a function of the interaction between participants which is mediated through the language. I will refer to this process as *discourse*. The language used to mediate the process can be recorded or transcribed and studied in detachment. This I will refer to as *text*: the overt trace of an interaction, which can be used as a set of clues for reconstituting the discourse. It is our only source of evidence about the linguistic rules used in the mediation of meaning.

But the text will not reveal how these rules are actually realized in the discourse process. It will indicate *what* rules were used but not how they were used, it will reveal what linguistic knowledge the participants have but not how this knowledge is actualized as communicative behaviour. Thus if we record an interaction we can subsequently note how the resultant text manifests certain syntactic features, how it illustrates the use of cohesive devices as discussed in Halliday and Hasan (1976) and the resources available in the language for organizing information so as to ensure propositional development across linguistic units. But text will not itself reveal the plans (Miller, Galanter and Pribram 1960) which have to be implemented to achieve the complex communicative task, nor which of these plans have been automated as routines in long term memory. Clearly the native speaker is not making conscious choices when he operates the basic rules of syntax: if he did his working short term memory would be too overburdened to make conceptual connections with his existing knowledge and so would be unable to service the discourse process (Levelt 1975). It has to be borne in mind that a focussing on linguistic forms as such will tend to inhibit the natural use of these forms for communicative purposes. The language learner has somehow to learn them so that they make no claims on his attention when he is using them. This, I think, has always been a central problem of language-teaching pedagogy. We might agree that what the learner needs to acquire is fluency in a foreign language rather than accuracy in its manipulation (Brumfit 1979). But if fluency is to be an ability within competence and not simply a facility of performance, it has to be sustained by linguistic knowledge which can be assessed by measures of accuracy and which can be held in reserve as a back-up resource for occasions when repair is needed in communicative activity. Fluency and accuracy are complementary and interdependent phenomena: the problem is to know how the dependency works in natural language use and how it can best be developed in the process of language learning.

So far I have been making reference to spoken communication. I want now to turn to writing. And I want to suggest that written discourse too represents an interactive process of negotiation. But whereas in spoken discourse this process is typically overt and reciprocal, in written discourse it is covert and non-reciprocal. Thus in a spoken exchange the participants alternate in open negotiation of meanings, as we have seen, each taking turns to contribute to the interaction. The writer, however, is solitary; the person to whom he wishes to transfer information is absent and often, to some degree, unknown. This means that the writer has to conduct his interaction by enacting the roles of both participants. Since there is no possibility of immediate reaction he has to anticipate what it is *likely* to be and provide for any possible misunderstanding arising from a lack of shared knowledge. The writer, then, has a basic conveyancing problem: he has certain information to impart for some illocutionary or perlocutionary purpose — to inform, to impress, to direct action and so on but he has to prepare the ground and set up conditions favourable to the reception of such information. He does this by continually shifting his function from initiator to recipient, from 'speaker' as it were, to 'hearer', enacting the interaction by playing the role of each participant. Consider an example: here is a text from Gombrich's *Art and Illusion*. (1961, p. 41)

> The Greek revolution deserves its fame. It is unique in the annals of mankind. What makes it unique is precisely the directed efforts, the continued and systematic modifications of the schematic of conceptual art, till making was replaced by the matching of reality through the new skill of mimesis.

This can be derived from the following discourse:

> *The Greek revolution deserves its fame.*
> Why?
> *It is unique in the annals of mankind.*
> In what way unique?
> *What makes it unique is precisely the directed efforts, the continued and systematic modifications of the schematic of conceptual art, till making was replaced by the matching of reality through the new skill of mimesis.*

Or again: this time a text from Gregory's *Eye and Brain*: (1977, p. 27)

> Almost every living thing is sensitive to light. Plants accept the energy of light, some moving to follow the sun almost as though flowers were eyes to see it. Animals make use of light, shadows, and images to avoid danger and to seek their prey.

This can be derived from the following discourse:

> *Almost every living thing is sensitive to light.*
> Give me an example.
> *Plants accept the energy of light, some moving to follow the sun almost as though flowers were eyes to see it.*
> You said almost every living thing. What about other examples?
> *Animals make use of light, shadows, and images to avoid danger and to seek their prey.*

And so the discourse is enacted by the writer shifting roles and so anticipating reactions like 'What do you mean?' 'So what?' 'Can you be more explicit?' 'Can you give an example?' and so on.

I have said that this conducting of covert interaction fulfils the essential conveyancing function of the discourse process. But it can also change the character of the information the writer wishes to convey. For although he may start out with some fairly clear idea of what he wishes to say, the very interactive process he enacts continually provides him with a different point of view which may yield insights and cognitive connections which he would not otherwise have perceived. The interaction not only *facilitates* the conveyance of information but also *generates* the thinking process. So it is that in writing one so frequently arrives at a destination not originally envisaged, by a route not planned for in the original itinerary. It is worth noting that when we instruct students to draw up a plan of an essay before writing and then to conform to it closely as they write we may be inhibiting the interactive process that generates written discourse.

The result of this discourse, this covert non-reciprocal interaction, is a text: words on a page. But written text differs from spoken text in a number of ways. For one thing, spoken text is of its nature transient and can only be recorded by outside intervention. When it is made permanent by tape or transcription some idealization interferes so that it is only a partial record of the discourse. In the case of written text, it represents a record not made by an outside third person observer but by the active first person participant. In this respect it is a true record. As far as it goes. For, of course, it usually represents only part of the discourse: it does not as a rule reveal the second person reactions which the writer anticipates by enacting the other participant's role, as it were, by proxy. There are, of course, exceptions. In some kinds of discourse, significantly those whose purpose is simple exposition, we find some textual record of the second person side of the interaction. The following, for example, comes from a popular account of the laws of physics:

> The law of conservation of energy says simply that in any isolated system the total amount of energy remains unchanged.
> *Is this true in the examples we have so far?* Take the case of the two balls recoiling elastically from a collision ... We saw that the balls' total kinetic energy was the same after the collision as before. *But what about the situation at the instant of collision?* At that instant both balls are stopped dead. In other words they have no kinetic energy. *Where has that gone?*
>
> (Milton A. Rottman *The Laws of Physics*)

One way, indeed, of characterizing the difference between

types of writing would be by reference to the degree to which the discourse is textualized. The textual record is never, however, complete: the vicarious second person contribution is always left to some extent presupposed.

Written text, then does not generally record the interaction itself but only the result of it. When the reader comes along, therefore, he has to create an interaction from the partial record provided: he has to convert the text into a discourse. The extent to which the reader's discourse corresponds to that of the writer will depend on a number of factors, some of which I will mention presently. For the moment let us note that written text is of its nature an accurate record of the writer's first person activity in the discourse he enacts although this does not therefore determine the reader's second person activity in discourse he derives from such text.

There is another difference between spoken and written text that it is important to mention. Spoken text is a direct and immediate linguistic reflection of the actual interactive process and is simply contingent on the discourse. Once a particular discourse is enacted in spoken exchange, its traces in text disappear unless recorded for some particular reason — for later analysis for example. So, in spoken exchange, the text as such does not matter to the participants: it is simply the consequence of the discourse. We do not usually concern ourselves unduly with fashioning spoken text because we recognize its temporary and non-recurrent character and we concentrate on the discourse process rather than the textual product. Hence spoken text tends to be untidy, to exhibit syntactic irregularities, incomplete and overlapping expressions, false starts and so on. With written text, however, the case is different. This is of its nature a record made by an actual participant to be used for the recreation of discourse. The text is not contingent but essential and must have existence beyond the discourse which it records. It is therefore an artefact, deliberately fashioned for the use of others. As such it has to meet certain standards of social acceptability. This means that it has to be tidy, correct, well formed. It must keep up appearances. The writer not only has to design his text so that it effectively records his participation in discourse and provides for the interaction of the reader, but also that it conforms to correct linguistic etiquette. Accuracy, in this way, becomes a necessary condition for fluency.

Of course, as with any other kind of social behaviour, constraints of correctness will vary in their force depending on the public one is exposing oneself to. The writer will be aware of them to a greater or lesser extent, according to who he judges his prospective readers will be. To return to a point I made at the beginning, one is not likely to agonize over correct textual composition when dropping a line to relatives. Writing a letter to *The Times* is a very different matter and might well involve reference to a manual of English usage, the *Oxford English Dictionary* and *Roget's Thesaurus*. The more public and permanent character of print commands respect for what is socially acceptable.

It follows, I think, from the textual and discoursal character of writing that I have been describing that the writer is confronted with two kinds of task, and (to refer to my title) runs the risk of two different kinds of failure. Firstly, he has to conduct a covert interaction with a presumed interlocutor and record his first person participation in such a way that the reader will be able to derive a coherent discourse from it. He has to produce a text which has appropriate discourse potential. This means that he must follow the cooperative principle, as described in Grice (1975), even though there is no actual person to cooperate with. Thus, if he *over*-textualizes, he will fail by being verbose: if he *under*-textualizes, he will fail by being obscure. At the same time, he has to produce a text which conforms to standards of social acceptability and which is correct and cohesive as a linguistic artefact. So it is that the writer's rendering of discourse as text is so much more difficult than the reader's interpretation of the text as discourse. For the reader can afford to be cavalier in his treatment of text: he will derive from it whatever information will serve his purpose in reading and so he will frequently ignore the directions for following the discourse which the writer originally enacted on his behalf. Some of these directions will be irrelevant since they are based on assumptions about the knowledge and purpose of the reader which turn out not to be applicable in particular cases. Typically the reader will focus on lexical items inferring and predicting meanings by reference to what he already knows and what he needs to know. And he can do this, of course, at considerable speed. Effective reading as a normal social activity is not a matter of completeness or correctness but of convenience and adequacy. But the writer must plod on, making allowances for all kinds of possible reactions, designing well-formed textual patterns which the reader may well ignore. The reader can afford to focus on lexis, only turning his conscious attention to syntax when this strategy fails to yield the information he needs. For the writer, on the other hand, engaged as he is in correct text composition, syntax must always be there to reckon with.

Let me now try to relate this discussion to pedagogic matters. Learning to write involves learning how to cope with the two tasks I have described. In the first place the student has to learn how to conduct a non-reciprocal interaction by adopting a dual participant role, anticipating the reactions of a presumed interlocutor. He must be aware of the function of language as a device for negotiating the transfer of information by reference to shared knowledge. This means that the student should always have some idea of who he is meant to be interacting with, of what shared knowledge he can assume, including a knowledge of conventions of rhetorical organization which characterize different types of discourse. He should have some idea, too, of the purpose of the interaction. This involves relating the act of writing to some preceding situation. For in normal circumstances we do not just sit down to write when the spirit takes us. We are impelled to do so by some previous event or state of affairs: a political outrage that calls for a letter to the Editor, a lack of funds that requires a request to rich Aunt Maud. Writing is a provoked activity, it is located in ongoing social life. The act of writing is not a wholly new start (to refer again to my title): it is a continuation. So the student should know who he is meant to be addressing and why. These are, after all, normal conditions for writing, and without them there can be no basis for interaction. You cannot negotiate anything unless you know who you are negotiating with and for what purpose and unless you know the conventions of the particular kind of negotiation you are engaged on. If these necessary conditions are not provided, then the business of putting words on a page becomes not a social activity but a language exercise: a manifestation of linguistic rules for display and not a realization of linguistic rules for communication. If the student does not recognize writing as a fundamentally interactive enterprise, then he will be forced to produce text which has no derivation from discourse: a piece of language existing in isolation for its own sake. Production of text for its own sake is not writing as a communicative activity but simply an exercise in linguistic composition.

This interactive aspect of writing is likely, I think, to represent a different sort of difficulty for L1 learners than for second or foreign language learners. Learning to write one's own language involves a shift in mode of discourse, from one which is reciprocal interaction through spoken exchange to one which is non-reciprocal and covert. It has often been suggested that the principal difficulty in learning to read and write has to do with the recognition of sound-spelling correspondences: hence, for example, ita (the Initial Teaching Alphabet). My own feeling is that this transfer of textual medium is much less of a problem than the transfer of discourse mode that I have referred to. To put it another way, I think the main difficulty has to do not with how language is manifested but with how it is realized in communication. With foreign learners, however, it may be that the central problem *is* textual rather than discoursal. If the foreign learners have already learned how to write in their own language, then they will have acquired the essential interactive ability underlying discourse enactment and the ability to record it in text. Their problem is how to textualize discourse in a different language. The teacher's task here is to get the learners to exploit their knowledge of the discourse process, acquired through their mother tongue, by realizing it through the linguistic rules of English. It is important to note that adult foreign learners of English come to the classroom with a great deal of experience of how language in general is used in communication. If we deny them access to that experience by presenting them with a model of language which is not congruent with it, then we impose learning problems upon them of our own devising. We must accept the possibility that many learning difficulties derive from the very pedagogy that is designed to solve them.

The first task in the learning of writing, then, relates to the production of text as a reflection of the discourse process. The second relates to the production of text as an acceptable well-formed artefact. Here again, I think, we have a difference between mother tongue and other tongue situations. The social pressure to conform by producing correct text in one's own language is familiar to anyone who has been subjected to formal schooling. We are made to feel the stigma of incorrect spelling and grammar from our earliest years. In the L1 situation correctness of text has the character of correct social comportment. If you get it wrong, you are likely to suffer some loss of status and what you have to say may not be taken seriously. There can be severe consequences for not conforming. But in the foreign language situation these social constraints may have little or no force since they do not belong to the learner's own society. The language is not his own and is not enmeshed in social values. It therefore becomes extremely difficult to eradicate those errors in written text which do not reduce its effectiveness as a discourse record. If the foreign learner has no sense of the social propriety of correctness in the foreign language, as is typically the case, then he will obviously find it difficult to achieve. The teacher may cajole, the examination threaten, but the essential social pressure is absent. The second-language situation is perhaps a different matter since here the language to be learned does, by definition, have a role to play in social life so there is the possibility of the learner feeling obliged to adjust his linguistic behaviour to the accepted norms.

Perhaps this is an appropriate moment to make an observation about creative writing as a learning activity in relation to the points I have been making. Exercises in creative writing can no doubt be justified in a number of ways but it should be noted that they can lead to an avoidance of the central problem of interactivity as I have described it because they encourage communion with self rather than communication with others, and represent writing as a personal rather than a social activity. Furthermore, they cannot of their nature come to terms with the issues of acceptability since originality is, by definition, not constrained by conformity. There is no formal way of distinguishing between the deviation of unintended error and deliberate violation of rules for literary effect.

The two kinds of task I have tried to describe can be related to two aspects of language as social behaviour. On the one hand, language use is communicative: it involves the conveying of information by interactive negotiation. On the other hand, it is indexical: it involves the presentation of self as a social person, and so reveals the extent to which one's behaviour is socially acceptable. In producing written text the communicative aspect presents a difficulty because of the non-reciprocal character of the interaction; and the indexical aspect presents a difficulty because one has to be particularly careful of one's linguistic comportment.

But now another problem arises. I spoke earlier of how a knowledge of linguistic rules is automated so as to leave the mind free for higher order communicative operations. Effective communication commonly requires the unconscious manipulation of linguistic rules. The mind can then engage with conceptual organization and negotiation because the lower-level syntactic plans have been automated, pushed down into long term memory, below the threshold of immediate awareness. What this automation appears in part to involve is a kind of idiomization process, whereby linguistic patterns are stored in the memory as whole units with potential communicative function so that they do not need to be composed on each occasion of use. The mind acquires a set of adaptable clichés. But if writing requires particular attention to correctness, as I have suggested, then there is the problem that unless syntactic rules have been thoroughly automated, then mental resources will be so preoccupied with achieving linguistic correctness that there will be little spare capacity for communication. In this case, very common in the second and foreign language situation, there will be a focus on the text for its own sake and its discourse function will be neglected.

I have tried to indicate certain difficulties about writing and the different kinds of failure that can arise in consequence. How we might cope with them in teaching English as a foreign or second language is another question. We need, I think, to devise a methodology which focusses on the interactive character of writing and develops in the learner an ability to produce text which derives from discourse and provides for discourse recreation on the part of the reader (see Widdowson 1979, Paper 13). At the same time, text-producing activities of this kind should provide incidental linguistic practice so as to ensure the automation of syntax. Only when a measure of automation has been achieved can one turn to the tricky question of how one can set up conditions of social pressure which will persuade the learner of the importance of appearances and of the need to behave linguistically in accordance with accepted etiquette.

Dr Johnson tells us that:

A man may write at any time, if he will set himself doggedly to it.

Perhaps; but it will help a man (and a woman, too, we should add) to know what kind of task he must set himself to, so that his doggedness can be directed in some way. In this paper I have tried to define this task in the hope that such a definition might help in the development of an effective methodology for the teaching of writing.

Part Two
The development of writing abilities

In the vast literature on child development, there is a long tradition of studies of the acquisition of language. Studies of the development of writing ability, however, are much less common, and most of those that are regarded as standard in the field tend to focus rather narrowly on the acquisition of the syntax of written discourse: see, for example, Hunt 1965, 1970; Loban 1963, 1976; Harpin 1973. Such studies, and especially the first two, have had an enormous influence in North America on the kind of research that has been undertaken into the development of writing ability; some of this is reviewed within in the introduction to the section on text and discourse (Part Three) and in Kameen's and Witte's papers in that section (Chapters 10 and 11).

The study of the syntax of student writing, of course, is necessarily product-oriented. However, the most innovative work currently being conducted in the field of development is process-oriented. The dissatisfaction with the limits of a product-oriented view of writing which is so evident in the preceding section has led many researchers interested in the development of writing ability to look at the development itself from a process-oriented perspective. Such a perspective means in the first place that researchers must be in the classroom and observe what happens as children learn to write. Such studies are represented in this volume by Donald Graves's study being conducted in the Writing Process Laboratory of the University of New Hampshire in Durham, N.H., and more particularly in nearby schools, where Graves and his team for several years have been watching, describing, recording and videotaping what goes on in the classrooms to which they have access. What is going on there, as this paper and many others that have reported on aspects of this project show (Graves 1979; Calkins 1980; Sowers 1979) is as remarkable as it was unexpected. It is important to note that this study is not an experimental study: that is, what the pupils being observed by Graves and his co-workers do has not been structured by the New Hampshire team; they are not testing the effectiveness of particular pedagogical techniques or experimental situations that they have devised. They are simply describing what they see and hear and read. To some, it will seem that this study represents a triumph of the Hawthorne effect: subjects who participate in experiments often perform better than expected simply because they are being observed. Certainly these students are being observed, and are doing remarkably well; and their success may indeed be due in part to their teachers' success in creating an enabling environment in which such development can take place, not least because of the presence of this particular team of researchers. But the students are doing something that all students have to do at the beginning of the development of their writing abilities: they are learning how to extend their already partially established oral linguistic abilities so that they can handle the quite different requirements of the production of a written text.

This extension of linguistic ability from the oral medium to the written is examined with great subtlety in Bereiter and Scardamalia (1982). Once again it is an area which ought to be of interest in second-language studies, because what is involved in both cases may be seen as a transfer of skills which are already at least partly established: from oral to written in the first-language situation; from the first language to the second in the other situation. Jones (1980a, 1980b) has begun the study of such transfer in relation to the writing abilities of adult learners of English as a second language.

However, what is involved in the transfer of such abilities in adult second-language learning is probably a good deal simpler and more local than what happens when children begin to extend their first-language competence from the oral to the written medium. For children learning to write, the transfer typically begins very early, when competence in the oral medium of the native language is still far from fully established, and when, as well, many years of physical, intellectual, cognitive, emotional, and moral maturation still lie ahead. Obviously these various aspects of development, in their turn, interact in complex ways with the acquisition and development of writing abilities. For man is a symbol-making animal, and language is primarily symbolic. In growing up and coming to terms with our world, we represent experience and ideation to ourselves in language. This productive, rather than receptive view of the use of language (it derives, of course, from Susanne K. Langer), is fundamental in recent work on the place of writing in first-language education, especially in relation to the use of writing for learning and knowing. It is an easy step to extend that kind of emphasis from specific fields of study to life in general, and this is a step which has characteristically been taken by leading British theorists, in their emphasis on writing from the earliest years on, on writing across the curriculum, on writing not as a way of giving teachers an easy way to determine what has been learned but rather as a way of learning.

However, once such a view of the development of writing ability is adopted, the study of development comes to be much more complicated. Consequently most of those who are working in development have shown considerable impatience with the kind of description of surface properties of the written product that can be seen in most work on syntax. On the other hand, the broadening of the scope of inquiry which the process-oriented emphasis requires is difficult to achieve. Consequently most of those who approach development in this way have regarded their work as, in Britton's terms (1979, p. 34), 'essentially a descriptive stage, an attempt to provide instruments by which development might be traced'.

That quotation is Britton's description of the first stage of the Schools Council project on the development of writing abilities, 11–18, the published report on which (Britton *et al.* 1975) is the context for so much of the work in this whole book, and above all for the work in this section. Almost all the other work going on in this field starts from the Schools Council project, and is concerned to extend its implications in various directions. Amity P. Buxton, for example, has been exploring writing at the same early years that Graves studies, but uses a set of dimensions explicitly derived from Britton's, though also an extension of them (Buxton 1981). Freedman and Pringle have been undertaking related explorations of development at the post-secondary level (Freedman and Pringle 1980b). Others, however, have been concerned to extend not the age range of the Britton studies but their scope: in their different ways, Wilkinson, Kirby and Kantor, and Odell are all concerned with what aspects of maturation to measure other than those already examined by Britton, and with how to measure them (Chapters 5, 6, and 7).

Yet other studies have been concerned with a third aspect of development: how students learn over time to replicate success-

fully the details of a particular mode of discourse which is culturally transmitted, the story (see, for example, Bartlett 1981, 1982).
The formal properties of a story are something that students have
to internalize to some extent before they can replicate them in
their own writing and story-telling. It is noteworthy that this, like
the syntax of the language, is something that students have to
work out for themselves on the basis of models. Moreover, in
both cases there is evidence for a developmental progression
which is obviously much more than a simple linear sequence. In
the studies of first-language acquisition it is clear that what the
learner is capable of learning at particular stages of development
may be quite different from what is there to be found in the available models. Now classic studies of this phenomenon include
McNeill (1966) and Chomsky (1969). If the process of maturation
in first-language abilities, then, can be seen as an increasingly successful attempt to analyse and thus to reproduce the grammar of
the first language, it is clear that there are very rigid constraints
on what is possible at any stage, and also that the production is
controlled during the immediate stages by grammars that may be
quite different from the adult grammar. So it is, presumably, with
the cultural norm which is the 'grammar' of a story. But this
mode is only one among many modes which have particular
norms in our culture; in all of them the same recursive cycle of
tacit analysis, partial replication, further analysis, and improved
replication takes place. When to the acquisition of the requirements of all these norms is added the acquisition of all the other
societal norms implied in Wilkinson's and Odell's papers, the
complexity of the development of writing ability is awesomely
clear.

In contrast to the vast scope of developmental studies of learning to write English as a first language, most studies of the development of second-language writing ability have a very local
character. In the literature on teaching writing to illiterate adults
(often referred to as teaching 'literacy skills'), the focus has been
on teaching these skills rather than on their development in the
individual. Most teaching of writing in ESL has been to adult or
near-adult students who are literate. It has usually been assumed
(wrongly, no doubt) that they already know what the process of
writing is all about. Consequently developmental studies have
been limited virtually entirely to the kinds of relatively small-
scale experimental and descriptive studies concerned with the acquisition of some particular skill (or perhaps merely some par-

ticular syntactic structure) as the result of an experimental or pedagogical treatment. (Kameen's paper in Part Three is an example of such work). No doubt much more remains to be done in the second-language field as a whole. For example, work on the interlanguage hypothesis (Corder 1967, 1973; Richards 1971; Selinker 1972) indicates that a developmental approach may reveal far more about learners' errors than that they had been caused by insufficient time devoted to memorization of word lists and verb forms. All of this research would suggest a very different approach to teaching writing, in which written production would be seen as going through a number of stages in the developing interlanguage. Developmental studies of writing in English as a first language should assist in the growth of theoretical work in this aspect of teaching writing to non-native speakers of English. However, the nature of most of the ESL teaching that takes place (to adults or near adults, over a very short period of time) is such that it will never have the same scope as first-language studies.

Developmental studies of writing ability in a second or third language in children have largely been absent from the research so far. However, the growing use of second-language immersion as a means of second-language teaching in additive bilingual situations is in the process of creating yet another field of developmental studies which will complicate the description of both first and second-language acquisition of writing abilities. Although there is now an extensive literature on many different aspects of the consequences of immersion programmes, the study of their effect on the development of first-language writing abilities has hardly begun (cf. Lapkin 1979) and to our knowledge there has been no formal study of the acquisition of second-language writing ability through immersion programmes that extends beyond the level of spelling and surface grammatical competence.

4 The growth and development of first-grade writers

Donald H. Graves

Steve is in first grade. At 9.10 a.m. he starts his unassigned paper on 'Sliding' and doesn't finish until 10.20 a.m. Steve is an average first-grade writer with average first-grade abilities.

In the midst of page three of his ten page writing booklet, he turns to a friend and says, 'Know when I hit a tree? I go sliding off. I go right off the sled and I hit myself on the tree.' On the first two pages, Steve has written general comments about sliding on snow. Now on the third page he finds through drawing and writing what he wanted to write about. He points to the drawing and comments to his teacher, 'Right here I hit the tree and I slid down the rest of the way.'

His teacher responds, 'Do you want to tell your readers about that? What happened when you hit the tree?' For the next fifteen minutes Steve calmly adds information and rewrites the page where he hits the tree. He even excludes two other pages in his booklet he now feels are unnecessary.

Most manuals and language arts texts for teachers suggest that Steve won't be ready to compose for a least another year. Many reason that a thorough knowledge of phonics, as well as a strong sight vocabulary is necessary for children before they can write. Writing is an ordeal for most adults. As an act of kindness they would spare six-year-olds the pain of labouring through sounds and letters at a speed of less than one word per minute. If writing is provided for first-grade children it is reduced to writing captions, copying, placing words in blanks, or writing the simple sentence.

I have long said we underestimate what children can do in the writing process. I didn't know what I was talking about. There was no way I could anticipate the meaning of this statement until I had time and funds necessary to observe children like Steve in the midst of their composing. Children have a natural urge to express, to make marks, to 'play' with writing, to experiment boldly with new ways to put messages on paper. By denying children the opportunity to write before seven, we lose out on a stage of development when children can make some of the most rapid and delightful growth in writing of their entire lives.

Steve and his teacher are unaware that most school curriculum guides suggest the delay in writing. Steve writes anyway. When he writes, writing becomes an adventure that leads him into a highly elaborate process of problem solving.

Steve's teacher does not try to save him from problems in the writing process. She does not intrude with a long list of anticipated writing problems usually encountered by six-year-olds. Indeed, if Steve knew what they were he probably would resist any thought of writing at all. His strong intent to write the details of hitting a tree, and playful asides about 'whopping a big tree and falling off into the snow', carry him through most problems of spelling, space, and language.

Steve believes others are interested in his messages. His playful, self-centredness provides a protective cloak for fearless experimentation. He solves most problems important to him without the aid of the teacher. But, when help is needed, Steve's teacher waits until he is stymied by issues that thwart his purpose in writing. She plays this role effectively because she knows both the order and importance of developmental issues Steve needs to solve.

Steve is one of sixteen children involved in a study funded by the National Institute of Education to document how — and in what order — primary children change composing, spelling, and motor behaviours during the writing process. Eight of the children are in grade 1, another eight in grade 3. They will be followed from grade 1 to grade 2, and grade 3 to grade 4. Primary emphasis has been placed on gathering information when children are actually in the act of writing. In this way, the problem-solving activities of children can be charted from grades 1 to 4.

This study of children's composing is not a controlled design. Rather, it is a case study of sixteen children — in grades 1 and 3 — who were chosen because of their differences on a pre-selected developmental composing scale. The study seeks to identify and describe what is involved in composing for young children in order to explain the 'why' of their behaviours during the writing process.

Each day three full-time researchers are with the children in their public school classrooms, carefully recording data as the children compose. Composing is broadly viewed from the child's painting, drawing, working with crayons, pens, pencils, to the composing of second, third, even up to ten drafts of a single selection. The data come from collections of all forms of composing, direct observation and video recordings of the children while writing.

This paper focusses on what some first-grade children do when they compose, the problems they solve, and our preliminary findings on the orders in which they solve them. Representative cases like Steve will be chosen to report data across many children in the study. Although it may appear that only one case is reported at a time, the data have support from the practices of other study children from similar developmental levels.

Teachers want to understand the dimensions of a child's development in the writing process in order to respond appropriately to the child's intentions. How hard it is to respond! The writing process is complex and children's behaviours are legion. Some sectors of development can be chosen for observation over others, however, thus simplifying the meaning of children's writing practices. So far the most useful sectors to observe are: the child's transition from oral to written discourse, use of time and space, and change from overt to covert actions. Let us examine these dimensions.

Choosing topics

Most first-grade children operate in a very narrow time frame when first choosing their topics. Initially the topic is chosen almost as the child picks up the paper. This child has no more difficulty in choosing topics for composing than in choosing topics for play. Soon the time frame changes. There is more delay in topic choice. The delay increases and for a time some children encounter major barriers in topic choice. This comes with the child's first major consciousness of audience. If children are given many opportunities to write they gradually pass through this phase to being conscious of many writing options. During the composing of one paper, they are aware of several topics to choose for the next.

Less than one minute after Eddie sits in the writing centre, he is busy working on his next paper. Eddie does not wrestle with topic choice since he will continue with the same theme of the last three weeks, 'The Good Guys and the Bad Guys'. Eddie writes as he plays, choosing the same theme until he tires of the subject. With each paper, the 'Good Guys and the Bad Guys' fight all over again in both drawing and print with shooting between them until the good guys finally win.

Just as Eddie is about to draw, the researcher asks, 'What will happen here?' (pointing to the space for drawing).

'I don't know,' Eddie responds. He rarely knows beyond the next action couplet in the drawing. The gun is drawn, the gun shoots, the plane explodes. Eddie supplies the sound effects to go with each salvo. The next episode is drawn, and the next, until a whole series of shots and explosions end in victory for the good guys.

Steve is more advanced than Eddie. He sat in the writing centre for several minutes mumbling, 'I wonder what I should write about? Let's see now; I can't think of anything. Oh, I know, I'll write about sliding in the snow.' Steve began by writing the title on the cover page 'About Slading'. Unlike Eddie, Steve writes *before* he draws. He can also speak several sentences ahead of what he will write before he writes it. The illustrations confirm rather than serve as a rehearsal for the writing. For six-year-old children there is a stage when long delays indicate a point of advancement. A rough sequence for topic choice development is contained in the following:

1. No delay.	Child draws immediately and then writes.
2. Short delay — 2 minutes.	Child writes and then draws.
3. Long delay — 5–10 minutes; complete avoidance of writing.	Child is usually close to seven and beyond. Audience has effect on topic choice. Child is much more self-conscious.
4. Little delay.	Child is aware of growing repertoire of topic choice. Is able to rehearse topic choice prior to act of writing.

Six-year-old Sarah, represented in the third category above, has a difficult time choosing a topic. She may label the cover with a title but the theme simply does not develop. To this point, topic choices have been easy for Sarah. She wrote about five books each week (total 220 words) on a range of familiar themes.

Themes followed certain characters, 'Woodsy Owl', or 'Chipper', for as long as three to five episodes, disappeared and reappeared again for another series. The text assigned attributes to Chipper: 'Chipper is nice. Chipper is beautiful. Chipper is loveable, I love Chipper.' Children did not often understand her affective, subjective stories and told her so. But Sarah paid little heed to their responses.

It is now April and Sarah's playfulness has ended. It has ended as traumatically as a child who first thought she was playing with kittens in green pastures and suddenly discovers that the kittens are lions and she is imprisoned with them in a cage. Topic and word choices are hard to manage. She now *hears* the words of other children when they say, 'What are you writing? That doesn't make sense.' Now Sarah says, 'I don't know what to write about; writing is hard; I'd rather do a workbook.'

Sarah has just turned seven. She is an able reader. It is almost as if she has just discovered that mother and father are Santa Claus. The masks have been removed. Conventions, rules, the opinions of others, now dominate her consciousness. Play no longer insulates. The empty page is indeed empty.

Tim has made the transition through the third stage. Audience became a *gradual* part of his writing process. Tim writes on a wide range of topics from Wild West stories to a trip on his father's tug boat. He is conscious of audience and steadfastly defends his content from the challenges of other children. Tim hears their critiques, yet defends his choices with information. Note Tim's responses during this conference:

CHRIS: You should have told what happened after you got to the Cape Cod canal.

TIM: What do you mean?

CHRIS: Well, we don't know how you got home. You left us stranded at the Cape Cod canal.

TIM: But this isn't about how I got home. Look at the title; it's about a tug boat ride, dummy. The tug boat ride was over when we got to the canal.

In summary, audience does affect topic choice. For some young writers, choosing a topic to please oneself is an easy choice. It is as easy as choosing what to play after school. Then there is a time when choices are difficult. Most children make easy transitions when many audiences are provided in the classroom. But for children like Sarah, it was difficult for her to leave the strength of her own self-centredness. The knowledge of audiences arrived abruptly. Change was upsetting. When children make the transition to a growing sense of audience, topic choices become easier; they are more secure in defending their content to others.

Changes from speech to print

When children compose they show us how they make transitions from speech to print. There are many tracks of development that can be followed to show how children make the change. Only a few of the factors have been chosen for review here: drawing and rehearsal, use of space, use of speech to accompany writing.

Drawing and rehearsal

If Eddie doesn't know what he will draw beyond a first step, he surely does not know what he will write before he has drawn. Drawing is an important rehearsal step, not only for the rest of the drawing but especially for the writing that follows. Once created, the drawing becomes an idea bank as Eddie keeps referring to it for the substance of his writing.

The drawing also helps Eddie change from speech to print. When Eddie was playing next to Matt in the block area moments before, Matt knew what Eddie meant when he said, 'This is gonna be the secret part where we keep all the bombs.' Matt can see what Eddie means before the situation tells him. But when Eddie writes, he must supply words to describe the situation in which the message will fall. If Eddie can draw before he writes, he creates the setting for the print, thus helping both himself and Matt who will read the paper later.

Drawing helps Eddie maintain control of his subject. It aids the choice and development of his topic. When Eddie can draw and control his subject, he writes more, gains greater practice in writing, as well as provides the setting for the teacher to help him with his paper. Content in the drawings usually exceeds the content in the writing.

Not all children need to draw before they write. More advanced children, like Steve, use drawings *after* the text has been written to illustrate a scene selected from the writing below. Still more advanced children do not need to illustrate at all, since the drawing takes time from revisions and more extended work on the text.

Use of space

When children first write, they are merely concerned with the ingredients of the message, not the order or placement of words on the page. In the figure below, Toni's words rise and fall across the page, with no spaces to show word separation. Speech runs together like 'hamaneggs' and rises and falls with pitch, stress, and intonation.

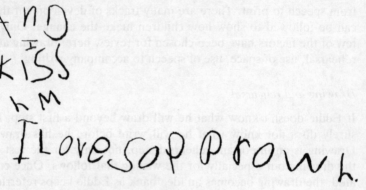

Translation: I love super owl and I kiss him.

Note Toni's message: 'I love super owl and I kiss him'. In this message Toni ran out of space on the right side and finished the line with a column of words down to the beginning of the line on the left side. The ingredients were present. Toni knew the meaning of the message. She assumed others could solve the problem as well.

When six-year-old Allison returned from a family wedding in New York, she wrote in columns, oriental style, with words going up the page. Direction was not important for Allison, only words emerging from other words.

Use of speech to accompany writing.

Most beginning writers speak as they write. Writing is silent and abstract and speaking keeps them in touch with the writing process. Note how Eddie speaks and writes:

sound line:	the		guh	guy	gut	gut	t	the gut guys
writing line:	the	g			r	t			s

Eddie says 'the', then writes it as shown in the writing line. He sounds 'guh', then writes a 'g'. The ratio of sound to speech is in much greater quantity than the symbols written on the page. Although Eddie sounds at about a 3–1 ratio over print, it is not unusual for other, more advanced first-grade children to sound at a 2-1 ratio. Some barely sound at all.

These data are gathered through a very sensitive microphone placed on the lapel of the child when the child chooses to write. The microphone is attached to a video system that shows just when the symbol is placed on the paper in relation to the sound as shown above. Even when researchers sit next to the child recording observations of writing practice by hand, it is impossible to get the murmurings and voicings of children in relation to the letters written on the page.

sound line: are are are are *sh* is *i*   *i* is *sh* shootin
writing line: R   A

Eddie has a very difficult time making inner language serve him in a process as abstract as writing. He sounds letters, and repeats them until he *hears* what is appropriate for what he wants to write. Indeed, he juggles so many types of sounding that he ends up with 'the good guys are is'. The struggle with the sounds of individual letters and words is so great that the syntax suffers.

When Eddie speaks to his friends, he gets confirming nods or negative reactions. But writing is silent. It sits on the page, passive, without sound. He therefore supplies the sound for the page, almost making it speak back to him. Occasionally he glances up at the picture to get an overall sense of the message, gives a sound effect as in a shooting gun, and then returns to the sounding and speaking of message components. It is difficult in this linear process of putting one word in front of the other on this page, to portray the many systems — thinking, sounding, writing that are occurring at the same time when Eddie writes.

Jenny sounds when she writes but her sounding is more advanced than Eddie's. Jenny has been writing longer than Eddie and draws on a richer oral language base to go with her writing. Jenny writes and sounds:

sound line: all, all, of, all of the, the, the, all of the reindeer
writing line: L oll ave   the

sound line: rein, *ruh*, rein loved them, all, of, them, the *muh, muh*
writing line: R   iendrer   lov e   m

Jenny draws after she writes and even edits 'them' to 'him' after rereading the sentence. Jenny is dealing with a broader message unit and knows as far as five or six words ahead what will be written on the page.

Chris does much speaking when he writes but it is strictly a *confirmation* of what is on the page. Chris does not sound out letter components; he merely says the word he will write, 'mechanic', then spells out loud, 'm–e–c–k–a–n–i–c'. Chris may murmur occasionally as he rereads, to feel the message on the tongue — to sense the aesthetics of sound, but this is all. Language also provides company for Chris when he writes, much as language works for a mechanic or carpenter in the process of assessing his work. A large share of Chris' language is procedural, 'Where is that fourth step? Oh, steps twelve and thirteen are dumb; I can skip those. This is a robot that anyone can make'. Note that the procedural comments are concerned with information, whereas Eddie's language emphasizes syntactical orientation and sounding of letter components.

Our analysis of spoken language in relation to written language is just beginning. Far more analysis is needed to understand the function of oral discourse when children write. Preliminary analyses show that most beginning writers use it and that there is probably a hierarchy of complexity to its function. Still, there are a few six-year-old children who do not use it at all. More work is needed to explain their writing behaviours.

In summary, language spoken at the time of writing seems to fulfil the following functions:

What do I want to say?	The child hears what he wants to say by speaking and then writes it.
How can I make it sound better? (feel better?)	Prosodics — stress, pitch, intonation patterns, emerge as the child repeats the message for the quality of sound.
Did I spell the word correctly?	The child sounds the word through in sequence after it is written.
How do I keep on track?	The child merely repeats the letters as they are written. The child seems to be keeping his place as the word is recalled more from visual memory than auditory memory systems.

What was I saying anyway? or What is the next word?	Child rereads out loud from the beginning ... up to current word and then adds on the new word.
What is the next step? (information)	Child consults drawing or makes a procedural comment. (I need more stuff about the planet.)
How much more do I have to do?	As the child gauges the material written; other pages are read, remaining pages are counted.
How can I let others know what is happening so far?	To friend: 'Look, when this sled comes down the hill it is going to hit this tree here.' This is usually a reference to the picture.

How do children change what they write?

When children revise they demonstrate the time frame in which they function in the writing process. Just as children show the time frame in which they operate by the way they rehearse before writing, they also show time operations by the unit and place of revision. For example, when Eddie changes a word, any revision is likely to come only as the word is just composed. Eddie was the same child who had to draw before writing and had little advance concept of his message beyond a few words.

Steve operates in a broader time frame than Eddie. He can tell at least a sentence ahead what will be written on the paper. Drawings follow writing. Finally, after he writes the last page, he is able to return to add or change information on pages written earlier. For example, Steve wrote in his 'Sledding' story:

I slad dawn hills a lot.

In his illustration done *after* the writing, Steve included details on how his sled hit a tree. Steve noticed this on rereading his booklet. He adds the following:

I het a tree and I go the rast of the way.

He is still dissatisfied, turns to a new page and changes his message again:

I lik slading dawn hills a lot. I het a tree and I go the rast ov the way dawn the hill.

Chris is the most advanced. He has a well-developed plan for composing his booklet on building robots and explains in advance the seventeen steps necessary for its construction. When the booklet is completed he removed two steps as stupid and unnecessary.

As children see ahead in their composing, they also review their products with a more expansive backward vision. Usually these children have successfully solved the major problems of handwriting and spelling and are composing at a sufficient rate (four words per minute and up), thus gaining a broader view of the entire composing process. Word by word writers have word by word visions both in forward and reverse time patterns. Children with a broader vision use broader time units and make more advanced semantical and syntactical changes. Chris lined out a word written ten minutes earlier from 'We *whipped* rocks across the water' to 'we *skimmed* rocks across the water'.

New information provides its own kind of problem for the young writer. More advanced six-year-olds soon are aware that new information presents problems of space and aesthetics. Note Chris' first encounter with the space problems attendent to new information in this conference with his teacher:

TEACHER: I see that you were able to put in the word 'may' to show that 'Brontosaurus' may travel in families. (Chris had been able to sandwich in the small word without erasing.) But you didn't say why they travel in families.

CHRIS: They travel in families to protect the young.

TEACHER: Do you think that is important information?

CHRIS: Yes, but there isn't any place to put it. (The writing goes from left to right over to the right hand margin at the bottom of the paper. Above this writing is a picture of a Brontosaurus.)

TEACHER: Look the paper over and show me where you could write it in.

CHRIS: There isn't any. (*voice rising*)

TEACHER: Look the *entire* paper over and put your hand on any space where there isn't writing or drawing. (There is space above the drawing.)

CHRIS: Well, I could put it up here (*motions to top of paper*) but it would look stupid. The other part is down here.

TEACHER: How could you show they were connected?

CHRIS: I could put an arrow down here pointing to the part that's at the top.

TEACHER: Good, but you'll need to connect the arrow with the top. This is what writers do when they are getting their books ready for the publisher.

Chris knew additional information would create a mess. Now his teacher has shown him how to control new information when there is a problem of space. She has also shown him that this draft is temporary, that rewriting is necessary.

Summary

At first, writing is a simple act for most first-grade children. Writing begins and ends abruptly. Problems are solved within a narrow time frame. They quickly choose a subject, pick up a pencil, draw, combine some sounds and symbols, and writing emerges. There is little premeditation to write, nor is the product contemplated once the paper is done. Just as in play, doing the paper is an end in itself. When children write in order to play they talk, make sound effects, laugh and end their actions abruptly. The sounds they make are highly complex, ranging from attempts to match sound and symbol, words spoken before, during and after writing, attempts to reorient a new word to syntax, to language used to 'play' with other children. These same children are unaware of the many problems they solve in the writing process: transitions from speech to print, placement of words on a page, or the matching of sounds and symbols. If words are changed, they are changed when they are written. Their self-centredness protects them from the opinions of others. They experiment without fear.

Children expand the time and space dimensions of their activity as they continue to write. Activity is less overt. There is less need for visual rehearsal. Drawings are more often done after the child has written. Overt language continues to accompany the writing but contains fewer sound effects or sounding of letters. Now the language is characterized by: the emergence of procedural statements, broader rereading for syntactical sense, minor sounding of letters, and the statement of words after they are written. Revision involves spelling and handwriting changes with the first addition of new information into the text. There is more conscious choice of the topic and the child grows in awareness of other children's writing and opinions but not to the point of responding to them.

Still more advanced first-grade children are less overt in language and illustration. They operate in a much broader space-time dimension. They may wrestle with topic choice but only to choose the best option. They rehearse inwardly. That is, they can rehearse topics without drawing or speaking well in advance of the commencement of writing. They may rehearse while reading, listening to conversation, or by watching television. There is a strong advance concept of what will be written on a paper, even to the point of sharing five to ten steps or several paragraphs. The audience factor is much stronger. These children can articulate the opinions of others and maintain their own positions. Drawing is no longer necessary; for a few it even disappears. Some may be completely silent as they write. If there is language to accompany the writing, it is usually procedural and confirmatory. These children are capable of revising both the content and language of their writing. They are sensitive to the need to add information provided they have solved the space problems accompanying revision.

First-grade children will write if we let them. There is an abundance of energy for expression that is waiting to be tapped. If we will only get out of the way, let children lead, then observe, follow and aid them intelligently, who knows what writing we will be privileged to read . . . and in a very short time.

5 Assessing language development: the Crediton project

Andrew Wilkinson

A problem of definition

The title of John Dixon's book *Growth Through English* represents a view of English teaching which nowadays many would subscribe to. English teachers have always felt a special responsibility for the personal development of their students, and the literature abounds with terms like 'growth', 'fruition', 'development', 'maturity'. These terms, however, are notoriously ill-defined. And there are clearly differences between the language of (say) a one-year-old, a five-year-old, and a ten-year-old. Development obviously takes place, but does not take place obviously.

With a view to obtaining a clearer picture of the language features of pupils at particular ages, post-graduate studies at the Language in Education Centre, University of Exeter, have been going ahead over the last three years. Currently a research team (Barnsley, Hanna, Swan) is devising scales of development beyond those tentatively outlined by Wilkinson and Wilkinson (1978) and Wilkinson (1978). The project at this stage is confined to written composition.

Some schemes of assessment

Traditionally, judgements on English compositions have been made under headings. Particularly on marking examination papers headings of the type Language, Style, Content and Mechanical Accuracy (principally spelling and punctuation) have been used. A fair amount of investigation into the reliability of examiners using the type of 'code' marking took place (Hartog and Rhodes 1936, being the classic) until Wiseman's work (1949) showed that 'impression marking' was just as reliable, faster and probably more valid. The impression markers were doubtless using internalized criteria derived from their experience; probably many of the code markers were doing this also and finding in the code system a simplified rationale for these.

What such criteria are, however, has not really been pursued, though there have been attempts to look beyond the conventional headings. In *Assessing Compositions* (1965) a team of LATE (the London Association for the Teaching of English) suggested five aspects of writing for consideration (in relation to imaginative composition): realization, comprehension, organization, density of information, relation of spoken to the written language. The group of teachers of Somerset L.E.A. organized to produce *Language Development Guidelines* (Jones 1978) suggested the following 'attributes of written composition' — originality, vocabulary, elaboration, organization, syntactic arrangement, spelling, handwriting and layout.

Interestingly, the headings for markers suggested by the Assessment of Performance Unit (which is attempting a national 'light sampling' in the U.K.) are strictly orthodox — orthographic conventions, grammatical conventions, style, structure, content. Each is to be rated on a three point scale. The order in which the headings are given and the equal loading of each seems to give an emphasis to the formal aspects of composition which has often been absent in recent years. Indeed any assessment system which operates across the board without knowledge of individual children will tend to operate on a 'skills model'.

Whilst useful for their particular purposes it is clear that none of these schemes are delicate enough to investigate developmental features in the detail we are interested in. To this end we have constructed the scales of development outlined below. But these are not designed as short-cut assessment instruments. They are intended to reveal unfamiliar aspects of written work, or at least some aspects which may have escaped conscious notice (though an impression mark may take them into account). They are scales of style, affect, cognition and morals. 'Language' seems an obvious omission but this is deliberate. So much work has been done in this area that it will be discussed briefly in the next section, and then left on one side.

Traditional linguistic measures

It is very late in the day to investigate development in purely linguistic terms, if by 'linguistic' we mean the objective 'count' measures which have been used, particularly by psychologists, over
the past fifty years. These include quantity (the number of words,
the mean sentence length). They include variety (the number of
different words, the variety of parts of speech — adjectives and
adverbs appearing to indicate greater maturity than nouns and
verbs). These two measures are, of course, calculated in relation
to the total words used. Obviously there is much more likelihood
of variety in ten sentences than in two. Thus, what is called the
type-token ratio is calculated — the number of words under study
(e.g. adjectives) being expressed as a ratio of the total number of
words. Again the use of unusual words has been regarded as significant (for instance, words not occurring in basic vocabulary lists
such as Thorndike's (1944)), as has also the variety of sentences
used (question, statement, exclamation, etc.). Often the occur-
rence of basic sentence patterns, or 'T-units', sometimes modified
by considering them as 'phonological' or 'communication' units,
has been employed. The degree of sentence complexity, counting
subordinate phrases and clauses, has been widely employed as a
measure. Thus Loban (1963) used a 'weighed index of subordination' giving one point for each dependent clause, and a similar
type of weighing for other subordinate features. There have also
been analyses using transformational and systemic grammar.
Coherence and completeness have also been included.

A study by Harpin *et al.* (1973) will serve as an example of the
types of analysis which might be used. This study, concerned with
writing development in the junior school, used the following measures: sentence length, clause length, subordination index, Loban
subordination scale, use of simple sentences, use of complex sentences, use of 'uncommon' subordinate clauses (all except adverbial clauses of time and noun clause objects), the incidence of
non-finite constructions in the main clause, general index of personal pronoun use, the proportion of first person and of third person uses, the proportion of personal pronoun uses other than as
subject.

If we may generalize from the results of numerous studies (for
summaries of the research see, e.g. McCarthy 1954; Carroll
1968) it seems that in preschool children language maturity is
marked by greater number of words, greater mean sentence

length, greater variety of words and parts of speech, greater use of unusual words, use of varied sentence types, greater complexity of structure, and superior coherence. However, we have to be cautious in considering these findings. Early researchers do not seem to have been sufficiently aware of the importance for it linguistic content of the situation in which the language was produced. Harpin *et al.* (1973) with junior school children find that their results agree with those of other research workers (p. 132) on the importance only of sentence length, clause length, and to a less extent on index of subordination. They point out that the most important source of variability in all measures is the kind of writing required.

'Count' measures as so used are very crude indicators of surface structure, and do not take into account meaning, though they obviously have had usefulness in for instance diagnostic and clinical situations. Other more important processes are going on than those merely of increase. The same vocabulary and structures are growing more meanings as the frame of reference of the child is enhanced. An awareness of style and an advance in analytical ability may in fact decrease the variety of words and structures used on a particular occasion.

The construction of models of development

There has been no previous work on the construction of models of development in the areas of style, affect, cognition and morals of the kind which the present research is undertaking. Britton's scale of transactional development, for instance, requires a single global judgement to be made of each piece of writing. The models we are devising enable one to make an analysis of details of written work from four different standpoints. Thus they are basically research instruments, but by attempting to lay bare the bases of judgement, it is hoped that they can bring about a greater awareness of the criteria by which readers do, or could judge composition work in a developmental context. It is for later work to simplify them for classroom use if that is the way they need to be used.

There follows a general description of each model. Under each heading in the final report the items in the model will be listed in hierarchical order, and each item coded, but for the purposes of this article that has been felt unnecessary. Instead, in a later section their operation on certain selected pieces of written work will be demonstrated.

Stylistic measures

Judgements are often made about the 'style' of children's written work. There is a difficulty of definition. Crystal and Davy (1969, pp. 9–10) distinguish four commonly occurring senses of 'style' — the language habits of a person, or of a group of people, the effectiveness of a mode of expression, and the idea of style as 'good' writing. The first two may be described largely objectively; the second two are partly evaluative. For our purposes we may perhaps equate the first two with the use of the appropriate register — the employment of a certain variety of language for a particular purpose in a particular situation. This is a feature which linguistics has sharpened up for us. The second two are derived from literary criticism, and assume a standard of 'good' or 'fine', or on the other hand of 'effective' writing — these are the ones which most often occur in teachers' judgements.

The first two definitions of style imply specific language for specific purposes, and thus no *single* concept of a good style. However, it is possible to specify certain stylistic universals — features which all styles must have in common, just as they must have language in common. These would seem to be:

Structure/organization
Concerned with the relationship of the separate elements to the whole organization. Development will be seen in terms of movement from perception of individual units to perception of the totality which they constitute.

Syntax
There will be a development from simple to complex, but the furthest point of development will lie in the control of the appropriate structures in relation to the semantic needs.

Verbal competence
There will be in general a movement from limited concrete vocabulary, perhaps with imprecise and general meaning, to a vocabulary which has greater precision, and uses abstraction and elaborates where necessary.

Reader awareness
The degree to which the writer can put himself in the place of the reader. Initially concerned with decentring, this category includes such aspects as the writer's 'orientation', the degree of elaboration and explanation to give the necessary context and understanding.

Cohesion

Cohesive devices are employed to maintain continuity between one part of the text and another. Just as grammar establishes the structural relativity within clause or sentence so cohesion establishes the semantic relationship within the text. The range of cohesive devices is set out in Halliday and Hasan (1976).

Appropriateness

Development is seen in terms of the writer's ability to adapt to the accepted style of discourse. Young children often write in oral modes, or mix spoken and written. At the other end of the scale a writer may well frustrate the reader's expectation for deliberate effect by breaking register.

Effectiveness

This universal concerns the success of the writing in communicating. In this sense it is the summation of the others. It is partly what Pope had in mind when he wrote 'In every work regard the writer's end' (*Essay in Criticism*, 1. 255), but we must beware of the intentionalist fallacy, that the quality of work is necessarily what the writer intended to make it. There can, of course, be no single criterion of effectiveness. In a narrative it may be the interest and suspense sustained; in an autobiography the realization of the writer's feelings and motives; in a set of instructions the success of the reader in installing the wall bracket, and so on.

Affective measures

Nowhere is the concept of growth more difficult to define than in the area of the emotions. It is commonly assumed that one is helping children towards maturity through language, but this never seems to be defined, certainly not in Holbrook's book *English for Maturity* (1961). A parallel article in the 1979 issue of *Language for Learning* by Harrison seems to go further in clarification than others have done.

For our purposes we see development in the affective mode as lying in three movements — one towards a greater awareness of self, another towards a greater awareness of others, and of their place in the environment, and a third towards an acceptance of reality and of imagination:

Self

Self expresses own emotions, becomes aware of these emotions, and evaluates them, recognizes their springs and complexities, becomes aware of motives behind apparent motives. Self becomes aware of self-image, and of how one appears to others.

Others

The awareness of others as distinct identities. To young children others appear as servicing agencies. There is a process apparent in some writing of others manifesting themselves as individuals, in terms of what they say and do and how this expresses what they think and feel. Degree of empathy displayed by the writer towards others.

Environment

An awareness of physical surroundings. These may not be noticed. They may be assumed as in a 'restricted code' situation. They may be responded to. They may be interrelated with the characteristics of self or other people.

Addressee

It is often argued that the writing to an unknown or not-envisaged addressee will be poor in quality since it lacks focus. Certainly the imaginative leap into the mind of another so that one grasps what terms have meaning for him is a kind of empathy which must characterize effective communication.

Reality

Basically this is concerned with how far a distinction is recognized between the world of phenomena and the world of fantasy, and the world of imagination, between magical and logical thinking; with how far the writer's own beliefs can come to an accommodation with external reality; with how far the literal-metaphorical aspects of experience can be processed in complexity.

Cognitive measures

Cognitive development has received more attention than affective development. Piaget's stages — sensorimotor, preoperational, and operational (concrete and formal) — are seminal in the field. Bruner suggests a movement from the enactive, via the iconic to the symbolic. All models offered agree on a movement from an undifferentiated world to a world organized by the mind, from a world full of instances to a world related by generalities and abstractions. The hierarchy of Bloom's cognitive domain (1956) from knowledge of specifics to synthesis and evaluation follows this progress in some detail.

Even so there have been few attempts to evaluate the cognitive aspects of writing, though Peel *et al.* (1971) have assessed the cognitive judgements made by pupils of writing in terms of describer and explainer thinking. Moffett (1968) comes nearer to the line we are pursuing when he classifies discourse into four categories:

what is happening — drama — recording
what happened — narrative — reporting
what happens — exposition — generalizing
what may happen — logical argumentation — theorizing
(p. 35)

He sees this in some relationship to Bernstein's codes:

The code differences run along the same line as the developmental shifts we have discussed; implicit; ethnocentric to individualistic, increasing choice, increasing consciousness of abstracting (speech being an object of special perceptual activity), increasing elaboration

(p. 58)

Drawing on and developing Moffett's categories, Britton (1971) in turn erects a hierarchy of 'transactional' categories from recording at the bottom (writing 'what is going on here and now') to the tautologic at the top ('the systematic combining of abstract propositions leads to new conclusions').

The model used in the present study is as follows:

Describing
There is a move from labelling and naming, via simple statements and incomplete information, to reporting of a complete sequence.

Interpreting
The development is from a simple explanation, or inference or assessment to a deduction drawing on a series of (e.g. causal) links.

Generalizing
The baseline would be a generalized concrete statement,

moving to a summation of a whole section, and thence to the generalizations implied by a classificatory system.

Speculating

The movement here is from inadequate to adequate simple hypothesis at the statement level, via exploring and projecting at the discourse level, to controlled and extended theorizing.

Moral measures

Although there is some disagreement between psychologists as to the number of stages a child passes through as he comes to internalize the morality of his culture, there is a general agreement that in early childhood 'anomy' or lawlessness gives way to 'heteronomy' or rule by fear of punishment, which in turn gives way to 'socionomy' or rule by a sense of reciprocity with others which finally leads to the emergence of 'autonomy' or self-rule. Kohlberg's three phases, preconventional, conventional and post conventional are elaborations of heteronomy-autonomy; Piaget (1932) emphasized socionomy replacing heteronomy at the end of the concrete operational period; Bull (1969) emphasizes the importance of all four, pointing out that even in adulthood evidence of earlier stages is apparent in all our thinking. The developmental model we are proposing is a cumulative stage model, not a discrete stage model in which earlier forms of moral judgement are totally superseded by more mature ones:

Judging, or naming, of self and others by *physical characteristics*, as though they carried moral force or by the physical consequences of actions.

Judging self/others in terms of *punishments and rewards* as the motive for action ('heteronomy').

Judging self/others according to *status and power*. Policemen good by status; witch bad by convention. Stereotypical thinking.

Judging self/others in terms of *conventional norms/rules*. Conformist orientation.

Judging self/others in terms of *intention or motive* regardless of status, power or results of actions.

Judging self/others in terms of *abstract universal concepts* rather than conventional or cultural norms.

Judgement in terms of a coherent *personally developed value system*.

The project design

The design of the project was to give the same four written tasks to children of seven, ten and thirteen. Three classes of pupils with about 30 pupils in each were chosen with the aid of the teachers. They were from a primary and lower secondary school in a market town in Devon, U.K. and both the choice of schools and the guidance of the teachers suggested that these groups were fairly homogeneous in terms of background and ability. Keeping the four tasks common across the age groups is necessary if one is to go further than the two Schools Council projects, and actually begin to answer the question; what are the features of writing development at different ages?

The tasks were:

1. *Autobiographical narrative*. 'The happiest/saddest day of my life' or (for 13 years olds) 'The best/worst experience I have ever had'. The audience posited is teacher as trusted adult. The function expressive-poetic. The content — the writer's choice on the principle of one day selectivity.

2. *An account of a process written from authority*. How to play (a particular game or sport). The audience posited is a layman, someone who wishes to learn the game. The function, expressive-transactional. The content — a game which the writer can play and thus may be able to explain.

3. *A fictional story*. The writer selects one of three photographs with the instruction 'Write a story for which your picture is one of the illustrations'. Function, expressive-poetic. The appeal is to a wider public. The writer begins with a picture containing two people in a dramatic situation.

4. *Discussion/persuasion*. 'Would it work if children came to school when they liked, and could do what they liked there?' The audience — peer group. Function, expressive-transactional. Pupils' own thinking stimulated by class discussion.

It can be seen from the tasks that they represent an attempt to vary audience and function; that two call for writing in role of the spectator, and two in the role of participant in the world's affairs. The choice was related to the models we are attempting to validate. Tasks 1 and 3, in that they call for writing in which values and attitudes towards people and events emerge, might be expected to bear on the moral/affective dimensions, tasks 2 and 4 to bear on the cognitive/stylistic dimensions particularly.

For reasons of space it is not possible to demonstrate fully here how far the models apply to specimens of all four modes at a three age levels. We shall therefore confine our discussion to the autobiographical narrative and the explicatory tasks.

Autobiographical narrative

Donna (7) *The happiest day of my life*

> One day I was Playing outside when I saw some boys and then they saw me and came up to me and called me names So I what in doors and when I whet out again they were Playing with a tyre and this Man had a new garig down the road and one of the boys rœd the tyre down to the other boy but he mercd it and it what right into the garig and the man told them off and then They whet home and when they whet to sunday school when they got home a Pilceman was their and he told them off

Style

The *organization* is of a series of events often linked individually but not as a totality. Significant and insignificant items are chronicled. The *syntax* is mainly simple sentences. In terms of verbal competence the generality of reference ('some boys', 'the man') illustrates at once the concreteness and impreciseness of much writing at this stage. *Cohesive devices* like *and*, *but* and *so* are used in an additive way. *The reader* is taken into account in that the orientation is clear — the motivation for the girl going indoors and for the garage owner's anger is clear. The *appropriate language* is apparent at the beginning where the written mode is employed ('One day . . .') but the style then becomes mainly oral. In terms of overall *effectiveness* the experience is imperfectly realized partly because of the inadequate command of the stylistic devices.

Affective

The piece expresses no feelings of *the self*; despite the title there is no 'happiness' in it; and there is little empathy for *the other* characters in the story. They are described from outside and what they say, think or feel is scarcely conveyed. There is some *awareness of audience* in the sense that adequate information is presented. But an imperfect grasp on *reality* is maintained, because (one suspects) the incident is manufactured rather than being a real or imaginatively real one.

Moral

The moral thinking is at an early level. The boys have done wrong and are thus punished by telling off, both by the garage owner and by a policeman, who represents the rule-based nature of society. What the writer has not yet realized is the distinction between an intentional wrong, and an accidental one — neither boy presumably intended that the tyre should trundle into the garage, and it seems unnecessarily punitive to involve the police in this incident.

Cognitive

Simple *reporting* of an early kind, *labelling* rather than naming people. She holds the temporal sequence at first but later the temporal markers deteriorate — did the incident occur on Sunday, did the policeman visit them on that day?

Francesca (10) *The happiest day of my life*

> The happiest day of my life was on a Sunday when we had to go out. I don't know were the place was I don't know what it was called. It was by a little stream, and there were trees growing we could climb to trees some were very high. There were rocks too with grasses growing on top. A hill which had a path leading a long side the stream. You could climb up and down the hill it was a rocky hill. But it had lot of trees to catch hold of to pull your self up. It was a long walk along the stream we walked about a quater of the way and quater of the way was about two miles. We got tired so we thought we should turn back there was a small water fall in the river. Because of some stones stuck in the middle of the stream there were bushes you could hide under, they were very big not many people walked on the path, there was another path on the other side of the stream. There were trees coving the path, but alot of light still came in. Then we got back we had to go home because the day was over.

Stylistic

The *organization* is loose but not uncontrolled, based on a leisurely chronological pattern. Apart from the opening sentence (expected under the circumstances) there is no overview; the day begins, proceeds, and ends. There are signs of ability to use the *syntax* for particular effects (e.g. the parallelism of 'I don't know where the place was; I don't know what it was called'). *Verbal competence* is represented in the exactness of detail ('there were trees covering the path, but a lot of light still came in'). *Appropriateness* of language is developing in the sense of a literary style; particularly she has discovered repetition ('a quarter of the way') as a *cohesive* device. Orientation to *audience* is clear; care is taken to display the context, to explain (for instance the reason for the small waterfall). The general *effectiveness* arises from the detailing of an obviously 'genuine' experience, though clearly the ordering of detail is slightly haphazard and unselective.

Affective

The experience essentially concerns self, though 'we' rather than 'I' is the pronoun used. Francesca states her feelings of tiredness; and there is implied a discussion with the *others* as to when they should turn back. She notes that the wood is empty of other people. Most noticeable on an affective measure is her response to the *environment*; it is described in careful terms and obviously enjoyed ('the bushes you could hide under' for example). This setting of the scene, and the various explanations shows an awareness of the needs of *audience* who cannot be expected to know the context. There is a sense of *reality* about the incident and its setting.

Cognitive

Basically a spatially organized reporting of the details of a place, within a simple overall chronology 'On a Sunday we had to go out' 'Then we got back we had to go home because the day was over'. She labels, because as she tells us 'I don't know where the place was...', yet goes on to describe the whereabouts of geographical features such as rocks and trees in some details. She does offer explanations within this 'there was a small waterfall in the river because of some stones stuck in the middle of the stream'. A good example of describer-thinking, organized spatially.

Moral

Moral judgements do not apply particularly to this piece.

Colin (13)

In 1971 I went for a holiday to Italy with the rest of my family. We went to Rimini (on the Adriatic coastline) and stayed at a small hotel called the Susie my birthday is in June and that year we had our holiday early. (last week of May 1st week of June) I was 5 then (nearly 6) and was passing through the phase in which I 'hated the Jerries' I often critised them calling them 'Stupid Idots'. I say I was passing through this stage in fact I had only been attacking the Germans for 6 months or so, this phase would generally have lasted several years. At the age of 5 I couldn't swim a stroke (I learnt to swim at 9 or 10) however Mum and Dad had no qualm's about me going of because the beech (a lovely golden sand) was a gently shelving one. At the time I had a small (one place) inflatable boat and padle, this was my chief joy, I would paddle around with it for an hour. The boat was a fairly stable

one. About two days after I had been given the boat I was gently pad-
dling it out toward the sea. the water looked shallow so I put my leg
over the side of the Inflatable and felt for the bottom The Inflatable
capsized and slowly floated away from me. My head bobbed up and
down and I saw the boat 3 ft away but I just couldn't swim even that
far I lifted my head above the water and tried to shout for help,
however it sounded more like 'Hel', and as my head sank below the
waves then my head was clear again and I shouted 'He' (the rest was
stopped as I swallowed a mouthful of water) then my foot touched the
bottom, the water was less than 4–5 ft deep! this time I didn't rise to
the surface on my own. (I would have drowned there and then) A
large broad shouldered man picked me out of the water with one hand
and pulled in the inflatable with the other, after querring wether it was
mine (by pointing to it and me and lifting an eyebrow). he then found
my parents put me down and conversed with my Mother at some
length in a foreign language. The Language he spoke was German.
from that day I have never attacked "the Jerries".

Stylistic

The *organization* of this piece is good. Past is related to present
experience. The details are relevant, and though one may predict
the ending it is held back and used suitably. The beginning is immediate and economical. The *syntax* is controlled, sentences
varying according to semantic needs (he seems to have recently
discovered brackets as a device and really celebrates this). *Verbal
competence* is indicated in the width of vocabulary, the exactness
of description, the absence of unnecessary detail for the most
part. He is in possession of a range of *cohesive devices* ('I say I
was passing through this phase' 'about two days after'). Sensitivity to *audience* is perhaps over obvious — the amount of information in brackets to ensure that the reader is in the picture could
have been dealt with in other ways, but otherwise there is good
reader/writer contact. The piece is very *effective* because the experience is so well realized in terms of what was felt, said and
done.

Affective

In this context the piece is of great interest. In terms of *self* it displays a recognition of the writer's own racial attitude, which he
can distance as a phase. Then, as a result of his experience he
comes to value *others*, in this case the German. There is a move
outward from an egocentrical position to *another* oriented one.
His observation of the German's sign conversation to discuss the
ownership of the inflatable ('by pointing to it and me and lifting
an eyebrow') is shrewd and appreciative. A normal device for
realizing others in composition is by giving their words. Here the

writer cannot do this, but gives the equivalent. There is consciousness of *environment*, with sufficient but not excessive detail. There is consciousness of a reader (we have already mentioned the parenthetical device). Fantasy moves to *reality* — the stereotype ('stupid idiots') disappears when he actually meets the human being.

Moral

The moral thinking is quite advanced. He can recall being at an earlier level where one judged Germans as stereotypes, attributing unfavourable attitudes to a whole race. He is able to distance that earlier attitude, and as a result of his experience see through the blinkers to the intentions and motives of the man who saved his life.

Cognitive

This is an elaborated narrative, in which explanations are offered for the incidents being developed. Beyond the incidental explanations are statements like 'I was passing through a phase' which represent a higher level of thinking, what one would call reflecting — generalizing with reference to external rules and principles.

Explanatory

Since the stylistic, affective and moral models have been applied in some detail to the biographical narrative writing for reasons of economy they will not be used again in this section, though the stylistic model would throw considerable illumination on the texts. The affective and moral models have little relevance to the 'How to play' tasks in the ways the pupils wrote them, but the cognitive model would seem to be very useful. We choose to discuss three compositions on the playing of football, but the range of topics was very varied — hopscotch and Monopoly for example.

Don (7) *football*

> first you pick the players Then One of players gos in goal and you score against him

Don gives us two well formed sentences, but they obviously contain only partial information. Such matters as rules, and the sense of context are absent. The structure is chronological as one would expect, and the viewpoint egocentric. However technical vocabulary (players, goal, score) is accurately used. The cognition is operating incompletely at describing level.

Andrew (10)

My favourite Game is football. It is well none all over the world. It is not Just a kids Game it is a Gown up Game to. there are lots and lots of teams in Britain. There is Liverpool and Exeter City and York City and West Ham United and Many more team these team meat up and Play against each over it. Ends like 3 v 1 and things like that. This is how you play. You have a field and up each end of the pitch you have a goal. And the field has lines. thing you got to do is score in the goals. I mean you have to kick a ball in the Net and Goal keeper got to you from doing this. You elevan Players on each side if you are playing Proffesinill. And Ill Tell you the Rules. If the ball goes off the pitch it is a throwing. And if you kick some man you have a three kick. But you kick some in the Penelty. And if you handell it you do same. I'll tell you the Bisians theres a Goal keeper and Theres Defenders, midfielders, Strikers, Wingers, Right Back, Left Back, and Theres more to and that how you play football. and if you pracktise you may play for a proffeinel, one day.

Andrew starts with a concrete personal statement, and then goes on to a generalization, 'It is well known all over the world' but it is not a generalization of particular relevance to the explanation of the game. He casts about, not sure which details to select. This indeed is one of his difficulties when he comes to the task proper. He specifies rules, but not comprehensively. His organization is partly chronological, partly spatial ('You have a field and up each end of the pitch you have a goal') though the two aspects are not well articulated. Lists of items (English teams and the names of positions) bulk out the piece. He goes far beyond Don but his thinking is still in the describing category.

Alan (13)

Alan writes a four page piece which has an overview, an introduction inserted, the main rules, and a list of basic skills. The piece is far too long to quote in full, so we will attempt to give some description by means of selective quotation.

The opening sentence goes straight to the aims of the game at the level of an overall evaluation:

The object of this game is to score in the opponent's goal.

Sets of rules follow about umpires, size of equipment and layout of the field. A drawing provided of the pitch presents 'a typical line up'. The main rules are then given, under sub-headings:

Offside is when a player has got one or no players in front of him when he is in the other half.
Penalties for fouls are given.

In part two Basic Skills are listed — control, shooting, heading, with an introduction:

> I think that the most important skills are passing the ball from A to B, control it when the ball comes to you and heading the ball when it comes at head hight or if you want to dive for it.

Arising out of the material is a general conclusion:

> Football is a popular game in Britain and has got a league containing 92 teams in four divisions.

The piece operates at the level of generalization. It provides complete information. Its organization is classificatory using abstractions as headings, and demonstrates a much higher level of cognition than either of the other two pieces.

Development in the biographical-narrative and explanatory modes

The passages quoted above seem to us to display some of the characteristics of the age range of their writer. They are quoted as examples only. One cannot generalize from them, nor indeed from the work of all three classes which we analysed. In what follows, where we have in mind also this larger sample of work, this limitation must be borne in mind.

Stylistically children of about seven may write short compositions with an additive structure, often incomplete, though their experience of stories will often give them a traditional opening like 'once upon a time'. Their organization will be chronological, and will often conclude 'And then I went to bed', but they will often omit locational markers. Cohesive devices will perhaps be confined to *and, so, then*. The mode will be spoken rather than written.

In the affective mode the seven-year-olds do not usually express their feelings explicitly, though the reader may infer some emotional states from the selection of the material from the stories. They are often egocentrical, though *he* or *she* may be used instead of *I*. They may have insufficient control of language to realize to the reader what they wish to say. If they write stories involving other people the characters may well be distanced and general as in the piece by Donna.

At the age of ten children may write coherent compositions still on a temporal principle, with more audience awareness and thus orientation elements. With their growing command some of them will have become fond of details, used insufficiently selectively. A variety of openings and conclusions may be observed. They may write with more confidence, in the first person cohesive devices, such as a more confident use of pronouns instead of repeated nouns, are often used. Audience awareness is greater, as represented by orientation devices.

The ten-year-old writer may express more feeling, but does not show a high level of awareness of his feelings. However, they are able to assess the general dispositions of other people, and to some extent represent this in the words they give them to speak. Such writers are also able to choose aspects of their environment for their significance in stimulating emotional impulse, though as yet of a shallow kind, and move easily into a fantasy land of wish fulfilment.

The thirteen-year-olds have often developed significantly stylistically, being able to organize their writing by a deliberate though not necessarily conscious preplanning. Structure does not need to be chronological; they can insert flashbacks or glances forward. Syntax can be subordinated to semantics. Verbal competence will have increased, partly because the sense of the various connotations of an individual word in different contexts has increased. Cohesive devices are more sophisticated.

In the affective mode thirteen-year-olds studied showed a marked development over the ten-year-olds. Many show an awareness of the complexity of emotions in themselves and an empathy with the feelings of others, often manifested by an ability to characterize them in terms of their speech and actions. In addition the writers are beginning to show an ability to select environmental factors, both social and physical, that are significant in the stimulation of the emotion. Perhaps most interesting of all, however, they are beginning to use writing as an opportunity to know their own feelings, and to come to terms with both the world of reality and the world of the imagination. Once having encapsulated these worlds in story as a form of self-expression they should be able to grow emotionally, having added to the development of their affective complexes; that is, to develop their understanding of the feeling aspect of living.

According to the cognitive model we have devised two dimensions of development emerge in the pieces analysed. One is the amount of information children can handle — from a partial account, which is descriptive, to full details with, in these tasks, explanation of the rule system. The other is the capacity for objectivity. Younger children may put themselves in the game and see it from a narrow viewpoint — e.g. as goal scorer. The older writer stands back, takes a more comprehensive view, including generalization and underlying explanations for performance. That is they see a game as a system, rather than as an instance of spontaneous behaviour.

Comment

Existing models purporting to describe development in language are inadequate. Most of them describe 'linguistic' skills, very narrowly conceived. One which sees language behaviour as a manifestation of human behaviour is needed.

The most advanced such model, based in functions, is that of Britton *et al.* (1975). It is effectively a cognitive model. It has no way of taking into account the moral or affective. Nor does it consider style; one of its two main divisions of language activity, the poetic, significantly fails to give any detailed account of this. The models we are offering attempt a mere comprehensive description, with which it will be possible not just to make judgements at sentence level, and not merely in general.

From our work it does seem possible to analyse the written work of pupils in a more objective way than has hitherto been thought possible. So often one hears comments to the effect that judgement is a purely idiosyncratic matter. Objectivity has, however, to be defined multidimensionally — the exclusive focus on a narrow range of skills such as spelling and punctuation can do nothing but harm. It would seem likely that many teachers are in fact using such a multidimensional model intuitively, equally that many others are not. The production of a category system is not intended to replace the teachers' experience by a machine, but to increase awareness of the bases of judgement.

We do not wish to talk of stages of growth in any over simple way. However, our work suggests that there are features which occur with older children and not with younger, essentially related to the learner's psychology, which mean that we can have proper expectations of 'development' with children within a broadly ranging age band. It is sometimes suggested that young children cannot handle 'transactional writing'. Judging by the response of some seven-year-olds to our transactional tasks, this may be because they are not asked.

Although linguistic tasks are specific to situations, and a writer may perform badly on one and well on another, on the evidence we have here it does seem that over a series of tasks expectations aroused in one will be fulfilled in at least some of the others. This matter, however, awaits further investigation.

As far as 'maturity' is concerned it does seem possible to offer some definition which is not merely subjective, but lies within the learner's psychology. This is not to say that it is not a cultural matter — obviously 'maturity' is a cultural concept. In terms of moral and cognitive development a good deal of research is at hand; in terms of affective and stylistic very little, so that the models offered here are very tentative. It is hoped that all four models will be found useful, if only to provoke disagreement.

6 Toward a theory of developmental rhetoric

Daniel R. Kirby and Kenneth J. Kantor

The teaching of writing in America has been dominated by a preoccupation with form. Specifically, writing instruction has been largely the explication of formulas for writing in one of the four traditional modes of discourse. Researchers have for the most part accepted these four divisions without question; much of the past research on written products has seen them as fixed entities, frozen in time and isolated from the composing process. These traditional product-centred notions of rhetoric, while sometimes helpful in classifying and analysing professional, adult prose have not been very useful to those researchers who wish to describe and explain the writings of immature and growing writers. Even more alarming, many teachers and writing texts continue to centre their instructional approaches in composition around adult standards of competence and form. Meanwhile curriculum consultants continue to assign writing tasks in random fashion to specific grade levels without concrete evidence of the appropriateness of such tasks for developing writers. Frequently these practices result in narrowing the focus of writing instruction to a formula or to a list of discrete skills. This fragmented, often futile approach to teaching writing has produced a widening gap between what educators think the child *should* be able to do and what they are developmentally *ready* to do, and has left us wondering about how one skill or process builds upon another.

By contrast, as Squire and Applebee (1969) suggest, 'the British success in creating a generation of writers through emphasis on creative expression offers an impressive demonstration that the ability to write does not have to be taught in any direct way and the cultivation of expressiveness can lead ultimately to a reasonable command of written English in its many forms'.

As researchers, we are convinced that the writings of children hold many developmentally significant clues to the actual processes inherent in growth toward writing competence. Such convictions, however, have left us without an adequate methodology to observe, catalogue, and order the clues. We are not as Bob Segar[1] suggests, 'working on mysteries without any clues'. Our problem is rather our inability to distinguish among the myriad of clues which lie there among the written words of children. If you have ever collected a large sample of student writings, you know of our consternation. There are too many things to respond to. It's an information overload. Out of this plethora of words, we wish to offer insights toward the formulation of a developmental rhetoric. Such a rhetoric would describe more accurately the signs of growth in written expression, speak to the interrelationships among these signs, and provide a model around which to build instructional strategies — a growth model rather than a prescriptive model based on adult standards.

Britton and his colleagues (1975) have offered us an important beginning point in their description of the functions of writing. Here expressive writing (writing about personal experience) is seen as the matrix out of which the more diversified transactional and poetic types of discourse grow. In transactional writing, writers act as participants in 'getting things done'; in the poetic function, they act as spectators standing apart from and reflecting on reality. The basic assumption of the Britton model is that developing writers do not give up expressive writing as a childish plaything; instead it is used to enhance the quality of explanatory, persuasive, and literary discourse. The process of becoming a mature writer is one of 'branching out', of developing versatility while building on established strengths.

Although the Britton model has been criticized for its separation of the transactional and poetic functions (Emig 1971), it remains the one most appropriate to an understanding of writing development. And unlike earlier theories, and, in Moffett's (1968) word, 'hallucinations', the Britton team conducted an empirical study, applying its theory to classifications in terms of function and sense of audience of over 2,000 school 'scripts' written by students ages eleven to eighteen.

Our present research attempts to extend the Britton investigations by looking at three additional variables: fluency, involvement, and invention. Essentially, our pilot study was designed for two purposes: (1) to develop an elicitation procedure which would encourage students to produce more diverse types of writing than the Britton sample and (2) to generate a range of rhetorical and discourse features which were observable in the writings of students at various levels of development.

Rather than conducting a *post hoc* analysis of a sample.of writings collected under conditions about which researchers have little knowledge, as was the case in the Britton study, we are examining writings produced in situations designed to serve our purposes more directly.

We have collected and analysed over 800 pieces of writing from 200 children in grades 4, 7, 10 and 12 to arrive at our pilot study conclusions.

These writing samples were collected using three distinct elicitation strategies: unplanned, planned and revised. *Unplanned* writings are short spontaneous writings, sometimes called free writings. Students were asked to write for ten minutes about anything they wished. Free writing was not new to them and they seemed comfortable with this unstructured writing task. These unplanned writings tended to be more like self-sponsored writing and were often primarily expressive rather than transactional.

Planned writings were those for which the teacher provided a stimulus for the writing task and discussed options which students might use to approach the writing task. The stimuli were designed to be mode-neutral, leaving presentational choices up to the writer. The researchers were concerned that narrow topics and more specific writing tasks used by many researchers in the past have often dictated process and closed down writer's options particularly in such areas as mode or function, audience and involvement. The intent of the study was to let the writer decide how to approach the writing task and then assess his/her strategies and performance in the light of those choices.

The researchers used as stimuli for the planned writings a film, 'The End of One' and a general topic 'Television'. The film was a short one without dialogue which depicts in loose narrative form the death of a seagull set against the backdrop of a garbage dump. The teacher discussed the stimuli with the students listing on the blackboard all ideas which the class generated for writing. This prewriting activity was essentially a brainstorming session in which the teacher reserved judgement and offered no help in selecting or structuring the topic.

I should mention here that we chose our cooperating teachers carefully. We looked for teachers who encourage writing in their classrooms and who have enlightened notions about the range of options for writing and strategies for teaching it.

Finally after a one week delay, students were asked to select one of their planned writings to revise and 'make better'. Pilot study observations indicated a wide range of revision behaviour. All of the revision data are being analysed in a separate study and will not be reported here.

We selected five variables which, on the basis of our pilot study observations, we believe to be developmentally significant. We have tried to represent these variables as existing on a continuum ranging from egocentrism to perspectivism; from centred-writing to writing which shows awareness of others. We define the end points of these variables using samples of student writing to illustrate immature and mature development. A major purpose of our longitudinal study now underway will be to determine the nature of the transitional stages for each factor, in particular the kinds of cognitive integration and differentiation taking place at various developmental points.

As with any two-dimensional representation, these variables are depicted in a linear diagram. We are convinced, however, that the development of these variables is not linear and that their patterns of interaction may be far more interesting and important than simply finding markers in student writings to document their presence.

The first factor, *fluency*, as a concept has thus far been applied and defined in two significant research contexts: *syntactic fluency* in both oral and written discourse, which analyses the student's ability to choose from a repertoire of syntactic options; and *oral fluency*, which focusses on the production process in oral communication.

Implicit in the work of both James Moffett and James Britton and any developmental rhetorical theory is a further application of fluency to a written context. These researchers theorize that written fluency is a necessary precondition or state of readiness without which a student is unable to explore the dimensions of abstractive altitude and rhetorical distance. In other words, a student must achieve fluency before he/she can control written language.

We see fluency as composed of three measurable elements: *vocabulary content*, or words as indicators of knowledge; *vocabulary fluency*, the ability to call forth words appropriate to expression, or the ability to marshall 'interior linguistic resources' as

Miller (1973) calls them, and *syntactic fluency*, the ability to use syntactic processes such as coordination and subordination to combine ideas within individual sentences.

A fourth component of fluency is less readily observable, and difficult to measure, but is no less important than the previous three. For the present we are calling this feature *authority*. Authority as it operates in fluency is the writer's sense of confidence with writing itself. Such confidence is often reflected in the writer's voice. As a writer develops a fluent, discernible voice, it is apparent that the writer is also experiencing a growing sense of authority. The writer speaks in less tentative language and seems more willing to take risks with the language.

In summary, the state of being fluent in writing is the ability to produce written language with ease, employing developmentally appropriate lexical and syntactic structures with a growing sense of self-confidence. The researchers are seeking to combine these four elements of fluency so as to create an objectifiable and developmentally accurate index of written fluency. Our investigation into aspects of fluency is only in the beginning stages. Initially we have been interested in the unplanned writing samples and what they reveal about the amount of written language students produce in ten minutes and the topics they choose to write about.

At immature stages, lack of fluency is reflected in halting, blocked expression; at mature stages, fluency is revealed in facile, confident language. Thus while the free writings reveal an expressive, often diary-like style at each level, the twelfth-grade writings show greater syntactic maturity (especially in use of embeddings) and greater ability to objectify thoughts and feelings than those of younger students.

At immature levels, as one might expect, when students are simply asked to write without stopping, their subject matter is frequently themselves. About one-third of all free writings at the seventh grade were expressive diary-like accounts of events, people, likes, hates, boyfriends, overbearing mothers and catty friends and former friends. Almost without exception the diary papers are written by girls. The papers bounce from topic to topic without much development. In most cases the author is at the centre of the paper, and she talks about subject matter without much concern for an audience. These diary papers sound as if the author is really talking to herself.

The second factor is *involvement*, or the extent to which the discourse reflects engagement in the writing task. At immature stages writing appears to be either 'hot' — reactive and highly subjective — or 'cold' — perfunctory and detached. Uses of connotative language give us clues to degree of involvement: seventh graders writing about sports use such descriptions as 'adventures of life', 'you get hit, smashed, kicked and have fun at the same time', 'you can be a star, hero, and everyone's number 1 player', 'full of excitement, action', and 'one of the greatest forms of entertainment there is', while other seventh graders writing about pollution referred to it as 'terrible', 'very bad', 'harmful', 'ugly', and 'one of the most unpleasant things in the world'. Note in particular how the reactive voice emerges in the following seventh-grade writing:

> Mans disrespect for nature is pathetic. How would you like it if you made a beautiful world and people started ruining it for no reason at all. Some people in this world don't even know what fresh air smells like because of pollution now isn't that crazy. Some people don't even know what little birds chirping sounds like because of noise pollution. Some animals die because of just pure old pollution. Here are a few examples of pollution doesn't it sound disgusting? Just tell me this, have you ever threw just one bubble gum wrapper out because you thought it wouldn't show to much, Well it does!
>
> (grade 7)

This tone may be contrasted sharply with that reflected in a twelfth-grader's essay, in which the writer gives three possible reasons for the death of the seagull (the garbage dump, old age, polluted water) but remains cool and non-committal as to his own position: 'Of course the choice is yours for I truly do not know what led to the gull's death.'

At mature levels we can see writing becoming more tempered, balancing the classical elements of reason and passion. Thus a ninth grader explains why he doesn't watch T.V. simply by listing the other activities that take up his time, a twelfth grader protests that her mother censors her T.V. watching ('She never seems to notice that some of her educational shows are filthier than the ones we want to watch.'), and another twelfth grader, in a natural conversational manner, comments on our T.V. watching society:

> I think that for the most part, television is a waste of time. I didn't pay much attention to it before. I just didn't watch it.
> After being in a bicycle-car collision a month ago and being confined to activities that don't require much mobility, I resorted to watching it some to occupy the idle hours. This, I believe, is the chief reason most people watch television. They can't, or won't take the effort to find something better to do.

Many times I have walked through the family room to find my parents sitting there talking about how absolutely asinine the program they are watching is, and how stupid it is every week. So I ask them why they watch it and the usual reply is 'Well, there's nothing else on'. The idea of spending the evening without the set going full-time doesn't even occur to them.

After awhile, you don't even notice it. It becomes a routine part of activities like homework, reading the paper, doing the laundry, grading papers, and in some homes, eating dinner. A lot of the time, I will come home and the television will be on, but no one will even be downstairs. Or my mom will have the T.V. on, but she will be vacuuming so that she can't hear what the people on T.V. are saying. I guess it gives some people an unnatural, spooky feeling to be in a family room without a television on.

(grade 12)

Some of the movement toward more tempered writing may be accounted for by a growing knowledge base and awareness of environment — older students are better able to cite illustrations and evidence to support their arguments. This phenomenon points to the third aspect of our theory, that of *invention*. In the classical sense, invention refers to finding a subject and discovering materials in external sources for the purpose of making a persuasive case. In the modern sense, however, we associate invention with creativity — originality, imagination, drawing on inner resources. We suspect that writing development has much to do with combining these two aspects of invention, reconciling inner experience with knowledge of the outside world.

Younger students, then, show a tendency to look within themselves for sources of material; many seventh graders, for example, said they liked T.V., sports and soap operas without giving very specific reasons. Some of them did acknowledge other authorities, as with one who cited her aunt's comment about why she would not want to be kept alive by a respirator, and a few cited personal experience as justification for arguments, as in the following discussion of commercials:

I think most commercials take too long. There are also too many commercials. And the most important thing is that there are too many commercials during a movie. Every 15 minutes there's 5 minutes of commercials. That's too much for me. And another thing is that some commercials are worthless. For instance the dog food commercials are worthless. (Mainly when you're watching a movie). I know the companies want more people to buy their brand. But really, most people don't care. Dog food is dog food! My dog has eaten many kinds of different dog food. And his health is the same as it ever was. Anyway, dogs will eat almost anything. And the same for other pet commercials.

But there is a good side to it. The commercials are long enough for you to get a snack for yourself. I like that because sometimes I eat alot.

(grade 7)

Several ninth graders showed an impressive command of characters and events on specific soap operas, suggesting again the impact of involvement. Students can bring many details to bear on a topic if they have a strong interest in that topic. In the same respect, the twelfth graders demonstrated an ability to use specific examples and illustrations to develop and sustain an argument; several of their writings on 'Man and Nature' and 'Why I Don't Watch T.V.' reveal this proficiency. Most important, however, is the ability to see relationships and make generalizations, as in this twelfth-grader's discussion of cartoons and soap operas:

Cartoons and soap operas are just great! I love them, they're my favorite kind of shows.

These two types of shows are quite similar because neither of them displays true reality. Cartoons just skip over reality and on to the fantasy world. Soap operas always overplay real situations. In cartoons there is always a hero that comes to the rescue at just the right time or some character that thinks he's the star of the show. These are just fun shows that help the mind to relax and enjoy a world of fantasy.

Soap operas do the opposite, they somehow manage to twist the mind until you're so involved that you just can't wait until the next day to tune in. Even if you only watch for five minutes, you're hooked and will want to find out if Marcia really is pregnant and if Brad really does have a brain tumor or if George really will make it through the critical operation.

The shows make you really appreciate your own life a lot more because you aren't the one with all of those terrible problems.

So to get away from it all with a T.V. set, cartoons and soaps are the way to do it.

(grade 12)

The writer's ability to point out connections between cartoons and soap operas, and to see soap opera characters as generalizable types rather than particular individuals reveals, we think, an impressive level of thinking, one which combines both the classical and modern aspects of invention.

This kind of writing also suggests that creativity is not limited to descriptive or narrative writing, as the classical rhetoricians held, but that expressive writing enhances the quality of explanatory or persuasive discourse, as Nancy Martin *et al.* (1976) contend in *Writing and Learning Across the Curriculum*:

Much effective writing seems to be on a continuum somewhere between the expressive and the transactional or somewhere between the expressive and the poetic. This applies to adult as well as to children's writing. What is worrying is that in much school writing the pupil is expected to exclude expressive features and to present his work in an unexpressive transactional mode. The demand for impersonal, unexpressive writing can actively inhibit learning because it isolates what is to be learned from the vital learning process — that of making links between what is already known and the new information.

Development of *command of function* (our fourth factor) thus has to do with being able to differentiate among and coordinate the modes of discourse for the purpose of establishing and sustaining one's intent. We found in our sample a wide range of discourse types, suggesting the kinds of transitions identified by the Britton team. Some writings were almost wholly expressive, as with a few personal reflections on loneliness; other writings revealed an impulse to inform or explain, as in a number of essays on the effects of pollution or the impact of television commercials. And many writings demonstrated a strong persuasive function, as in this argument by a ninth grader concerning violence on T.V.:

> The parents of many young adults say, 'Violence on T.V. should be banded.' They, the parents, think that, what the young ones see on television has an awful affect on the way he behaves in society.
> I am quite sure that some of the children will get the wrong idea by what he or she sees on T.V., but if their parents had brought their children up in the way that they should go, violence would have almost no affect on the way they look at society, and the parents would not have to worry about their children seeing something on T.V. and going out and doing it.
> I think this is a good idea for the parents that, as the parents and children see a man robbing a bank and getting killed or sent to prison, they should tell their children 'see what happens when you do something wrong'.
> On the other hand there could be a robber who gets away with a large sum of money and the police never catches him, it could give them the wrong idea, that robbing a bank is an easy way of getting money and never get caught.
> It is the parents responsibility to see that their children don't get the wrong idea about the things they see on T.V. If a child doesn't see these things on T.V., but sees them on the street where no one is there to tell them 'this is the wrong thing to do' they might grow up and think it's right to kill or hurt someone because they were not told that it is wrong to kill or hurt someone etc.
> The parents that say that violence on T.V. should be banded, must

not be raising their children at home, that way they should go in life. If they did violence on T.V. would be helping, not hurting their children with society.

(grade 9)

While some might dispute the logic of this argument, there is little doubt as to the strong moral tone and sense of purpose in the writing, suggesting important aspects of development.

Finally, a few writings showed a movement in the direction of poetic discourse, as in a poem about death by a twelfth grader. While only a small number of students chose to write in this mode, we are pleased that at least a few were willing to take the risk of doing so in a school setting.

Command of function is, of course, intimately tied to the fifth aspect of our theory, *sense of audience*. We see development here as characterized by a movement from concern with self to awareness of others' points of view, from a subjective orientation to a wider perspective marked by what Flavell (1968) has called role-taking. At immature levels, we see students primarily discussing things they like or don't like, or beginning their writings by assuming the reader knows the context to which they refer: 'When Calvin said there was too much killing in television . . . ' or 'I think I got a different impression of the film'. Signs of growth appear, however, as writers address their audience directly ('Just tell me this, have you ever threw just one bubble gum wrapper out because you thought it wouldn't show too much', 'Have you ever thought about death? (If you have did it frighten you?')). Perhaps more significantly, we can see instances of writers acknowledging points of view other than their own: 'Although some people say it's wrong to show violence to small children . . . ' 'Some people don't like sports on T.V. . . . ' 'But there is a good side to it. The commercials are long enough for you to get a snack for yourself.'

Two points concerning sense of audience should be made. First, sense of audience may be largely intuitive, existing more below the level of consciousness than at the surface, and this makes the factor difficult to assess. We must depend to a great extent on 'shadows' to give us insight into deeper processes. Secondly, since the teacher is, as the Britton team concluded, the major audience for most school writing, we need to encourage teachers both to provide opportunities to write to peer group or wider audiences and to broaden their own range as audience, especially to encourage the 'child to trusted adult' and 'pupil to teacher, particular relationship' sense of audience categories. Many of the writings we collected suggest a positive movement in these directions, as they reveal personal voice and a willingness to take imaginative risks.

Perhaps the most interesting part of our research is the study of interactions and relationships among the five variables we have identified. We suspect that each factor operates to some extent in any given piece of writing and influences the others in a variety of unique ways. Given some knowledge about the nature of these interactions, we may at some time be able to construct profiles of individual writers at various stages of development, which will in turn enable us to predict performance on specific writing tasks.

The Schools Council Research Team in Great Britain made an impressive start in identifying important developmental processes in writing. Some of us in the Colonies are now eagerly joining them in that effort.

Notes

1. Segar, Bob, from song 'Night Moves', ASCAP, 1978.

7 Redefining maturity in writing

Lee Odell

A little more than a decade ago, Francis Christensen set us thinking about a question that seems particularly appropriate now that
so many people are concerned about writing and the teaching of
writing. The question is this: What do we mean by 'mature' writing? Obviously, this question is important; our answer to it will
determine how we go about teaching, evaluating, and doing research in writing. What is less obvious — since we are energeti-
cally going about the business of teaching, evaluating, and doing
research — is that we still do not have a good answer to the
question.

We do have some well-documented answers about the development of 'mature' syntax. Particularly through the work of Kellogg
Hunt, we know a great deal about the ages at which writers are
likely to begin using a given syntactic structure. And we know
which features of syntax are most indicative of 'syntactic fluency'
or 'syntactic maturity'. That is, we have a good notion about the
syntactic patterns one is likely to encounter in the work of adult
writers — both professional and non-professional. This information about syntax (as provided by Hunt 1965; Christensen 1967;
and others) has implied one definition of maturity in writing, a
definition which has influenced teaching, research and evaluation. But useful as this definition is, it is troublesome because it is
uninformed by a theory-based definition of what constitutes a
mature person. This view of growth in writing ability lacks a clear
relationship to a theory of cognitive or personal development.

One of the first people to try to establish this relationship was
James Moffett, who equates growth in writing ability with the
progression from a relatively egocentric state (in which one is
able to address only limited audiences about only a few kinds of
subjects) to a relatively decentred state (in which one is able to
address a variety of audiences about a variety of subjects). Mof-

fett's work has led to substantial improvements in the way writing is taught. And it has helped us understand the kinds of tasks a mature (i.e. relatively non-egocentric) writer should be able to perform. But Moffett does not help us identify the specific cognitive processes that are reflected in relatively egocentric writing or in relatively decentred writing. Thus even Moffett can lead us to make distinctions and overlook important similarities between pieces of writing. Consider, for example, the following two letters. The first appeared several years ago in the Ann Arbor (Michigan) *News*.

> To the University of Michigan — so-call Student body.
> What, if I may ask as a tax payer and a person who pays taxes to support a bunch of Hoods, beer slops, punks, and you name it U. of M. has it including the commie Profs.
> I put (3) three sons through college and not one was a bunch of pigs like you birds . . . [rather, they are] men with good honest jobs, homes, and families. If even one of my son's had come home and said he was going to burn his draft card, I would have took him apart piece by piece, then stick him back together and he would have been glad to enlist then, and I would not have cared if he ever came back.

The second letter is excerpted from J. P. Marquand's novel *The Late George Apley*. The central character of the novel is addressing his son:

> Dear John: I suppose a father always writes advice to his son upon the important moment of his entering college and I am no exception. A large part of your future life will be influenced by what you do this next year. The habits and ties you form will be with you always. At least, they have been with me, and I want you to do the right thing. There is a great deal of talk about democracy. I thought there was something in it once but now I am not so sure.
>
> . . . .
>
> Sometimes it seems to me that you are reticent in talking to your parents. You are making a great mistake, John, for I really think that I could be a good deal of help to you. I am still quite well-known around the Club, you know, and your first object must be to 'make' the Club. I believe that everything else, even including your studies, should be secondary to this. You may call this a piece of worldly counsel but it is worthwhile. I don't know what I should have done in life without the club. When I leave Boston it is my shield. When I am in Boston it is one of my great diversions. The best people are always in it, the sort that you will understand and like. I once tried to understand a number of other people, but I am not so sure now that it was not a waste of time. Your own sort are the best friends and you will do well not to forget it.

Clearly, these letters are different in important ways. And our current notions of mature writing would let us readily point out these differences. The letters are, as Moffett would lead us to note, addressed to different audiences. George Apley's letter is addressed to a single, relatively well-known person whereas the other is addressed to a large group that the writer appears to have little direct knowledge of. Further, the 'Dear John' letter is, by Hunt's definition, syntactically more mature. The mean T-unit length is greater (17 words per T-unit versus 16 words per T-unit in the letter to the University of Michigan student body) and the 'Dear John' letter contains a greater number of nominative absolutes.

But despite these differences, it seems to me that the two pieces are similar in important ways and that our usual notions of maturity do not lead us to see or be concerned about these similarities. For example, both writers concern themselves solely with their own values and feelings. And both assume that the audience shares (or should share) those feelings. Certainly neither letter suggests that the writer has considered such questions as these:

How does my audience feel about the subject at hand?

How does my audience feel about me?

How are my audience's feelings/values/experiences different from mine?

What justification might my audience have for those feelings/values?

What kinds of arguments might my audience see as persuasive?

Moreover, both letters reflect a very simple view of the world.

1.   There are only two classes of people:
     (a) those who are in the Club/those who are not.
     (b) those who are hoods and beer slops/those who have good honest jobs.
2.   There is only one acceptable way to act: join the Club/join the army.
3.   The consequences of actions are very uncomplicated and inevitable: if the writer's son joins the Club, all will be well; if the writer's son burns a draft card, then the only recourse is physical punishment and that punishment will inevitably have only one result — the son will be 'glad' to enlist in the army.

We may acknowledge that the 'taxpayer and a person who pays taxes' may have derived some therapeutic benefit from his letter to the University of Michigan 'so-call Student body'. And conceivably there are audiences for whom each letter might be effective. But whatever else we may say about these two writers, the thinking reflected in their letters seems terribly egocentric. Other people (i.e. their sons) exist chiefly to do as the writer instructs. Other points of view virtually do not exist; certainly, neither writer takes any serious account of values, experiences, feelings other than his own. Furthermore, at least for this particular piece of writing, each writer assumes there is only one way to view the subject at hand, and each writer assumes there is no particular need to accommodate the needs/interests/values of his audience. In this implicit definition of egocentricity, I am obviously drawing not only on these letters but also on the work of Jean Piaget (1968), who would appear to have described both of these writers in his comments on children's egocentrism. A child, says Piaget, is likely to display 'an egocentric attitude, in which the incorporation of objects into his own activity prevailed over accommodation' (remodification of behaviour as a result of experience) (p. 18). 'Rather than extricating himself from his own point of view in order to coordinate it with the viewpoints of others, the child remains unconsciously centred on himself' (p. 21). Further, Piaget notes, young children are likely to have a very simple view of reality; they tend to focus on only one aspect of an experience. (We may think of Piaget's experiments in which young children insisted that the amount of water changed when transferred from one container to another simply because the children focussed solely on one aspect of a container — e.g. height — and ignored others — e.g. diameter — that would contradict or modify the child's initial perception.)

These references to Piaget's work raise several concerns:

> Piaget has devoted more attention to children's thinking about impersonal phenomena than to their ability to examine feelings and values;

> Piaget has emphasized stages of cognitive development and has limited each stage with a particular age level;

> Piaget's discussions of cognitive ability are not based on analysis of written products;

> Piaget has worked with relatively young children, whereas many English teachers work with adolescents and adults.

As to the first two concerns, I shall simply stipulate two assumptions: (1) cognitive activity includes the examination of personal feelings, values, and reactions as well as more impersonal phenomena; (2) for purposes of research in writing, it may not be useful to associate stages of cognitive development with particular age levels; my experience suggests that a writer may display greater cognitive maturity in some rhetorical situations than in others. As to the usefulness of written products, we must acknowledge an important limitation. We cannot assume that a piece of writing reflects all the intellectual work that went on during the process of composing. I do, however, assume that a piece of writing reflects ways of knowing, strategies for understanding one's topic and one's audience. By analysing a piece of discourse, we cannot conclude that a writer is egocentric, but we can determine whether egocentric thinking is reflected in the piece of writing at hand.

Finally, with regard to the issue of cognitive development in late adolescence and adulthood, we may take some encouragement from William Perry's study of undergraduates at Harvard College (1970). Put briefly, Perry found that many of these undergraduates had entered Harvard with a rather simplistic view of knowledge — especially the knowledge they were to acquire in their college course work. Entering freshmen were likely to feel that their instructors had access to an authoritative, correct view of their subject matter. An instructor might present conflicting views or puzzling information to 'make us think'. But eventually, if one worked hard, he or she would come to understand that authoritative view. Somewhat later in their college careers, these students were likely to adopt a more relativistic stance: There is no 'truth'; all views are equally good, so who are you to tell me what is right? By the time they had graduated from Harvard, it was not uncommon for students to come to a somewhat different philosophical position: Reality is complex; compelling alternative views exist. Yet one can weigh and assess these and make a reasoned judgement.

My first point, then, is that people can continue to develop cognitively, well into their adult years. People can change in their view of knowledge and, consequently, in the ways they think about experience, feelings, values, and ideas. My second point is that this development is important to one's growth as a writer. Indeed, I suspect that what often appear to be 'writing problems' may be cognitive problems; at least some of these problems may appear because writers (at whatever age) have not learned to go beyond their egocentric, overly simple view of a subject or have not come to understand that their audience is someone who may not see the world as the writer does and who must, therefore, be accommodated in a variety of ways.

Although it is true that we never completely escape our own personal view of things, it is possible to recognize degrees of egocentricity in writing. To see my point, consider these two pieces of writing, done by eighth graders, in response to this assignment:

> The school board is considering setting up co-ed gym classes, so that — in some sports at least — boys and girls would be able to compete on equal terms. A woman has written a letter to the editor of the local paper claiming that co-ed gym is a bad idea and that most students are opposed to it. Write a letter to the school board in which you state your position on this matter and try to persuade them to accept your position.

One student wrote the following:

Dear Editor,

I disagree with the Lady. Its nor fair to us girls that we have to miss out on some of the things that the boys do. It's not fair. Us girls want to show the boys that were every bit as good as the boys. I think if we want to do this they have to give us a chance by having the girls and boys doing the same on the Phyal fitness. Its not fair I don't think for the boys to do more than we do. But if they want coed than have it all coed instead of spliting classes up when it comes to contact sports. Girls can play contact sports to can't they. Give us a chance!

Another student wrote this:

Dear Editor,

Last night in the Tonawanda news paper I read a letter from a parent saying she thinks it is a bad mistake for boys and girls to be together in the same gym class. She also said she bets all the students at the Junior High feel the same way she does.

I disagree with her because I feel the girls will try harder to keep up with the boys and so be more physically fit. Also, the girls have the oppertunity to compete against some fine athletes and learn more. If we have to have coed gym and swimming it should be all coed even in contact sports. I also think we should have a say in what we want to do, not what other people make us do.

The End

The thinking reflected in the first letter seems somewhat more egocentric than does the thinking reflected in the second. The first writer appears to assume that the reader has the same knowledge she does (i.e. that the reader has read the previous letter) and can call it to mind with little prompting from her (the only cue she gives is the capital *L* in *Lady*). The second letter, by contrast, reflects no such assumption. The writer paraphrases, accurately, the main points advanced by the person she is arguing with. By doing so, she provides a context for her views, a context that her assigned audience might not otherwise be aware of.

Another way in which the first writer seems egocentric is that she simply asserts her value judgment ('it's not fair') and to justify that value judgment simply refers to what 'us girls' want. Of course, that justification is persuasive only if one has the same values as 'us girls' and if one is willing to make the rather simplistic assumption that getting what one wants is necessarily fair and desirable. The first writer also sets up a hypothetical sequence which allows for no alternatives, no deviation: 'if we want to do this, they *have* [my italics] to give us a chance . . . .' The second girl's argument is not a great deal more complex: If the girls have gym with the boys, they will (with no explicit exceptions or complications) learn more and become more physically fit. But at least this second writer presents an argument based on something other than her own personal wishes. Her basic assumption, about the desirability of girls being physically fit, could easily be shared even by someone who was not inclined to favour the specific programme that 'us girls' want.

This analysis lets me suggest some of the ways in which 'mature' — i.e. decentred — thought might be reflected in writing. Recognizing that the audience is different from himself or herself, the writer:

1. provides an appropriate context for his/her statements;
2. bases his/her arguments on values the audience is likely to share.

Extrapolating from the negative examples of the 'Dear John' and the 'To the University of Michigan . . .' letters, one could speculate about other features of 'mature' writing. This writing might show an author trying to:

1. anticipate and respond to objections/questions the audience is likely to have;
2. recognize the legitimacy as well as the limitations of other points of view on a given subject;
3. acknowledge, where appropriate, the limitations of his/her own point of view, indicating what his/her theories can *not* explain, taking note of and trying to reconcile evidence that appears to contradict one's ideas or feelings.
4. recognize the complexity of the subject at hand, attending to more than one single feature of an experience.

As I shall suggest later in this article, this definition is, at best, limited. But I hope that my discussion thus far will let me justify this assertion: Written products may reflect not only a writer's conclusions but also strategies for developing and testing these conclusions; we may be able to base our definition of *mature writing* at least in part on our understanding of mature thinking. My main concern in the rest of this article will be to identify ways in which all of us who teach writing can contribute to the redefinition of the term *mature writing*. Further, I shall try to show that our work can take the form of small·scale studies that will let us contribute to basic research in our field and, at the same time, get on with the day-to-day business of improving students' writing. But before describing these studies, I want to anticipate several problems that could misdirect and trivialize both teaching and research.

The first problem is that, as is always the case for researchers and teachers of writing, we must be careful about what we try to conclude from a single piece of writing. It does seem reasonable to try to determine whether a given piece of writing reflects relatively mature thought processes. As we identify some of these processes, we may be able to see more clearly how we can help students explore and convey their ideas more adequately. But it seems foolish to use our analysis of one or two pieces of writing to label a writer as egocentric. As I suggested earlier, a writer's performance can vary widely from task to task. People who think and write with some maturity in one context may not do so in other contexts. Moreover, labels — *all* labels — have ways of becoming self-fulfilling prophecies. Students have a way of meeting our expectations. If we say 'Of course little Johnny can't write. He's still very egocentric, you know', we may find little Johnny does what we expect and persists in not learning to write.

Another problem is that one might be tempted to equate non-egocentric writing with impersonal, bland prose in which the writer never refers to him/herself, never takes a stand but, rather, continually acknowledges that 'there are two sides to every issue' and concludes only that 'there are no easy answers'. In investigating cognitive maturity in writing, we must remember that the use of passive-expletive constructions or careful avoidance of first person pronouns cannot hide the fact that all writing is produced by an *I*; a person whose feelings, values, and choices shape what is being said. Further, we must remember that even the most complex issues require writers to take a stand, make some personal commitment. The question for teachers and researchers alike is whether a writer's choices and commitments reflect a degree of mature thought and perception concerning the subject at hand.

A third problem is that recognizing egocentrism in writing is not so straightforward a matter as is, say, computing mean T-unit length. In one rhetorical context, a feature of organization or content may suggest egocentricity and yet in another context may suggest relative maturity. This point is illustrated by two pieces of writing done by high school students of 'average' ability. The first piece was written in response to this assignment:

> Write about a loss you experienced as a child. Tell what you lost and how you felt about the loss. Through your writing help your reader understand what the loss meant to you.

In talking about the loss of a prized toy, one student wrote:

> After saving my allowance for a couple months, I ventured to the local hobby shop to purchase a brand new Hot Wheels. The make of the toy was a Paddy Wagon. Alot of kids in school were involved in the same hobby I was, so I brought the toy to school. During our lunch period I took out the toy and was showing it around the table. After everyone had seen it I put it in my lunch bag. Forgetting the toy in my lunch bag, I threw the bag in the garbage as I was leaving the cafeteria to go to my class. When I got to my next class I realized what I did but it was a lost cause. The car toy was gone for good.

The second piece of writing was done in response to this assignment:

> Choose a place or object that you know very well and describe it so clearly that even someone who had never seen this place/object would be able to recognize it.

One student chose to write about 'a little patch of woods, a half mile down the road from my Aunt's house, in South Carolina, where I used to sneak away to have cigarettes when I was younger'.

> I would tell my mom I'm going for a walk and go out the door. I'de walk down the driveway, and take a right on the road. The walk is about half a mile long, or until a wooded section appears on the right hand side of the road. When you look to the right you see a path tracked in the red clay, leading upward into the woods. By simply following the path, through viny trees, and well spaced shrubs, you come to a fairly open area, about the size of a car. Lying on the ground, there should be about two hundred rotting cigarette butts. The woods are fairly thick, and if you're a kid it's a good place to sneak off to, because I never got caught.

Both of these pieces contain a good bit of personal narrative. Yet this narrative may suggest egocentricity in one but not in the other. In the piece about the loss of the car, the narrative — admittedly not a very skilful or complex one — provides a context that enables a reader to have some sense of what the toy meant to the student. This narrative suggests that the writer has some awareness of the kind of information the audience will need if the writer is to accomplish his assigned purpose. By contrast, the second narrative seems to reflect much less awareness of the audience's needs. The narrative doesn't provide the information an audience would have to have in order to recognize the place the writer used to go to sneak a smoke.

A final closely-related problem in redefining *mature writing* is that our definition may have to vary according to the kind of writing one is doing. Consider, for example, the following excerpt in which a student skilfully conveys the perceptions and reactions of a novice, out-of-condition hiker who is trying to keep up with a well-conditioned and apparently relentless hiking companion.

> The red pack bobbed ahead of me, always the same distance, always just out of reach, teasing me on. Only twenty minutes out and my lungs were burning. I swung my arms, loping up the trail like an orang-utan, each hand in turn clutching for the invisible handle that would pull me on. 'Tell me when you want to rest.' 'Ha!' I laughed back proudly and spent the next three minutes gasping to make up for that extra air I had wasted. Don't talk, just climb. Breathe. My breath came and went in fast, deep rasps. 7000'. I wasn't breathing. I was viciously sucking the air into me, as if through a pillow. I was a sieve, the air running through me, too thin to feel, gone and lost before I could soak it up. The slow ache from my chest creeped up, tightening around my throat. Couldn't swallow. No time. Just breathe. Teeth ached. 'if I ever stop,' I thought, 'I'll never move again, I swear.'

Earlier in this article, I listed a few of the qualities that might distinguish relatively mature writing from relatively egocentric writing. Clearly, 'The Red Back Pack' does not display many of these qualities. For instance, nothing in the student's essay suggests that the writer has considered other points of view concerning her experience. She never, for example, makes any reference to what the wearer of the red back pack might have thought about this experience. Indeed, the writer deals so extensively with her own perceptions that it would be easy to consider this narrative the product of very egocentric thinking. Yet I not only think this a very effective piece of writing but also believe it represents relatively complex, mature consideration of the experience. This relative maturity becomes apparent when we contrast this piece with another piece of personal experience expressive writing.[1]

> Yesterday, my boyfriend and I went to a big dance in Detroit. When we walked into the place, it was real noisy because everyone was talking and dancing. The dancing area was a lot bigger than most of the other ones I've seen, but the air was filled with smoke that would choke a horse. While looking around, my boyfriend noticed a few of his friends across the room, so we went over there, and he introduced them to me. They were the coolest guys! After talking a while with them, Fabian came up to me and asked me to dance. I just about died! I thought I was going to faint, but I pulled through. He's the most!

As do so many unsophisticated writers, the writer of this account deals in global, unexamined impressions: The friends were 'the coolest guys'; Fabian was the 'the most'; on meeting Fabian, the writer 'just about died'.

In fairness to this writer, we must acknowledge that reflecting upon our reactions and impressions is always difficult, especially when we are convinced of the inherent, self-evident rightness of our impressions. But this reflection upon the self-evident, this attempt to break up a global impression by considering the varieties of detail that comprise the impression — this is part of what separates the 'Red Back Pack' essay from the piece on the dance. The author of 'The Red Back Pack' doesn't just say 'this is awful, I hurt'; she focusses her attention on the diverse aspects of her experience: the burning of her lungs, the movements of her hands, the effort involved in breathing, the ache in her chest, throat, and teeth.

One reaction to these two essays is simply to note that one writer has used many more details than has the other. That, of course, is true. But such a reaction should not obscure the possibility that those details may be the product of a relatively mature thinking and perceiving process that is not apparent in the essay about the dance. Unlike the student who wrote about her reactions to a dance, the author of 'The Red Back Pack' shifts the focus of her attention to different aspects of her experience and manages, thereby, to capture the richness and detail of her experience. Assuming that 'The Red Back Pack' reflects relatively mature thinking, I want to reiterate a point I made earlier. It might be that we will have to modify our definition of cognitive maturity to suit the type of writing we are concerned with. Otherwise, our definition of 'mature' persuasive writing might not enable us to identify, say, mature personal experience writing.

I raise this problem, and those that precede it, because we have only begun the work of re-defining the term *mature writing*, and it seems best to proceed with some care. With this in mind, I want to propose several types of inquiry that may help us re-think our definition of mature writing.[2]

One kind of study would require us to identify the 'mind at work' in writing done by our own students. We might rely on a combination of theory and intuition to identify one group of writings that seem to reflect relatively mature thinking and another group that seem to reflect relatively immature thinking. We would then analyse this writing to see whether we could detect patterns of thought which appear in the one group but not in the other. This is essentially the procedure I have followed in discussing contrasting pieces of student writing earlier in this article. (For other approaches to this sort of analysis, see Odell 1977; Ohmann 1962.)

Instead of, or perhaps in addition to, analysing the written products of our students, we might examine their composing process by having them 'compose aloud' as they write. Several teachers and researchers (Emig 1971; Flower and Hayes, forth-coming) have found that student writers can verbalize their thoughts, reactions, uncertainties as they write. Apparently, even very unsophisticated writers can give a useful report of their com-posing process (Perl 1977).

Whether analysing pieces of student writing or transcripts of students' composing aloud, we might ask at least two kinds of questions:

1. Do students at one age level appear to use cognitive process-es that are rarely or never used by students at another age?
2. Do some of these students display cognitive processes that are consistent with what psychologists (Flavell 1977; Piaget 1968) tell us about mature or immature thought?

Answers to these questions will help us understand how cogni-tive maturity (or immaturity) is reflected in students' writing. Moreover, these answers can guide our work with students. For example, I have already noted one of the important processes re-flected in the essay 'The Red Back Pack' was a skilful shifting of focus. We have some basis (Goswami 1979) for thinking that stu-dents can be taught to shift focus and thereby improve their de-scriptive writing. This evidence, combined with other studies that show we can influence the cognitive processes student writers en-gage in (Odell 1974; Young and Koen 1973), leads me to make this suggestion: as we identify the cognitive processes that are characteristic of our more mature student writers, we may be able to help less mature writers engage in those processes.

Another type of study would require us to assign writing tasks that we felt reasonably confident required a specific kind of cognitive maturity. For example, Carl Bereiter *et al.* (1979), recently conducted a study in which they assumed one aspect of cognitive maturity was the ability to re-formulate one's conclusion about a given set of facts, expanding and revising that conclusion so as to accommodate new information. Participants in the study were asked to describe what was going on in a picture, 'a cartoon scene of classroom disorder: two children are having a pea shooter fight, another has just sat on a tack . . . and a large bee is flying out the window'. Some of the participants were shown only the complete picture, but others were shown the picture in four successive 'exposures', each exposure being designed so as to give a different impression of what was going on in the picture. For example, the first exposure showed only one child in pain and a bee flying out a window. This exposure clearly allowed the interpretation that the bee had stung the child. Subsequent exposures gave slightly different impressions; not until the fourth exposure did participants see the full picture and, thereby, get the most comprehensive view of what was going on in the picture.

For Bereiter *et al.*, the important question in this study was: Do writers at different ages revise their initial impression so as to account for new information? That question is important to all of us since the act of writing about a complex piece of literature or exploring a challenging subject may require writers to re-examine and reformulate their initial impressions. Furthermore, the format of the experiment by Bereiter suggests ways we might combine classroom teaching and research. Assume, for example, that we want students to write about a character in a literary work — *Macbeth*, let us say. We might ask students to read up to the point where, near the end of Act I, Lady Macbeth urges Macbeth to murder Duncan. In their reading, students would identify all the statements that give some insight into Macbeth's character. Once students had identified those statements, we might ask students to free write about their initial impressions of the character Macbeth. We might have students repeat this process at several points during their reading of the play. Having completed this process of reading, note taking, and free writing, students would be in a position to write an essay about the character Macbeth. Their notes and free writing would serve as preparation for that essay. These same notes and free writings, combined with students' essays, could become the subject of our own research. In examining the work of a small number of students, we might ask ourselves such questions as these:

1. Which students seem most (or least) able to re-formulate their initial impressions?
2. In what ways do their initial impressions change (or fail to change)?
3. What difficulties do students have as they engage in this process? Can we use the work of more successful students to give direction to the work of less successful students?

By analysing the work of small numbers of students we might add to our knowledge of the cognitive processes of students at a particular age level and, at the same time, see how we might modify our teaching so as to help all students at a particular grade level engage in more complex conceptual activity.

One final possibility for research would be to examine the writing of adults, particularly those adults who are not professional writers but who frequently have to write as a part of their work in business or government. My own contacts with such writers suggest three pleasantly surprising conclusions: (1) many people do a great deal more writing than one might expect; (2) these writers are frequently willing to discuss their writing — once they discover that we respect what they do and are not simply looking for 'mistakes' in grammar, usage, etc.; (3) many of these writers approach their writing with sophisticated strategies that suggest cognitive maturity. For example, in examining the letters, memos, etc. of a worker in a government agency, I realized that this worker had several rather different ways of asking people to do something. In one memo she had said 'The Agency Director requested that I send you this form for completion'. In other memos and letters, her requests were likely to take different forms: 'Perhaps you could...' or 'Please send...' During an interview, I asked the worker how she came to say 'The Agency Director requested...' rather than 'Please fill out this form' or 'Perhaps you could fill out this form'. Her response:

> I suppose I could have said please complete this.... (pause) Do you know [the person her memo was addressed to]?..... He's kind of abrupt. So he's just not the kind of person that you say 'Please complete this' to; he's not that type. 'The Agency Director requested...' that's all he needs.

A similar sense of her audience underlay her decision to say 'Please' or 'Perhaps you might', in other contexts. This awareness of audience also appeared in many of her other choices about what she would say or how she would say it. As the worker herself pointed out, she had learned to make her choices almost instinctively. She said she rarely sat down and carefully plotted her strategy before writing. Yet her writing makes it clear that she did in fact have different strategies and that her use of those strategies parallels her understanding of her audience. Her awareness of her audience and her sensitivity to the different needs of different audiences suggests a cognitive maturity that one might not find in the work of students or, perhaps, even in the writing of less experienced workers (cf. Kroll 1978).

Inevitably, we will find that adult, non-professional writers possess varying degrees of skill; their writing and their comments about their writing may reflect varying degrees of cognitive maturity. Indeed, we may find that a particular writer may exhibit more egocentrism in doing some writing tasks than in doing others. Nevertheless, analysis of the thinking of adult writers provides one more way we can understand the relation between cognitive maturity and maturity of writing. And as we discover some of the conceptual processes that guide the writing of skilful adults, we may be able to teach our students to engage in those processes.

This last suggestion may make me seem to encourage teachers and researchers to ask a version of what Piaget has reportedly called 'the American question': If we can identify some of the characteristics of 'mature' thought, is there some way we can speed up the process of maturity, some way to train younger writers to avoid egocentrism altogether and make their writing display only those qualities one would expect to find in the work of older writers? Although I may seem to be treading a very fine line, I think we must avoid entrapping ourselves and our students in the implications of this question. For one thing, egocentrism appears to have its uses. Even very mature writers may, at some point in their composing process, find it helpful to be egocentric. For example, the free writing proposed by Peter Elbow (1973) may lead one to make intemperate or ill-considered statements that would not appear in a final draft. Yet that free writing, with all its potential for — even encouragement of — egocentrism, is for many writers a useful part of the attempt to understand what they wish to say about a given subject.

Another reason for being leery of 'the American question' is that are limits, surely, to the demands we may place upon students at a given age level. At each stage of one's development, there are important experiences that should not be bypassed. In other words, twelve-year-olds deserve a chance to be twelve-year-olds. Furthermore, egocentric language must have some uses — otherwise children would stop throwing temper tantrums and professional reviewers of the arts would stop writing vituperative, polemical reviews. And we would stop reading those reviews.

But even while rejecting the implications of 'the American question', I still wish to argue that all of our efforts to teach writing must be informed by our sense of what is possible for mature writers. As we explore the ways cognitive maturity is manifested in writing, we may find that what is possible and desirable may differ according to the particular group of writers or the type of writing we are working with. But as we identify the cognitive processes that are possible and desirable, we shall be able to expand our definition of 'maturity' as it applies to writing. And in so doing, we may also assist our students (and perhaps ourselves) with the problem that is the theme of this conference, the problem of learning to write.

Notes

1. My comments about expressive writing in this context reflect James Kinneavy's definition of the term rather than James Britton's. That is, I intend the term to refer to writing in which one articulates one's ideas and feelings in a deliberately crafted manner that is intended to make those ideas and feelings accessible to someone other than oneself.

2. For additional suggestions for research, see Loren S. Barritt and Barry M. Kroll's 'Some Implications of Cognitive-Developmental Psychology for Research in Composing,' in *Research in Composing*: *Points of Departure*, Charles R. Cooper and Lee Odell, (eds.) Champaign, Illinois: National Council of Teachers of English, 1978.

Part Three
Text and discourse

This section begins with a study which provides a context for all the remaining papers in it: James Kinneavy's (Chapter 8) synoptic analysis of what researchers in the first-language field will immediately recognize as the most extensive and also the most influential attempts to situate a piece of writing with respect to the person of the writer and his aims, the intended audience, and the modes within which such aims can be realized for such an audience. As Kinneavy shows, the four rhetorics he analyses are to a very large extent compatible with one another; moreover where they do not overlap, they usually complement each other. That there should be so much congruence between these four systems is itself a testimony to the strength of the tacit tradition underlying the development of the new rhetoric, for, as Kinneavy notes, the four systems were to a large extent developed independently.

Still more remarkable, therefore, is their silence about precisely those formal aspects of written texts that are most familiar in current-traditional rhetoric. The disinclination to focus on the surface of the composed text is, of course, symptomatic of the strong reaction in the new rhetoric to the preoccupations of the immediately preceding generations of rhetoricians. Their attempts to codify rules which would guide novice writers during those parts of the process that are accessible to conscious monitoring and control (in effect, the revising and editing stages) came to be interpreted in the continuing degeneration of the tradition as rules to be followed during the process of writing. So, for example, since a thesis sentence and a complete sentence outline can be extracted from any successful piece of completed argumentation, it was argued that their formulation must constitute a distinct stage in the prewriting process. New rhetoricians are unanimous in their rejection of this confusion between the product and the process for, as Donald Murray has frequently argued, you can't infer a pig from a sausage.

All the four systems that Kinneavy analyses take a much more distant view of the surface of the finished piece of writing, and place it in a much larger context. In all of them, to begin with, writing is situated in the underlying semiotic structure of the triangular relationships between writer, subject matter and audience. In all of them, the aims of discourse are elaborated in terms of the pragmatics of communication. And in all of them the concern with the structure of the finished piece of discourse goes far beyond the traditional division into four modes (to say nothing of the traditional emphasis on 'formal expository writing'), to provide a detailed taxonomy of the modes of discourse in English-speaking cultures. The scope of such studies is thus very broad.

Apart from such wide-ranging studies, the rapidly increasing body of research examining the development of children's ability to produce narrative (see, for example, Bartlett 1981, 1982), and the kind of work on oral discourse represented in Coulthard (1977), there has been very little discussion in the first-language context of the way English discourse is organized, and still less in relation to written prose. As Richard Larson points out in a bibliographic review of studies dealing with form and structure in contemporary rhetoric, 'form in complete essays has not been the subject of much theoretical investigation' (1976, p. 45), and written text, as an autonomous entity, has also received little attention in its own right.

Complicated as Kinneavy's synoptic view of the written product is compared to the traditional view, its complexity is vastly extended when it is looked at from a second-language point of view, as we shall see. Probably it is to this very extension that the fairly narrowly conceived limits of most second-language work on text are due. On the whole, those working in English as a second language have been much more concerned than those working in the first-language field with the linguistic analysis (broadly conceived) of the formal properties of discourse. In this volume we have already seen such a concern in Widdowson's paper, and it is to return in Part Four, in Johnson's. At first sight it looks as though there has been a tacit agreement not to extend research much beyond a linguistically sound revision of the current-traditional approach, with its analysis of the product as the starting point for teaching.

Apart from its sensible caution, however, that restraint is not without theoretical foundation, given the fact that so much of the instruction in ESL that takes place is given to adults, often adults already highly educated, who need to learn English for some specific academic or professional purpose. Widdowson, in particular, has been concerned to show that the underlying discourse structure of much scientific writing, whatever its language, is basically similar, so that an adult learner who is already master of a particular field needs to learn only the more local and relatively superficial aspects of text that are English-specific (see especially Widdowson 1979, pp. 19–61).

Nonetheless other researchers have begun to push the second-language field away from this narrower interest in the surface properties of discourse in its immediate sociolinguistic context to a larger and more rhetorical conception of the place of writing. For the constraints imposed by the English modes of discourse, as Kinneavy and his fellow investigators have analysed them, are to some extent culture-specific. (This fact is perhaps still clearer if one compares the norms of the English narrative, as Bartlett (1981, 1982) analyses them, with the norms of narrative in other cultures). Insofar as the English modes of discourse are culture-specific, those for whom English is a second language have to learn them, and their difficulty in doing so will presumably be all the greater if the tacit constraints imposed on them by the rhetorical norms of their own culture are radically different. This possibility is the subject of Robert B. Kaplan's paper (Chapter 9).

Prior to the emergence of work on text and on discourse, Kaplan's contrastive rhetoric hypothesis was virtually the only alternative to the structural view of why second-language learners 'get it wrong' when they sit down to write. Contrastive rhetoric is closely related to contrastive linguistics in that it deals with contrasts between languages; it is also related to rhetoric as this has developed as an aid to written composition; and it has links with discourse analysis insofar as it concerns itself with the writing process (Houghton 1980). Kaplan's early articles dealt with the problem of finding an explanatory hypothesis to account for the differences between the writing of students from other countries (who were entering U.S. colleges and universities in increasing numbers in the 1960's) and the writing of their English-speaking counterparts. The differences, he believes, are related to rhetorical patterns typical of students' first languages. The most complete version of his theory is to be found in Kaplan (1972); it is based on the weak version of the Sapir-Whorf hypothesis.

In the paper in this volume, Kaplan extends his work and continues to suggest that 'the problems a second-language learner grapples with are not purely linguistic and probably cannot be solved by purely linguistic means'. In this he agrees with Widdowson, and claims that stress on sentence syntax does not prepare the non-native speaker either to write or to read English texts. He develops his definitions of *topic* and *focus* as controlling mechanisms in a discourse, stating that the treatment language teachers have provided of illocutionary values in the study of discourse has been inadequate largely because of a lack of understanding of these mechanisms. The treatment offered here of *focus* and its function fits with Widdowson's assertions about writing as an inter-active process. However, Kaplan goes further and states that focus is culture-bound and that it is this factor which creates 'a tension between the apparent relationship of ideas to topic and the possibly inappropriate realization of focus through intersentential syntax' in the written production of the second-language learner.

Work is proceeding at a relatively slow pace in this area, and no wonder, given its demanding and complex nature. The selection of texts to be studied contrastively is a very difficult problem, as is the linguistic analysis to be employed. Both these factors may contribute to differences or contrasts perceived, and so interpretation of results may be at times unclear or unsatisfactory. Nonetheless it is a field which has a great deal to offer, and it will be interesting to observe developments as the work of linguists on both sides of the Atlantic converges, and discourse analysis continues or overlaps with contrastive rhetoric.

The culturally determined rhetorical expectations which are Kaplan's concern are, of course, a feature of audience, though not a feature that Kinneavy, working entirely from a first-language perspective, has any reason to discuss. Kameen's paper (Chapter 10), although it is concerned as Kaplan's is with the syntax of the English written by second-language learners, returns us to a concept of audience which is much narrower than Kinneavy's conception, and all too familiar in a first-language context as well: the audience provided by the teacher or instructor who reads and grades a student's written production. What Kameen's study shows is that the grades assigned by experienced ESL instructors correlate highly with particular features of syntax that other researchers have shown to be significant markers of developmental progression in first-language student writing. This discovery has obvious pedagogical implications.

The field that Kameen touches on here is the one area of first-language studies which is an obvious exception to the preceding generalizations about the lack of interest, in first-language studies, in the surface properties of the written product; for the investigation, above all from a developmental point of view, of the syntax of student writers (as the following paper by Witte (Chapter 11) amply attests and documents) has become a major research industry in North America. In Britain, the key study is that reported in Harpin (1976); for most North Americans the key figures in this area of investigation are Walter Loban and Kellogg Hunt. Beginning in the early 1960's, Walter Loban (1963, 1976) followed a group of children through their schooling from kindergarten to grade 12, tracing the syntactic changes in both their oral and written language. Over the same period, Kellogg Hunt (1964, 1965a, 1965b, 1970, 1977) was describing the grammatical structure of both student and mature writing, using a transformational analysis. This analysis involved a specification of many syntactic features, but the breadth of Hunt's work has been obscured by the prominence many later researchers have given to the new unit of analysis that Hunt introduced, the 'minimal terminable unit' or T-unit (i.e. the main clause with all its attached dependent constituents), which Loban had called the 'communication unit'. Various measures relating to T-units have been shown to be a more accurate index of 'maturity' than the sentence, and it has therefore come to be widely used as a measure of linguistic development in general as well as of the success of specific pedagogic strategies, especially sentence-combining exercises.

For over the same period of time, researchers were experimenting with the effects achieved by teaching transformational grammar, or by having students practice sentence-combining. The most influential of these studies (Mellon 1967, 1969; O'Hare 1973; Daiker, Kerek and Morenberg 1979) have all confirmed that such exercises not only increase the syntactic complexity of student writing, as measured by the T-unit (so that students who have received such instruction seem to learn to write like older students), but also improve the overall quality of the students' written production, as measured holistically. Moreover, both O'Hare's study and subsequent research have shown that such effects are achieved when there is no direct formal instruction in grammar: sentence-combining practice is enough in itself. Given the overall improvement in the quality of writing, there are once again obvious pedagogical implications.

On the other hand, as Witte is concerned to show, there are serious questions which have yet to be answered about the use of the T-unit to measure either syntactic maturation as it shows in student writing or the effect of particular instructional techniques. It is clear from this paper that even in so basic and so long and intensively studied an aspect of language as syntax, much research remains to be done. Even more is that true of the other aspects of written discourse that Widdowson, Johnson and Kaplan point to. More than any other in this book, this section shows where first-language researchers stand to gain from the kind of research that is going on in the second-language context.

8 A pluralistic synthesis of four contemporary models for teaching composition

James L. Kinneavy

Rhetorical theory at the present time is in a similar situation to that which linguistics faced at the end of the 1950's shortly after the publication of Chomsky's *Syntactic Structures*. Linguists at the present time are asking themselves if the ensuing slaughter was worth it. The vicious attacks on previous and competitive grammars made by some advocates of transformational grammar may in the long run prove to have done more harm than good.

In a similar manner there are at the present time several competing theories in rhetorical theory facing each other in gladiatorial manner. To avoid useless, even harmful carnage, it might be useful to look at the compatibilities of the various theories before engaging in a display of their incompatibilities. We are not yet ready, in other words, for the purifying war which Kenneth Burke continually refers to.

In an attempt to show some critical compatibilities among current models of the teaching of composition, I have here chosen four different types of models and attempted to analyse their common traits and to place them in a meta-system which exploits their several strengths and yet allows each to preserve its autonomy. The first is that of James Moffett, *Teaching the Universe of Discourse* (1968) — a model heavily used in elementary and secondary schools in the United States. The second is that of James Britton, *The Development of Writing Abilities (11–18)* (1975), quite influential in England and the United States at the secondary level. The third is that of Frank D'Angelo, *A Conceptual Theory of Rhetoric* (1975), a text which has exercised more influence at the beginning college level composition course in the United States. The last is my own *A Theory of Discourse* (1971), a theory which is meant to cover all levels but which has been most influential at the secondary and college levels in the United States.

The choice of these four texts does not mean to exclude the possibilities of incorporating other current theories or models into the proposed meta-system. For example, I believe that the proposed meta-system is compatible with the work of Richard Young in tagmemics, with that of Ross Winterowd in language and style, with that of John Trimble also in style, etc. But I have chosen these four systems because of their stark similarities. An international conference on the teaching of writing presents many of us with problems of literacy which are common to the entire English-speaking world. It seems more advisable at such an initial meeting to avoid contentious division and to emphasize communities of aspirations.

The similarities which these four models possess are of different kinds. In the first place, all of the four invite a theoretical examination because all of the four respect theory. Three of the four (Moffett, Kinneavy, and D'Angelo) use the word 'theory' in the title or subtitle of one of their major works. Indeed, all four of the books which I propose to examine would probably be classed as theoretical, as opposed to nuts-and-bolts classroom practical textbooks. On the other hand, none of these four writers has been afraid to test his theory out in the classroom. Moffett has written a massive series called *Interaction*, intended to be used from kindergarten to high school. D'Angelo has written a freshman composition text for college based on his theory. Kinneavy has used his theory with immigrant children from Mexico, with the elementary and high school guidelines for language arts in Texas, and with two advanced composition texts for college. Britton's theory has been influential in England, the United States, Canada and Australia.

This combination of theory and practice contrasts, on the one hand, with writers like Kenneth Burke who have not written classroom texts and, on the other hand, with many practitioners like Trimble and Coles who articulate practice but shy away from theory.

A second reason for the choice of these four writers is the endeavour on the part of each for a certain measure of comprehensiveness. Although Moffett maintains that his is 'not a completely systematic and consistent theory' (1968, p. 211), and Britton (1975, p. 17) acknowledges that his system is as yet only two-dimensional and other dimensions remain yet to be developed, and D'Angelo remarks that his system is not 'a complete theory or even a complete methodology' (1975, p. 1), and Kinneavy has only developed two of the six dimensions of his model,[1] nonetheless each is secure enough with the general goals and outlines of his system to advocate extensive practice at several levels.

Thirdly, three of the four are explicitly based on the semiotic structure of the relationships among writer, reader, and subject matter. As will be shown shortly, Moffett, Britton, and Kinneavy use this structure in virtually every segment of their work. And D'Angelo's construct is not inconsistent with this base.

Fourthly, all four of these authors believe that composition is best taught with examples of full discourse. The concerns with mechanics, sentence structure, style, even invention and arrangement are best seen in the act of handling a full discourse. Moffett (1968, pp. 205–206) decries what he calls the particle approach; Kinneavy (1971, p. 23) prefers the holistic over the meristic approach; D'Angelo states that 'the sentence and the paragraph are more important as they relate to the complex network of relationships that link them to the longer discourse' (1975, p. 27). Britton makes the same point by what the logicians would call the argument *ex silentio* — he simply ignores the particles and molecules which the three Americans feel they have to mention.

Finally, the four theories are all unabashedly conceptual. D'Angelo places the word in his title; Moffett (1968, p. 211) lists thinking as his first goal; Kinneavy uses the term 'logic' instead of the traditional 'invention' for the major section of each of his chapters. And, again, the British don't have to apologize for thinking.

These fundamental arguments make it possible to posit each of these constructs in a single meta-system which emerges stronger than any of the individual parts.

The basic semiotic structure of the four theories

It is probably no accident that three of the four theories are explicitly rooted in the basic semiotic structure of the so-called communication triangle. Moffett's *Teaching the Universe of Discourse*, which appeared in 1968, incorporated essays printed in several vehicles between 1964 and 1968.[2] Kinneavy's *A Theory of Discourse*, which was published by Prentice-Hall in 1971, was first copyrighted in 1966 in a mimeographed version. And Britton's research team, which was to publish its results in 1975, first began its work in 1966. These three works, then, were all reaching conceptual realization in the late sixties. At that time the semiotic structure of Charles Morris had reached almost axiomatic acceptance in many areas of language study.[3]

In any case, these three authors consciously use this trinity of author, audience, and subject matter. As Moffett says, 'The structure of discourse, and therefore the superstructure of English, is this set of relations among the three persons' [i.e., I, you, it; (1968, p. 10)]. As we will see, Kinneavy and Britton (following Jakobson) add language to the trinity. But this basic structure is at the core of all three theories.

Let us look at the structures in some detail. Moffett's structure is explicitly grounded in two dimensions, the I-thou relations and the I-it relations. The I-thou relations yield the 'orders of discourse', the types of media situations which obtain between author and audience as the two become further and further separated in space and as the audience grows to include several and then finally unknown masses. I have attempted to summarize these on the horizontal axis of the graph Figure 1.

This dimension of Moffett's theory is heavily indebted to Piaget's notion of a decreasing egocentrism in the development of the self (see Moffett 1968, pp. 17, 24, 148). Piaget's notion of an increasing order of abstraction is also used in constructing these kinds of audience situations.

The secondary dimension of Moffett's theory is represented vertically in Figure 1. It is an attempt to address the I-it relation.

Figure 1 Moffett's kinds and orders of discourse

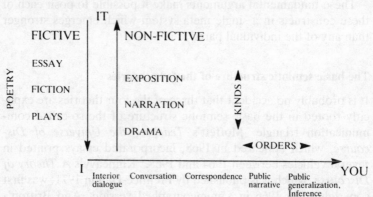

Here the major question is 'what', since the issue has to do with the subject matter. Even more than in the first dimension, Moffett uses the notion of abstraction. He applies the notion of abstraction, this time deriving from both Piaget and Korzybski his main criteria and applying them to the traditional forms of discourse; description, narration, exposition, and argumentation. He substitutes drama for description and then arrives at a continuum of time abstractions: drama records 'what is happening', narrative reports 'what happened', exposition generalizes about 'what happens', and argumentation theorizes about 'what may happen'.

As in the first dimension, the movement of development for these 'kinds' of discourse is away from the self and towards the more abstract 'it'. These kinds of discourse are in the nonfictive areas. In the area of the fictive, the order of progression is reversed — this explains the direction of the arrows in Figure 1 (on the inversion of the literary, see Moffett 1968, pp. 151, 153).

We will return to Moffett's system. In the meantime, however, let us look at Britton's. Britton used Moffett in some of his categories, in fact in both of his dimensions. Britton's system is also

Figure 2 Britton's two dimensions of discourse

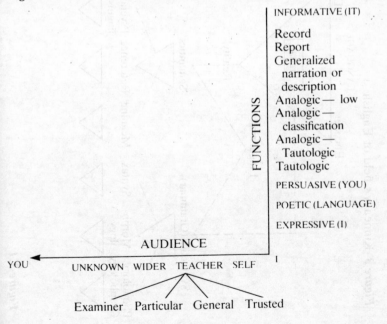

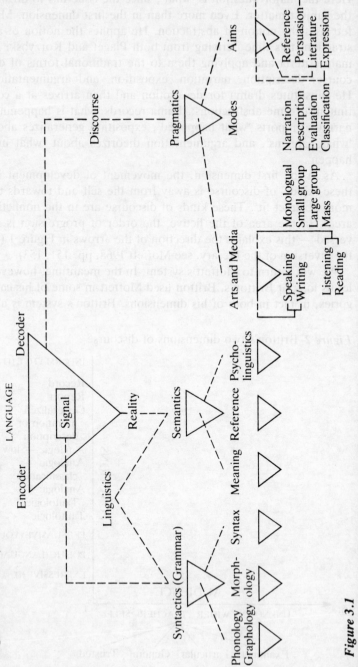

Figure 3 Kinneavy's field of English

Figure 3.1

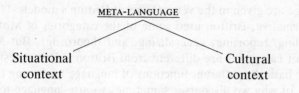

Situational context	Cultural context
Considers such problems as:	Considers such problems as:
Personal and social motivations for speaking, reading, etc	Large social reasons motivating science, propaganda, literature, etc.
Immediate personal and social effects of discourse.	Large social effects of science philosophies, literature, propaganda, etc
Proxemics	Taste in literature, propaganda, science, etc.
Kinesics	
Haptics	Comparative ethno-science, ethno-literature, ethno-rhetoric, ethno-etc
etc	
	Traditions
	Genres
Figure 3.2	Period characteristics

two-dimensional, as he says. The first dimension addresses the question of audience. The audience which Britton's team was analysing were the audiences found in the 2,122 themes written by 500 boys and girls from schools throughout England; the students ranged in age from eleven to eighteen.

Britton's audiences are also arranged in a scale moving from the self to the teacher to the unknown audience. I have attempted to summarize the main categories in the horizontal scale at the bottom of Figure 2. It is obvious that the general direction of the scale closely parallels the I-thou scale of Moffett.

Britton's second dimension, however, differs significantly from Moffett's because he asked a different question. Instead of asking 'what', he asked 'why'. Because he asked 'why', and because the traditional forms of discourse were at least in part answers to 'what', Britton (1975, pp. 3–6) rejected them and turned to other categories. He eventually settled (pp. 13–17) on the semiotic framework suggested by Jakobson and Hymes. The simplified (and yet expanded) answers to the question of why we use language are given in the vertical axis of Britton's models. Under the informative, Britton used some of the categories of Moffett (recording, reporting, generalizing, and theorizing). But Moffett's major categories are different from Britton's. Britton established four basically different functions of language answering the question of why we discourse: sometimes we use language to express ourselves, to verbalize our consciousness; sometimes we use language to construct 'patterned verbalization[s] of ...[our] feelings and ideas' in literary genres; sometimes we use language 'to influence action [and] behaviour'; sometimes we use language to impart or acquire information (1975; the quotations are from the summary statements after the Index).

Let us now turn to a third model of types of discourse. A look at Figures 3.1 and 3.2 will indicate the general structure of Kinneavy's model. He starts out with the communication triangle, which was implicit in Moffett's treatment and is explicitly drawn as a triangle in the last edition of *Student-Centered Language Arts and Reading, K-13* (Moffett and Wagner 1976, p. 15). But Kinneavy's (and Britton's) includes language as a fourth component.

Following Charles Morris, Kinneavy established grammar as the field which specifically studies the language, semantics as the field which studies the capabilities of the language to refer to subject matters (to mean), and discourse study as the field which studies the actual full communications of users of the language.

Under discourse study, Kinneavy parallels Britton's functions of language with his aims of discourse. And indeed one of the sources which Kinneavy used was Jakobson, the same source as Britton. Kinneavy's aims and Britton's functions of language are the same in the general categories. Kinneavy addressed the question of removal from audience in his categories under 'Media'. Here he classifies media as monologual, small group, large group, or mass. It is again clear that the classification principle is the same as in Britton and Moffett — increasing removals from the self in the direction of a larger and then unknown audience. We will return to these various audience classifications later on. For the time being, let it suffice to point out that Britton's audience dimension has some parallels with Kinneavy's media categories.

Kinneavy addresses the question of 'what' the subject matter is in his 'modes' of discourse. He follows Moffett in starting out with the traditional forms or modes of discourse and, like Moffett, he makes some substitutions. He retains description and narration but substitutes two new categories, classification and evaluation, for exposition and argumentation. I will go into the reasons for these changes somewhat later. However, at the present time I would like to point out that the aims of discourse are attempts, like Britton's, to answer the question 'why' we discourse; the modes are attempts, like Moffett's, to answer the question 'what' we discourse about; and the media are attempts, like Britton's and Moffett's, to determine the kinds of audiences addressed in discourse.

It is at the dimension of modes of discourse that D'Angelo's model can be seen to relate to the other systems. D'Angelo's system is a series of topics, a series of 'what's', for topics are subject matters which we discourse about to use for arguing, at least in the traditional meanings of the term.

D'Angelo's model is presented graphically in Figure 4. This graphic presentation is not, like the graphic presentations of Britton and Moffett, a graphic rendition of a verbal presentation; D'Angelo himself uses these branchings to illustrate his theory (1975, pp. 42–49). He first divides the topics into logical and non-logical. The logical are then divided into static, progressive, and repetitive — a trilogy he says he derived from Kenneth Burke (D'Angelo 1975, p. 42). The static categories reflect the more traditional topics which are associated with Aristotle — and they also are quite similar to description and the subdivisions of classification in Kinneavy's modes. The progressive logical topics (with the exception of syllogistic progression) are related to narrative, found in both Moffett and Kinneavy in the 'what' categories. Syllogisms have to do with function in both Kinneavy and Britton. Finally, D'Angelo's non-logical topics do not seem to be 'topics' in the usual senses of the term at all. They are related, says D'Angelo, to the right hemisphere of the brain; it is also obvious that some of them derive from Freud. If there is any relationship to the other three systems, it must be in the areas of self-expression, literature, and persuasion, that is, in the function or aims of language.

Finally, before taking a more careful look at some of these subdivisions, it might be pointed out that Moffett and Kinneavy both consider the range of the language arts: speaking, listening, writing, and reading. Moffett adds thinking as a coordinate to these (an ominous suggestion), whereas Kinneavy maintains that there is a separate kind of thinking in each of the modes and aims.

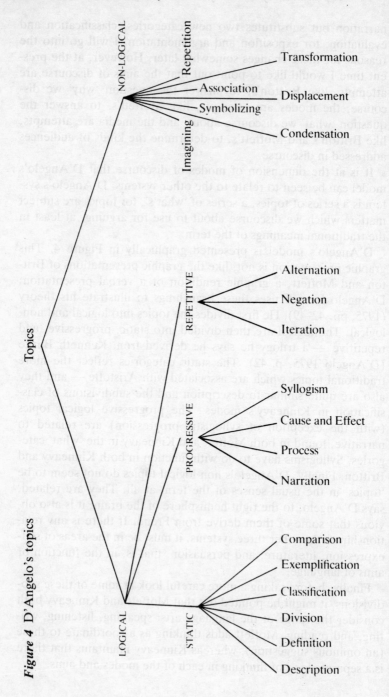

Figure 4 D'Angelo's topics

The functions of language

What is the composite picture given us by the synthesis of the four systems when we consider the functions of language, as Britton calls them, or the aims of discourse, as Kinneavy terms them?

Britton's study brings to the theoretical categories of Jakobson, Urban, Hayakawa, Aristotle, Russell (all used by either Britton or Kinneavy) the support of empirical testing. These basic categories do exist and the writing chore does change when the function changes. Further, Britton's study gives empirical support to the basic contention of Britton and Kinneavy — that function is one of the major dimensions of language study.

Britton (1975, p. 31) and Kinneavy (1971, p. 393) both agree on another fundamental, which however does not receive much empirical proof in the British experiment. Both give priority to self-expression and both maintain that all other functions start with the self-expressive. Britton further suggests that 'it is what the writer makes of these expressive beginnings that determines his thought processes as the written text is produced' (1975, p. 31). The nature of this influence in the composing process has yet to be examined.

The developmental movement among the functions would certainly seem to suggest a priority of the expressive. In some respects Britton's study illustrates this, at least at the informative end of the spectrum. The developmental dimension found both in Moffett and Britton is entirely lacking in Kinneavy and D'Angelo. Both of their models might be called Brunerian in the sense that neither posits a developmental sequence for any of the components of the model. This is certainly an area in which Moffett and Britton can add to Kinneavy and D'Angelo.

However, the small proportion of the expressive writings to the other functions (5.5 per cent of the sample; Britton 1975, p. 141) in the Britton experiment is not reassuring. If self-expression is the most important and the psychologically prior function of language, it would seem that it would occur more frequently than the Britton studies suggest. One can only shudder to suspect what might have been the findings in some American schools.

What remains to be done with the expressive function? We need to know what types of activities will foster the expressive function in all of the language arts throughout the entire gamut of psychological development from childhood to adulthood. In early childhood, possibly some of the best suggestions will come from the types of activities suggested by Moffett, particularly in his *Interaction* programme. This will require a re-examination of Moffett from the point of view of the explicit recognition of what is only implicit in his work at the present time. Other writers on early childhood and childhood can also be profitably used. The intermediate, junior high, senior high, and college years need to be similarly analysed and provided for. The Dartmouth and York conference suggestions will often prove useful in this area. At the college level, the work of Macrorie (1970), Elbow (1973), and Kelly (1972) will point the way. The philosophical framework of Sartre, Heidegger, and Hegel (used by Kinneavy) can provide general guidelines (see Kinneavy 1971, Chapter VI).

The poetic function is clearly recognized by all four theorists. Probably because English departments throughout the world are departments of literature primarily, the literary function is given some careful attention. Nevertheless, the decline from a high of 24 per cent in the sixteenth year to 7 per cent in the eighteenth year, as seen in the Britton experiment, is also ominous. In America it is quite certain that many of the students will never write a literary piece after their high school years; maybe this is also true of other English-speaking countries. Of course, the poetic function is also satisfied by reading and listening as well as by writing — and literary readings are a solid core of English requirements throughout the English academic world.

Nevertheless, from the creative (rather than receptive) point of view, the poetic function seems at the present time somewhat in eclipse. In America, at least, both at the high school and at the college level there is not the large scale encouragement of poetic and fictive writing that existed some thirty or forty years ago.

The persuasive function seems the most neglected of all the major categories. In the Britton study (1975, p. 146) only 1.6 per cent of the scripts were judged to be persuasive. Moffett does not even give it a place in his categories, though he does discuss rhetoric for a few pages (1968, pp. 115–116). In his *Student-Centered Language Arts and Reading* and in *Interaction* he gives some slight attention to propaganda, usually in a defensive manner. D'Angelo did not provide for persuasion in his conceptual theory, nor in his first edition of the freshman text; however, in his second edition there will be a section devoted to persuasion. Kinneavy (1971, pp. 211–306), on the contrary, devotes almost one-fourth of his book to this function.

In the real world, as opposed to the academic, persuasion is omnipresent. The average New York family, according to a marketing director for General Foods Corporation, is exposed to 1,518 ads from newspapers, magazines, bus and subway posters, radio and television ads *every day* (Kinneavy 1971, p. 267); these figures do not count the educational, the political, the religious, etc., types of persuasion encountered by the individual every day. Indeed, it might be maintained that the persuasive is the most dominant of all functions.

In any case, there has to be much careful work at all levels of the developmental spectrum on the persuasive function. Probably the Aristotelian framework can provide the analytic guidelines, but they have to be modified and adapted to the modern era (see Kinneavy 1971, Chapter IV, passim).

The informative function comprised 62 per cent of all the samples in the Britton experiment. The subdivisions, however, show something quite peculiar. Classification, a subdivision not even provided for in the theoretical framework, came to be the dominant category. As Britton says, 'In point of fact, though, it is not merely the informative writing in the sample which is dominated by the classificatory level: it would be more exact to say that classificatory writing predominates in the sample as a whole' (1975, p. 165).

It is strange that a category not even identified as a major area would come to dominate the entire sample. The fact that this category was imported from Moffett's 'kinds' of discourse, those answering the question 'what', seems to suggest that the analysis might have slipped to a 'what' level instead of a 'why' level.

This problem leads into a consideration of the modes of discourse. But before we discuss them, a few remarks on the functions of language still remain to be made.

The major categories of the experiment of Britton correspond fairly closely with the major categories of Kinneavy generically, as has been pointed out already, but in the area of Britton's informative and Kinneavy's referential functions, they even correspond specifically. Britton's lower level functions of recording, reporting, and generalized narrative or descriptive information correspond to Kinneavy's informative aim. The middle level of speculative corresponds quite closely to Kinneavy's exploratory. And the analogic and tautologic correspond to Kinneavy's explanation or proof (analogic being inductive and tautologic being deductive). The term 'tautologic' seems somewhat ill-advised under a general class of informative, since a tautology is precisely not informative [on this point see Kinneavy (1971, p. 109) quoting Wittgenstein: 'It is no less remarkable that the infinite number of propositions of logic (mathematics) follow from half a dozen 'primitive propositions'. But in fact all the propositions of logic say the same thing, to wit nothing' (1961, p. 89).] This was one of the considerations which led me to use 'referential' for this general class rather than informative.

Britton and Kinneavy both agree on the concept of a dominant function. The raters in the Britton experiment (1975, pp. 106–107) also came to substantial agreement on this matter. Britton also remarks that crossing over in functions within a given theme often characterized immature writers. Kinneavy, analysing more sophisticated prose for the college level, notices the presence of a dominant aim and the use of subservient aims to support the dominant aim; for example, much modern advertising incorporates information for purposes of persuasion, literary works often have very successful persuasive themes, etc. Kinneavy (1971, pp. 60–64) therefore analyses coordinate, subordinate, and interfering aims.

The modes of discourse

Kinneavy, in analysing what he calls 'modes', Moffett, in analysing what he calls 'kinds', and D'Angelo, in analysing what he calls 'topics', are all asking a question like 'What is this subject matter?' And Kinneavy and Moffett both go to the traditional forms (now often called modes) of discourse for their answers to this question. We have seen their adjustments of these traditional categories. In the Anglo-Saxon world at least, this tradition was probably most influenced by Alexander Bain. Bain's categories, however, are rarely fully reproduced in textbooks, for in addition to the usual four (narration, description, exposition, and argumentation), Bain also included poetry and persuasion in his forms of discourse. Bain's categories, therefore, were categories for the aims or functions of language as well as for the subject matters. Indeed, exposition frequently and argumentation always are aims or functions of language rather than aspects of subject matter (for a more lengthy treatment of this issue see Kinneavy, Cope, and Campbell 1976a, Chapter I).

Yet Bain's categories did partly answer the question of 'what'. Let us take a look at narrative. Narrative is a subcategory of Britton under information. And narration is a major category of Moffett in his nonfictive kinds of discourse. Yet Britton certainly does not rule out narrative in his poetic discourse, nor Moffett in his fictive and poetic kinds of discourse. And if one looks carefully at many of the examples of expressive writing given by Britton, it is clear that a good number are little narratives. Finally, the parables of Jesus in the Bible, the lives of the saints, the medieval exempla, and many other religious, political, and educational stories are obviously narratives. It seems clear, therefore, that narratives can be used for any of the major functions.

The same is true of description. There are scientific and informative descriptions, there are persuasive descriptions, there are literary descriptions, and finally there are expressive descriptions. The same is true of classifications and definitions. And the same finally is true of evaluation (for the examples of all of these see Kinneavy, Cope, and Campbell 1976a, Chapter I).

Classifications obviously loom large in Britton's sample. And if one generically includes definition, division, classification itself, and comparison (with all of its subdivisions) in D'Angelo's chart, it is obvious that this category is by far the largest in D'Angelo's system. In his static logical topics only description and exemplification would be excluded.

Excluding exemplification for the time being, then, D'Angelo and Kinneavy agree on the basic inclusions for static topics: description and classification (with its subdivisions). D'Angelo and Kinneavy also agree that static topics should be coordinate with dynamic topics (D'Angelo calls them progressive). And narration, process, and cause and effect are issues which Kinneavy addresses in his chapter on narration.

Moffett's system obviously can absorb without much trouble some of these elements. Narration is central to his system, to Kinneavy's, and to D'Angelo's. Classification presents no problem, for Moffett's analogic (used in exposition) is classificatory in nature, as Britton's adaptation shows. Description is more of a problem because Moffett has explicitly repudiated description as a mode. Nevertheless in his teacher-training texts Moffett frequently uses descriptive materials. There is a long section on 'Sensory Writing' in *A Student-Centered Language Arts Curriculum* (1976, Chapter 13, pp. 183 ff.), which is predominantly descriptive in nature. In any case, description is not incompatible with his system — and that is all that I am arguing in this instance.

Britton's system is different. However, since he has included classification, narration, and description under information, he is at least not averse to seeing these modes used in one component of his system. And I have pointed to instances of narration used throughout the different functions. The same holds for description. Consequently, although Britton has repudiated the traditional modes (as have Moffett and Kinneavy as they are usually presented), it would seem that some kinds of modes are compatible with Britton's functions.

I believe that Moffett, D'Angelo, and Kinneavy have made a strong enough case for the conceptual nature of the activities in these modes to justify their separate consideration from the functions or aims. Kinneavy's philosophical framework for the differences among the various modes (see Kinneavy, Cope, and Campbell 1976a, Chapter I) will hopefully placate the legitimate critics of the traditional modes. In addition to the philosophical argument the historical argument has some plausibility. In antiquity, the issues (*staseis, status* in Greek and Latin) were separated from the purpose or function; this held true in the Renaissance. And the Ciceronian *status* are the real ancestors of the modes as Kinneavy presents them, rather than the system of Bain.

Technically speaking, the modes can be looked upon as the semantics of discourse (what discourses mean or refer to), while the functions of discourse are the uses or pragmatics of discourse, and arts and media are the syntactics of discourse (see Kinneavy 1971, p. 30 ff.). There really is a distinction between what one is talking about and why one is talking about it.

If one grants this, then the developmental sequences for the modes at all levels have to be worked much as those for the functions. Here, however, much of the work has been brilliantly done by Moffett. Even description is covered by much of the work he suggests. What no one has yet done is to approach evaluation developmentally and pedagogically. Although it was a component of the historical rhetorical *status* in antiquity and the Renaissance, it dropped out of consideration in Bain's and Reid's treatments of the modes in the nineteenth century. Kinneavy has tried to reintroduce it. It is not theoretically incompatible with any of the systems I am here examining.

Considerations of audience

The least controversial component of the meta-system which I am proposing today should be the audience component. As I have already pointed out, Moffett and Britton and Kinneavy all have substantially the same structure in their general considerations of audience. Britton's and Moffett's were designed with a psychological development in mind, whereas Kinneavy's was simply designed to try to cover comprehensively the various kinds of authors and audiences in different media situations. Moffett's system is very elaborately worked out for different grade levels; and for ages eleven to eighteen, Britton's is also (though only for school situations).

There is a mild conflict of realism versus idealism in the two systems of thought. Britton's sample (1975, p. 192) ends up with two of the categories (directed to the teacher) constituting 92 per cent of the sample. This is a realistic presentation of the facts as they are in England (and probably in Canada, the United States, Australia, etc.). Moffett (1968, p. 12) denigrates this tendency and has organized his whole programme of interaction around the use of small groups as much as possible. I would hope that the move in Moffett's direction in this matter could be as decisive as possible.

Moffett and Kinneavy generally tend to incorporate more than the usual school situations in their models. And this is true of their treatments of audience. It is also true of their treatment of the relationship of speech to writing. Both of their models are models of discourse generally, not just models for writing. Consequently their models must be interpreted in this light.

One aspect of audience which Kinneavy has isolated for consideration has to do with the relationship of audience to function. Britton (1975, pp. 185–187) has made some remarks on this matter. But Kinneavy (1971, pp. 127–128, 173) has tried to focus on the specific nature of the scientific audience, the informative audience (pp. 93–94), the persuasive audience (pp. 241–245) — in a word has argued that in mature writing the audience differs considerably from function to function.

Conclusions

If this presentation has been effective, certain working assumptions about the teaching of writing might be accepted in the meta-system of Britton-D'Angelo-Kinneavy-Moffett (to revert to an alphabetical order).

1. Four of the major contemporary rhetorics are compatible with each other and can be incorporated into a meta-system which profits from the strengths of each component system but yet respects each component system.

2. The meta-system comprises an interest in the functions (or

aims) of language, the modes of discourse, and the different kinds of audiences for which one writes or speaks.

3. The operative conceptual processes for at least the functions and modes of discourse are different. Consequently a different type of intellectual chore is presented by these different types of assignments. These differences in no way prevent or discourage the overlap of these kinds of discourse.

4. The psychological developmental sequences for the presentation of these various types of discourse and audiences are critical for a workable educational programme. The research of Britton and Moffett is a healthy beginning in this area and needs to be supplemented in some areas. Without such a supplement, Kinneavy's and D'Angelo's systems are Brunerian systems without level adjustments.

5. These four authors favour the holistic teaching of composition over the isolated teaching of parts of the theme (such as grammar, paragraph, etc.).

6. Although the school situation must be realistically respected, the teaching of composition ought to be related to the situational and cultural contexts of the student whenever possible.

7. The empirical evidence of Britton, the psychological bases of Moffett and D'Angelo, and the philosophical and critical foundations of Kinneavy give such a meta-system a strong plausibility.

Notes

1. His *A Theory of Discourse* (1971) and *Aims and Audiences in Writing* (1976a) expand his theories on the functions or aims of language. His *Writing — Basic Modes of Organization* (1976b) expands his theories on the so-called modes of discourse. Another expansion of his theory will be given below.

2. Chapter I appeared in the *Harvard Educational Review*, XXXVI, 1 (Winter, 1966) 17–28; Chapter II appeared in *Continuity in English* (Champaign, Ill.: NCTE, 1968); Chapter III appeared as *Drama: What is Happening* (Champaign, Ill.: NCTE, 1967); Chapter IV appeared as 'Telling Stories: Methods of Abstraction in Fiction', ETC: *A Review of General Semantics*, XXI, 4 (1964); Chapter VI appeared in *Papers of the Yale Conference on English* (New Haven: Office of Teacher Training, Yale University, 1967). Chapters V and VII are largely original.

3. For the references on this point see Kinneavy (1971, p. 13 ff.).

Contrastive rhetorics: some implications for the writing process[1]

Robert B. Kaplan

In his longish essay 'On Difficulty', George Steiner attempts to develop a taxonomy of difficulties that beset the reader of literature. He writes:

> Very often, probably in the great majority of instances, what we mean when we say that [a text] is 'difficult' does not relate to conceptual difficulty . . .
>
> Far more often than not we signify by 'a difficulty' something that 'we need to look up'. . . . The word may be archaic: when . . . we meet with mighty *dints* in *The Knight's Tale*, we may no longer know what Chaucer is telling us . . . . The expression can be arcane and technical: it might not be immediately apparent to the reader just what 'bliss' T.S. Eliot promises when he qualifies it as *pneumatic* . . . . Frequently, the poet is a neologist, a recombinant wordsmith. . . . Writers are passionate resuscitators of buried or spectral words. . . . The below-ground vocabularies and syntax of slang, of argot, of taboo-usage, are sometimes almost as extensive and polysemic as those of mundane discourse.
>
> 'Looking things up' does not stop because the context pertinent to a major . . . text is that of the whole ambient culture, of the whole history of and in the language, of the mental sets and idiosyncrasies in contemporary sensibility. . . . In some time, in some place, the difficulty can be resolved. Conceivably, the distance between a culture and certain texts can grow so drastic that *everything has to be looked up* . . . . Granted time and explicative means, even *everything* can be looked up. I suggest, therefore, that we label this first class of difficulties as 'epiphenomenal' or, more plainly, as *contingent* difficulties. . . .
>
> Contingent difficulties are the most visible, they stick like burrs to the fabric of the text. Yet we may find ourselves saying 'this is . . . difficult' . . . even where the lexical-grammatical components are pellucid . . . .
>
> The poem in front of us articulates a stance towards human conditions which we find essentially inaccessible or alien . . . .
>
> The difficulty which we are up against is of a class which I propose to call *modal* . . . .

Heir to Rousseau, our culture professes to know less but to feel more than any before it. We may have to look up even the most elementary of scriptural, mythological, historical, literary or scientific terms and references; but we claim confident empathy with Benin bronzes, the shadow-drama's of Indonesia, the ragas of India and every genre and epoch in Western art . . . . We are ashamed to concede any modal inhibition, to confess ourselves closed to any expressive act however remote from our own time and place. But this ecumenism of receptivity is spurious . . . .

Contingent difficulties arise from the obvious plurality and individuation which characterize world and word. Modal difficulties lie with the beholder. A third class of difficulty has its source in the writer's will or in the failure of adequacy between his intention and his performative means. I propose to designate this class as *tactical*. The poet may choose to be obscure in order to achieve certain specific stylistic effects. He may find himself compelled towards obliquity and cloture by political circumstances . . . .

There is a dialectical strangeness in the will of the poet to be understood only step by step and up to a point. The retention of innermost meaning is, inevitably, subverted and ironized by the mere fact that the poet has chosen to make this text public. Yet the impulse is an honest one, arising from the intermediate status of all language between the individual and the general. The contradiction is insoluble. It finds creative expression in tactical difficulties . . . .

Contingent difficulties aim to be looked up; modal difficulties challenge the inevitable parochialism of honest empathy; tactical difficulties endeavour to deepen our apprehension by dislocating and goading to new life the supine energies of word and grammar. Each of these three classes of difficulty is a part of the contract of ultimate or preponderant intelligibility between poet and reader, between text and meaning. There is a fourth order of difficulty which occurs where this contract is itself wholly or in part broken.

Because this type of difficulty implicates the functions of language . . . I propose to call it *ontological*. Difficulties of this category cannot be looked up; they cannot be resolved by genuine readjustment or artifice of sensibility; they are not an intentional technique of retardation and creative uncertainty (though these may be their immediate effect). Ontological difficulties confront us with blank questions about the nature of human speech, about the status of significance, about the necessity and purpose of the construct which we have, with more or less rough and ready consensus, come to perceive as a poem . . . .[2]

Let me apologize both for the length of the quotation and for the pastiche I have made of Steiner's logic and development, and try to explain why I have taken such a liberty. My topic is contrastive rhetoric; that is, I am concerned with the notion that speakers of different languages use different devices to present information to establish the relationships among ideas, to show the centrality of one idea as opposed to another, to select the most effective means of presentation. It seems to me that Steiner shows how difficult the reading of a text in one's mother tongue may be. It seems to me, further, that Steiner's conceptualization of a category of difficulty named *ontological* — based on the nature, essential properties, and relations of being — should be of the greatest significance to second-language teachers because it should suggest to them that the problems a language learner grapples with are not purely linguistic and probably cannot be solved by purely linguistic means.

Now let me call your attention to another article 'Defining Complexity', by Joseph Williams, which deals with some features of English writers. Williams writes:

> ... The clearest style is one in which the grammatical structures of a sentence most redundantly support the perceived semantic structure. The more consistently the grammatical structure reinforces — or reflects — the semantic structure, the more easily a reader takes up that semantic structure.
>
> It is not always possible — as demonstrated by the way in which this sentence opens — for us to write sentences in which every agent occurs in subject position and precedes what it does; in which what that agent does is expressed in a verb directly following a subject/agent . . . .
>
> But it is possible for us to come far closer to this kind of maximally redundant pattern than most writers in fact do . . . .
>
> Those structures that have come to be known as rheme-theme or topic-comment sequences coincide with subjects and noun/agents and the verb phrases that follow. The topic is that element in the sentence from which the rest of the sentence flows. The topic ordinarily communicates the most familiar, the previously mentioned, the implied ideas. In most languages, the topic regularly coincides with the subject. But even in English, it need not:
>
> In regard to style, there are still many unknowns. The topic is *style* but *style* is not the subject. The topic is regularly the first noun in the sentence, but again, it need not be:
>
> In this paper, style has been the main subject. *Style* is not the first noun, but it is still the topic.
>
> The comment expresses the new ideas, ordinarily that which cannot be deduced from what is assumed or already mentioned. And the end of the comment, the end of the clause, emphasizes that new information most strongly . . . .
>
> On the basis of some preliminary evidence . . . it appears that a series of consistent topics is judged to be more clearly written than a series of sentences in which the topic is not consistently selected. And when we reinforce a consistent topic with a consistent nexus between subject and agent, with a consistent nexus between verbs and what the agents do, then the style appears to become the clearest and most efficient of all . . . .[3]

142   *Robert B. Kaplan*

If Mr Williams is correct, it seems safe to posit that English expository style is (or should be) marked by the kind of redundancy
he describes both at the sentential and at the intersentential
levels. However, the fact that English style should be so marked
does not suggest that the styles of expository prose in other languages ought to be so marked; indeed, preliminary investigations
in a number of other languages and dialects — the Spanish of
Puerto Rico, the French of Eastern Canada, the Arabic of Cairo,
the Mandarin of Taiwan — suggest that the expository characteristics those languages are quite different. Those preliminary investigations further suggest that there is a great need for the examination of intersentential syntactic, semantic, and pragmatic
characteristics in the extended written prose of all those languages and others, including English.

So far I have offered you very little that is original or new, having spent most of my time in extended quotation from the works
of others. But this paper is not to be entirely a trick done with
mirrors reflecting the brilliance of others. The rest, I fear, will be
less reflective and less brilliant.

In the remainder of this paper, I want to say a few things about
the way in which English expository prose seems to be organized
and a few things about the mechanisms that seem to function in
it. Most of the notions expressed in what follows are derived from
a study of rhetoric in contrastive situations; that is, not only from
an examination of what non-English speakers do when they try to
write in English, but also — though to a more limited extent —
an examination of what speakers of other languages do when they
write in their mother tongues. Though I will discuss some examples drawn from spoken language, those examples will be used
only to illustrate a particular point and not as the basis for drawing
conclusions about written language.

A number of studies over the past decade have touched on the
English rhetoric of non-English speakers and the rhetoric of other
languages. Although it is not possible in this brief paper to survey
all of the work that has been done nor to trace the origins of the
notion of contrastive rhetoric, I want to claim that the contrastive
study of rhetorics has been most productive in throwing light both
on what does happen in English and on the problems that non-
native speakers have in acquiring English. I want to claim that, to
the extent that courses in English as a second language, at least at
the advanced level, continue to stress sentence syntax, such

courses do not prepare non-native speakers either to write or to read English texts. Indeed, if — as I have suggested above — at least part of the problem faced by the language learner is ontological (it is, I think, already conceded that part of the problem is essentially epistemological), then clearly any approach which deals only with linguistic fact is not likely to be enormously successful. You will find, lurking about the edges of my argument, some tinges of the weak version of the Sapir-Whorf hypothesis — a notion that seems to me far more significant at the discourse level than at the level of the sentence. While I do not speak much of the paragraph as such, please think of the paragraph not as a typographical but as a discourse unit. Try not to think of sentences at all.

Recently, during a visit to Australia, I was introduced to a brand new ESL textbook which had, as its opening exercise, something like the following rather traditional dialogue:

P: Oh, Spiros, is that a new photo?
S: Yes, Philia, it is.
P: Is it a photo of your sister?
S: Yes, it is a photo of my sister.
P: Is she young?
S: Yes, she is young.
P: Is she short?
S: No, she is tall.
P: Is she fat?
S: No, she is slim.
P: Is she pretty?
S: Yes, she is very pretty
P: May I see her photo?
S: Yes, you may.
P: Thank you.

Note that this text consists of 15 utterances and that it contains 65 words; that is, there is an average of 4.33 words per utterance. Note too that there is a very high proportion of redundant information (intentional) in the nature of the exercise, since it provides practice in answering yes/no questions which require subject/verb position shifts.

My concern is not with the quality of the dialogue as dialogue or as teaching device; my concern is with what is happening in terms of real language. (Note that the whole dialogue could have been avoided — or telescoped — by establishing that a photograph existed and then simply asking to see it, as Philia finally does in her seventh question.) Though this particular example is stilted, repetitive, and quite far from the realities of conversation, it does operate on the basis of questions and answers. Let me call attention to the fact that, absurd as it is, the dialogue conveys a modicum of information, but let me also note that the same information might have been conveyed in a number of other ways, e.g.:

My name is Spiros. I have a new photo of my sister. She is tall, slim, and very pretty. I will show this photo to my friend, Philia.
(4 syntactic 'units'/28 words — average 7 words/utterance)

My name is Spiros and I have a new photo of my tall, slim, very pretty sister which I will show to my friend, Philia.
(1 syntactic 'unit'/25 words)

The latter two versions, while they contain all of the basic information, obviously will not serve as devices for practising answers to yes/no questions. But they illustrate the notion that written text may consist of a series of assertions responding to stated or implied or assumed questions. Without raising the issue of the possible variety of assertions in English, or in any other language, I want to contend that an assertion may be composed of three elements:

ASSERTION

Subject + Attribute + Modifier

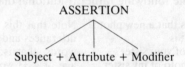

$$\text{Subject} \rightarrow \begin{Bmatrix} \text{Agent} \\ \text{Object} \\ \text{Sub-class} \\ \text{Individual} \\ \text{Subject} \end{Bmatrix} \quad \text{Attribute} \rightarrow \begin{Bmatrix} \text{Function} \\ \text{Characteristic} \\ \text{State} \end{Bmatrix} \quad \text{Modifier} \rightarrow \begin{Bmatrix} \text{Identity} \\ \text{Class} \\ \text{Object} \\ \text{Modifier} \end{Bmatrix}$$

Further, by definition, a modifier has one of two possible functions; either it adds information to a subject, an attribute, or a whole assertion, or it restricts the meaning of a subject, an attribute, or a whole assertion. A modifier may either be preposed or postposed. Clearly, modifiers vary both in their grammatical designation (relative clause, prepositional phrase, adjective, etc.) and in their semantic function (causal, temporal, instrumental, locative, etc.), but what is primarily at issue here is function, not form. To illustrate:

agent/function	she was talking	(to a neighbour)	clas(modifier)
object/function	she was shot	(with a gun)	obj(modifier)
subject/ characteristic	she will be exhausted	(tomorrow)	(modifier)
subject/state/ identity	she is my mother	(my angel)	iden(modifier)

individual/state/ class	she is a teacher	(of chemistry)	clas(modifier)
sub-class/state/ class	principals are teachers	(sometimes)	(modifier)

The issue, however, does not concern assertions *per se*; rather, it concerns the ways in which assertions get stuck together into discourse, particularly written discourse.[4] Isolated assertions have *syntactic/semantic* value and a modicum of *propositional* value; contextualized assertions have a modicum of syntactic/semantic value, somewhat more propositional value, and *illocutionary* value. For example, the assertion 'Your tie is crooked' has some value simply because the lexical items *your, tie, is* and *crooked* all have some denotative semantic meaning and the arrangement of those lexical items has some syntactic meaning (the arrangement 'tie is your crooked' would not have syntactic meaning, while the arrangements 'your crooked tie is' or 'is your tie crooked' would have different syntactic meanings). In isolation, the utterance is solely dependent on these features, but once the utterance is contextuated, the pronouns may take on definite reference, and the utterance will acquire some propositional value because a number of suppositions will become identifiable:

I exist (whoever I am).

You exist (whoever you are).

The tie exists.

The tie is your property (or at least is presumed to be on your person).

It now becomes possible for the person addressed (you) to report to a third person the utterance I made, e.g. 'Kaplan said, "your tie is crooked".' This report merely quotes exactly my words; it attributes no additional value or interpretation. It is possible for the person addressed (you), in reporting the event, to add interpretation, e.g. 'Kaplan announced in a loud voice to the assembled multitude that my tie was askew.' or 'According to Kaplan's biased view, my tie was crooked.' or 'Kaplan deeply offended me when he called attention publicly to the fact that my tie was crooked.' None of these interpretations call into question the truth value of the initial assertion (though it is of course possible to do so, e.g. 'Kaplan said my tie was crooked when in fact it wasn't.'). What has happened in all of these interpretations is that a supposition has been added to the basic set enumerated above; namely: It matters that one's tie is crooked. The development of the context so far has presumed a 'regular' social context; but other sorts of social contexts are of course possible. If the speaker (Kaplan) were a Master Sergeant addressing (you) a private soldier, or if the speaker were a father addressing a young son, both situations in which roles are hierarchically defined, the value of the utterance would be quite different, and the reporting would in all probability be different, e.g. 'Sgt. Kaplan called attention to my crooked tie and I straightened it at once.' or 'Dad told me my tie was crooked but I straightened it before anybody saw it.' The point is that in both of the latter situations the initial utterance is no longer an observation of a true event, with or without interpretation; rather, the initial utterance becomes a command to correct the situation. In the 'regular' situation, the person addressed (you) is free to respond 'It's none of your damn business.' or 'Stuff it in your ear.' or 'Gee, thanks, I'll fix it.' but none of these responses is appropriate in the hierarchical situation. What has happened is that still another supposition has been added; namely: There is a role relationship between you and me that will filter what I say and how you may respond to it.[5] Given this accretion of layers of meaning, performance errors or dialect variations in the initial utterance (which affect the syntactic/semantic value of the utterance) have lower significance, e.g. 'Your tie's crooked.' or 'You tie crooked.'

This problem of lower significance, obviously, is more complicated than I have suggested. Units like the following, though they may be more distressing to teachers than to laymen, nevertheless have a somewhat greater impact on communication:

I am speaking Russian at home.
The student that I was speaking to him explained me the problem.

The distinction made by Burt[6] between 'global' and 'local' errors (where global errors 'significantly hinder communication' and local ones don't) is an attempt to deal with the problem, but the criteria simply do not hold up under analysis. Thus, for example, 'tie is your crooked' contains global errors which hinder communication, but 'tie wore I yesterday' containing similar global errors interferes with communication less than 'I wore my tie to the jointing' (where *jointing* means *wedding*) in which the error is local because it interferes only with a single constituent. It seems clear that any attempt to define extent of interference in communication must include more than linguistic criteria (cf. Morrissey 1979).

In a discourse, the bunches of individual or linked assertions of which the discourse is composed carry semantic/syntactic, propositional, and illocutionary values, and the values interact in important ways. In the past, language teachers have provided relatively good instruction with respect to the semantic/syntactic value of assertions, somewhat less effective instruction with respect to propositional values, and none at all with respect to illocutionary values. In part, the reluctance of teachers to deal with the illocutionary values stems from the fact that those values may be exophoric (as in the illustration of the Master Sergeant talking to a Private, where the role relationship provides the major cue to the fact that the assertion is not an observation but an indirect command) or endophoric, or cataphoric, or to some degree some combination of these. It is difficult in the classroom situation to deal with the exophoric because the classroom, by definition, inhibits some common varieties of exophoric contexts. Even in dealing with the endophoric and cataphoric, however, the treatment has been inadequate because the nature of the controlling mechanisms is not well understood. In a discourse, two principal controlling mechanisms are *topic* and *focus*.

Topic obviously is a loaded term. I do not mean it in the sense in which it is used in the Czech school, by scholars like Firbas, in the sense of theme and rheme, topic and comment;[7] nor do I mean it in the syntactic sense in the context of *topicalization*. I mean to use the term in the sense of 'aboutness', but that is not a particularly pleasing word. I have toyed with coinages like *topos, krinein,* and *cernere*, but they are not very satisfactory either; indeed, the problem is more complicated than is suggested by the mere coinage of a new term. In frustration, I have determined to use *topic*, despite its potentially confusing semantic accretion.

Topic is relatively easy to define; it is the dominant notion that governs a sequence of discourse. As I have pointed out elsewhere,[8] topic is either definite or generic, and definite topic may be of four types; anaphoric, associative, occurring in a larger context, or occurring within an immediate reference. To oversimplify, perhaps, in a given string of discourse dealing with the relationship between dogs and their masters, one would be startled to find an assertion about sub-arctic weather patterns or about U.S. foreign policy in Southeast Asia. To a large extent, topic is maintained through a longer semantic chain by the use of simple repetition or synonymy. For example, in a discourse whose defined topic was language universals, one would expect a lexis chain which might include such items as *formal, form, shape, substan-*

tive, substance, material, etc. (see Appendix I, p. 156).

While topic may be relatively easy to define, *focus* is very difficult. Tentatively, *focus* is that set of operations which permit the reader/listener to recognize the prominence of certain information. The operations may be syntactic, e.g. grammatical subordination, grammatical parallelism, passivization, relativization, apposition, nominalization, clefting, etc. These operations are conventionally examined within the context of a sentence, but since discourse focus has to do with establishing intersentential coherence, it becomes necessary to look at them as they operate in discourse.

> The literal meaning of an assertion is independent of its structure: the same assertion can appear as an independent sentence, as part of a compound sentence, as part of a parallel structure, or as an additive modifier. But the role it plays in a composition, its relationships with other assertions, can be affected by different structural possibilities. For example, parallel structure is a means of showing commonality among two or more assertions. In contrast to this structure is independent structure. A fundamental advantage of independent structure is as a means of emphasizing an individual assertion.[9]

In many languages, fronting is one important device for achieving focus, though this is probably less true in English. In some languages, any NP as well as many kinds of adverbs can be swung around in front of the subject — e.g. in SVO languages like Hebrew — and can thus be put in focus. The point, however, is that it is fruitless to examine such sentences out of context, since without a context they appear merely as random alterations of the basic structure. Whether fronting *per se* is significant, there can be little question that *positioning* plays some role in determining what is in focus (and indeed what the *topic* may be). In the following examples, the same clause is embedded in various positions. In the second, third, fourth and sixth instances, the clause is clearly out of focus, while in the first and fifth instances it is in focus but there is some question of the topic in the first (which seems to be 'I' as opposed to 'you', rather than the whole structure).

> *I bought some bananas*. What did you buy?

> My wife and I went to the supermarket yesterday. While I *bought some bananas*, she did the rest of the weekly shopping.

> The kidnapper was described by witnesses as a tall, well-dressed man *who bought some bananas* before he forced the manager's wife into his grey Volkswagon bug with the California licence plates.

We had time to kill, so we went into one of those little mom-and-pop corner grocery stores. She, being practical, bought a newspaper, and *I bought some bananas*. Then we got in the car and began driving to Melbourne.

When I was in Brazil last year, *I bought some bananas* which made me ill.

It was I *who bought some bananas* while the market was being robbed.

To illustrate the point in another way, the following assertions need not be presented as a discourse, though certain discourse presentations are clearly more efficient and perhaps more effective.

1. He advanced slowly.
2. His ears were pricked up.
3. His head turned from side to side.
4. He was expectant.
5. The trail broadened.
6. His quarry came into view.
7. His pace quickened.
8. His ears lay back.
9. He made a final headlong rush.
10. He covered the last eighth of a mile in seconds.

He advanced — slowly at first, with ears pricked forward, looking expectantly from side to side, then rapidly as the trail broadened and his quarry came into view, finally in a headlong rush, with ears laid back, covering the last eighth of a mile in seconds.

In the contextualized example, the pronominal reference which occurs in the itemized list vanishes, and the assertion breaks up into three parts controlled by the rate of advance — *slowly at first . . . then rapidly . . . finally in a headlong rush* — but the relative rate (*slowly, rapidly, in a headlong rush*) is overlaid with the temporal chain (*at first, then, finally*). The basic assertion is simply *he advanced*; everything else is modification. Focal modification elucidates rate; the temporal chain is backgrounded, and the physical information (*ears pricked forward, looking expectantly, ears laid back*) still further subordinated, while other modifiers are still further backgrounded. Thus, there appear to be a number of levels of information:

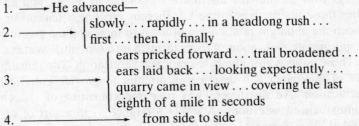

1. ——→ He advanced—
2. ——→ { slowly . . . rapidly . . . in a headlong rush . . .
          first . . . then . . . finally
3. ——→ { ears pricked forward . . . trail broadened . . .
          ears laid back . . . looking expectantly . . .
          quarry came in view . . . covering the last
          eighth of a mile in seconds
4. ——————→ from side to side

The hierarchical arrangement of the information is totally absent in the simple listing of the facts. It is controlled by the syntax in the final one-sentence version.

I want to contend that, since focus is in part a syntactic phenomenon, the non-native speaker cannot deal with it precisely to the extent that he/she does not control intersentential syntax. To put it another way, one may look at topic as essentially semantic and at focus as essentially syntactic; topic is present in the deep structure, but focus can only be realized in the surface structure as a manifestation of deep-structure topic. Again, I am guilty of oversimplifying in order to make my point. One must distinguish between purpose or function on the one hand, and the devices used to achieve that purpose or function on the other. It seems likely that the function of *focus* is essentially pragmatic on the part of the writer; it is he/she who has a reason for making one part of an assertion more prominent than another in terms of the relative importance with which he/she views them. There is no syntactic or semantic reason for doing so.

Thus, focus is more *culture-bound* because it is realized through the finite possible alternatives available in the syntactic system. Perhaps having said that it is again necessary to introduce some further clarification. One must distinguish between what is *culture-bound* and what is specifically *language-bound*. The phenomenon described here is in a sense *language-bound*, because some languages have formulaic devices for topic establishment and syntactic manipulations for focus establishment. Phenomena which are more clearly culture-bound can be better illustrated by such notions as the relatively greater or smaller tolerance in some languages for parallelism, for lexical repetition, for tangential inclusion in the rhetorical development of an argument. What I am trying to suggest in using the term *culture-bound* is that the realization of focus occurs in the surface structure and is thus more subject to cultural preference; it is, then, perhaps easier to deal with in a pedagogical sense, because the non-native speaker brings with him/her the alternatives available in the L1 and applies those alternatives in the L2, thereby creating a tension between the apparent relationship of ideas to topic and the possibly inappropriate realization of focus through intersentential syntax.

These notions are subject to empirical verification. The remainder of this paper will describe an attempt to provide empirical verification. An instrument was prepared consisting of sixteen contextualized assertions. A whole utterance — in a sort of extended cloze format — was deleted from a context of two or three sentences. Respondents were to select the *best* alternative from among three to complete the text. The items included sentences in which the subjects were postponed by using preposed place holders, passives, normal SVO sentences, sentences in which direct/indirect object position was inverted; in short, a number of the sorts of structures that are said to manifest focus. The distractors were designed to alter focus while the preferred choices maintained the focus of the original. The instrument was pretested on a group of fifteen naive native speakers, and confirmation was obtained for the preferred choices and for intentional ambiguities.

The instrument was then administered to a group of sophisticated native speakers (N = 48), and to a group of foreign students (N = 146). The native-speaker group consisted of new teaching assistants employed to teach in the University's Freshman Writing Programme. This group, all graduate students, consisted of 42 per cent males and 58 per cent females (a slightly skewed sample); the mean average age of the group was twenty-eight, and the age spread was from twenty-two to forty-eight. All members of the group held a Bachelor's degree, and twelve members of the group (25 per cent) had had one or more years of graduate study. While the majority of the group had taken more or less traditional undergraduate study in English (literature), the group contained eight individuals who had studied Linguistics, five who had studied Dramatic Writing, two who had studied Comparative Literature, and one each who had studied Classics, Education, Journalism, Philosophy, Slavic Studies, and Television Arts.

The non-native-speaking group consisted of all students enrolled in the advanced level in the University's American Language Institute (that is, all who were present on the un-announced day on which the instrument was administered). Roughly half of the group had had at least one prior semester of ESL at the university while the remainder had previously studied English either in their home countries or in special English programmes elsewhere in the United States and had been at the University an average of three months at the time of the experiment. The population consisted of 59 per cent graduate students, and roughly 80 per cent was male. The mean average age was thirty and the age spread was from eighteen to forty-six. Approximately 40 per cent of the group was studying Engineering of some type (e.g. aerospace, chemical, civil, electrical, industrial, mechanical, petroleum, etc.) and the remainder was widely scattered over some forty-five academic majors. Approximately 20 per cent of the group were

Farsi speakers; the second largest group consisted of Arabic speakers (e.g. from Algeria, Bahrain, Kuwait, Lebanon, Saudi Arabia, the Trucial States, etc.), and the third largest group consisted of speakers of Chinese (e.g. both Cantonese and Mandarin, from Hong Kong, Taiwan, and other areas in Southeast Asia). The remainder was scattered over some sixty languages (e.g. Bhasa Malay, French, Finnish, German, Japanese, Korean, Russian, Spanish, Tagalog, Urdu); thus, it was not possible to undertake any sort of language specific correlations.[10]

The instrument is included as Appendix II, pp. 158–161. The results showed that in ten items the native-speaking population clustered on the items originally designated as the preferred choices. Six items had been designed to be ambiguous. In two of those items, the native-speaking population chose the two preferred alternatives equally, but in four items native speakers chose one item two to one over the other. The non-native-speaking population distributed quite differently; indeed Chi^2 analysis of the data (with 2 degrees of freedom) showed significant differences between the two populations in thirteen items. A detailed summary accompanies the instrument in Appendix II. The data show not only significant differences between the populations with respect to preferred choice, but significantly different distribution among the distractors.

Another experiment is currently under way to determine to what extent the differences demonstrated here may be a function of the recognition of a hierarchical arrangement of information from generalization to specification. An instrument consisting of a dozen long pieces of prose (each approximately 150 words and eight to ten sentences) with whole sentences deleted has been prepared. Subjects will be required to replace the missing assertions from among a set of four choices in which the distractors will to varying degrees violate the order of specificity established in the text. The instrument will be administered to some three hundred subjects, roughly one-third native speakers. Pretesting suggests that the instrument has great promise.[11]

The following claims seem to be justified: First, in a written discourse there is a 'head' assertion which contains the topic, and the topic comes from the deep structure of the discourse. This 'head' assertion is different from all other assertions in that its NP must, being the onset of a discourse, carry *new* information (whereas it is generally conceded that the subject NP of most sentences carries *old* information deriving from prior assertions in the discourse). The topic expressed in the 'head' assertion is carried through the remaining assertions through the operation of focus. Focus is expressed in syntactic terms in the following assertions; that is, focus determines which available alternatives will be chosen.

Second, the native speaker and the non-native speaker differ in their ability to determine what suppositions may be shared between speaker/writer and listener/reader in a given communication situation. Third, native speakers and non-native speakers differ in the strategies they bring to bear on the development of any given topic through the intersentential syntactic choices they are able to make. These choices seem to be directly tied to the realizable syntactic alternatives available in the native speaker's L1; thus, the non-native speaker not only uses the intersentential syntactic alternatives available from the L1 but also uses those alternatives in the framework of the rhetorical (cultural) preferences of the L1. In itself, knowledge of the sentential syntax of the L2 does not seem to be of much help, though clearly it is a precondition to any sort of manipulation of the intersentential syntax. (It is possible, however, that both the amount of sentential syntax and the kind of sentential syntax to be taught need to be re-thought with respect to the functions necessary to deal with intersentential syntax.)

There are thus two problems: First, to the extent that the set of realizable intersentential syntactic alternatives is shared between the two languages, the non-native speaker will be able to maintain focus, but to the extent that the two sets are mutually exclusive, focus will disappear or at least weaken. Second, since the alternatives fall in the range of *what everybody knows*, and since the initial formulation of topic also is predicated upon *what everybody knows* in the sense that the writer/speaker must know what presuppositions are shared with the reader/listener, it seems clear that native speakers and non-native speakers will demonstrate quite different abilities in topic formulation as well as in focus maintenance.

While the centre of attention in this paper has been on topic and focus and some elements involved in the range of available alternatives, there are, as I have pointed out elsewhere,[12] other mismatches between any two given rhetorics. For example, languages differ in the amount of non-direct inclusion they will tolerate in various forms of discourse, and they differ in the amount of pronominalization permitted as well as in the distance permitted without relexification. As Ts'ao has suggested,[13] in some languages, where topic is explicitly marked, the need for pronominalization may be abridged by the strength of topic domination. Larkin and Shook contend that English and Cantonese differ at least in the way relative clauses are positioned (postposed in English, preposed in Cantonese) and therefore in the amount of information they may bear.

> ... English is basically right branching and Cantonese is always left branching. A very important implication of the left-branching nature of Chinese relative clauses is that Chinese speakers cannot tolerate excessively long relative clauses, because short-term memory is strained by having to hold all the modifiers before getting to the thing being modified.[14]

Obviously, this is an area that requires a great deal more study. But essential to any such future work is the recognition that there is such a thing as intersentential syntax and that it deserves study in precisely the same degree of depth that sentential syntax has already been studied. It also demands recognition that illocutionary value in discourse is at least as significant as syntactic/semantic and propositional value and that it derives not only from exophoric causes but from topic and the way in which topic is maintained through focus. It demands recognition of the fact that focus is managed by making choices among available alternatives in the syntax. As Göran Hammarström has suggested, 'units and relations between units are the basic linguistic facts to be described'.[15] And *units* are not necessarily 'sentences'.

Notes

1. I wish to express my gratitude to a number of colleagues who have reviewed this manuscript during various stages of its development. I am particularly grateful to Ruth Berman for her helpful comments.
2. George Steiner, 'On Difficulty', *On Difficulty and Other Essays* (New York: Oxford University Press, 1978), pp. 19, 20, 27, 28, 29, 32, 33, 35, 40–41.
3. Joseph M. Williams, 'Defining Complexity', *College English*, Vol. 40, No. 6 (February 1979), pp. 603–605.
4. Written discourse consists of sets of assertions stuck together, and those assertions may, in fact, be answers to implicit or explicit questions. In the simple example from the dialogue with which this paper starts, by way of illustration, the assertions can be elicited by questions other than those developed in the dialogue:

What do you have?	I have a photo.
Is it new?	Yes.
What is it of?	My sister.
Can you describe her?	Yes. She is tall, slim, and very pretty.
What will you do with the photo?	Show it to my friend Philia.

I have a (new) photograph (of) my sister (who) is tall, slim, and very pretty, (and I will) show it to my friend Philia.

But note that a different set of questions will elicit a different dialogue:

What do you want?	*I have a photo.
	I want to show my new photo to Philia.
What's new about it?	*Yes. [NB: *new* can only be introduced if it occurs in the prior reply.]
	It was taken only yesterday.
What does it show?	*My sister.
	How pretty my sister is.
Can you visualize her?	Yes. [But the answer is redundant.]
What will you do with it?	Show it to my friend Philia. [But the answer is redundant because the information was given in answer to the first question in this series.]

(I have) a photo of my sister (which) was taken only yesterday (and which shows) how pretty she is. I want to show (it) to Philia.

5. Clearly, there is also more involved here than the pragmatic impact of roles; there are important anthropological and cultural factors as well. For example, there are cultures in the world in which the existence of a photograph is unlikely, not for technological reasons but for other kinds of reasons stemming from cultural taboos, and there are societies in the world in which the wearing of a tie is totally foreign — the California sub-culture being one case in point.

6. Marina K. Burt, 'Error Analysis in the Adult EFL Classroom', *TESOL Quarterly*, Vol. 9, No. 1 (1975), pp. 53–63; see also Marina K. Burt and C. Kiparsky, 'Global and Local Mistakes', in *New Frontiers in Second Language Learning*, ed. J. Schumann and N. Stenson (Rowley, Mass.: Newbury House, 1974).

7. See the quotation from Joseph Williams above for an example of this usage of the term *topic*.

8. 'On the Notion of Topic in Written Discourse', *Australian Review of Applied Linguistics*, Vol. 2 (May 1978), pp. 1–10.

9. Bennison Gray, *The Grammatical Foundations of Rhetoric: Discourse Analysis* (The Hague: Mouton 1977), p. 190.

10. Language specific correlations have, of course, been undertaken, cf. entries in the bibliography for Kaplan, Newsham, Santana-Seda, Santiago, Strei, etc.; see also Shirley Williamson, 'English in Parallels: A Study of Arabic Style', unpublished paper read at the 1978 California Linguistics Association meeting.

11. This work is being carried on by Ms Ann Martin at the University of Southern California and will appear in her forthcoming doctoral dissertation in the School of Education.

12. 'Contrastive Rhetoric: Some Hypotheses', *ITL*, Vol. 39–40 (1978), pp. 61–72.

13. Ts'ao Feng-fu, 'A Functional Study of Topic in Chinese: The First Step Toward Discourse Analysis', unpublished Ph. D. Diss., University of Southern California 1977.

14. 'Interlanguage, The Monitor, and Sentence Combining', unpublished paper read at the Los Angeles Second Language Research Forum, October 7 1978, p. 3.

15. *Linguistic Units and Items* (Berlin: Springer 1976), p.v.

Appendix I

Language universals, Chomsky suggests, are of two basic types, *substantive* and *formal*. *Substantive* universals represent the fundamental 'building blocks' of language, the *substance* out of which it is made, while *formal* universals are concerned with the *form* or *shape* of a grammar. An analogy might make this distinction clearer. If, hypothetically, Eskimos were born with an innate knowledge of igloo-building, they would have two kinds of knowledge. On the one hand they would know in advance that the *substance* out of which igloos are made is ice and snow just as thrushes automatically know that their nests are made of twigs, not bricks or worms or glass. On the other hand, their innate knowledge of igloo-building would include the information that igloos are round in *shape*, not square or diamond-shaped or sausage-like, just as thrushes instinctively build round nests, not ones shaped like bathtubs.

Italics have been added to this text to pick up the first-level lexis chain; obviously, there is a second-level chain made up of such words as *made, ice, snow, twigs, bricks, worms, glass, round, square, diamond-shaped, sausage-like, bathtubs* where the first seven items relate to substance and the remaining five items to form. Almost 15 per cent of the total word count in this bit of discourse is made up of lexical items which are fairly directly related to the notions of form and substance which occur in the topic assertion.

It is, of course, possible to construct discourse which has a lexis chain giving the appearance of 'free association':

> Once upon a time there was a lovely young princess who lived in a castle in a far off mythical kingdom. The castle was designed by her uncle Hernando who was an architect in a nearby city. He was also a fine family man and was once an excellent swimmer. He competed against Johnny Weismuller many times during the late 1920's. This was the time of the great depression during which many huge fortunes were lost. Fortunes that occasionally equalled the amount of treasure brought back from the orient many centuries ago by Marco Polo. Or perhaps the total salaries, operating expenses, and advertising budgets of the Kansas City Chiefs, Radio City Music Hall and Darlene's Dancing Dalmations. Next door to Hernando's office was a tattoo parlour. Many of our country's brave young fighting men went there for tattoos of their mothers, Barney Google and Eleanor Roosevelt. It was these same young men who displayed such courage on Bataan and Iwo Jima. The courage that made this country safe for you, me, our children, zoo animals and restoring old Hudsons as a hobby.

> [*Broomhilda*]

One fully expects, based on the traditional opener (once upon a time) and the focus on *lovely young princess* in the first sentence, that the princess is the topic. But the second sentence picks up *castle* as its focus from the position of object of a preposition in a modifying phrase in a relative clause — a position pretty far out of focus normally. The third sentence picks up *Uncle Hernando* also out of the position object of a preposition. There is, without doubt, a lexis chain in this discourse, but it is a 'lunatic' chain because the focal items are picked up out of normally out-of-focus positions.

Appendix II

1. To tap a private telephone line is not technically a very difficult process. / — / There are several steps in the process.

   $Chi^2 = 37.559$; d.f. = 2 (·001 level)

   a. Private telephone lines may be contrasted with party lines.

   NS = 0%; NNS = 7%

   b. It is, however, essential to have the right equipment.

   NS = 6%; NNS = 49%

   c. *Tapping* is a process whereby it is possible to listen in on someone else's conversation.

   NS = 94%; NNS = 43%

2. As far as mathematics is concerned, he was a complete failure. / — / His lack of ability was a constant source of frustration to him in his science major.

   $Chi^2 = 10.758$; d.f. = 2 (·01 level)

   a. He was very bad in athletics.

   NS = 0%; NNS = 5%

   b. He was, however, very good in athletics.

   NS = 0%; NNS = 14%

   c. In fact, he had trouble with simple arithmetic.

   NS = 100%; NNS = 81%

3. Looked at politically, it was not an easy problem. / — / In addition, popular opinion outside

   $Chi^2 = 15.702$; d.f. = 2 (·001 level)

the party structure created an additional dimension.

a. The economic issues were very com-
   plicated.   NS = 13%; NNS = 27%

b. Party loyalties were a constant
   issue.   NS = 87%; NNS = 57%

c. Of course, what is easy for one per-
   son may be hard for another.   NS = 0%; NNS = 16%

4. Geographically, ethnically, and linguis-   Chi^2 = 6.359; d.f. = 2
   tically, the Ryukyu Islands are closer to   (·05 level)
   the Japanese mainland than to their
   neighbouring islands. / — / But it might
   be better to suggest that the distance
   from the southernmost tip of Kyushu to
   the main body of the Ryukyus is less
   than 800 miles, while the nearest point
   in the Philippines is more than 1,000
   miles away.

   a. With respect to geography, the dis-   NS = 66%; NNS = 46%
      tance to Tokyo from Okinawa is less
      than 1,000 miles.

   b. Japan has a long history of activity   NS = 0%; NNS = 1%
      in Southeast Asia.

   c. The neighbouring islands include   NS = 33%; NNS = 52%
      Taiwan and the Philippines.

[NB: Several native speakers admitted that they had difficulty with this item because they were unfamiliar with the basic
geography of the region.]

5. It was Mary's birthday. / — / And her   Chi^2 = 1.814; d.f. = 2
   sister gave her some perfume.   (No significance)

   a. I gave her a rose.   NS = 100%; NNS = 97%

   b. A rose was given to her by me.   NS = 0%; NNS = .05%

   c. She received a rose from me.   NS = 0%; NNS = 2.05%

6. The boy who was here drank the milk.   Chi^2 = 23.419; d.f. = 2
   / — /

   a. He arrived at 6.00 p.m.   NS = 2%; NNS = 6%

b. He was very thirsty.   NS = 50%; NNS = 79%
c. It was sour.   NS = 48%; NNS = 14%

7. The boy who drank the milk was here.   Chi² = 8.771; d.f. = 2
   / — /
   a. He arrived at 6.00 p.m.   NS = 98%; NNS = 80%
   b. He was very thirsty.   NS = 2%; NNS = 16%
   c. It was sour.   NS = 0%; NNS = 3%

8. The milk was drunk by the boy who   Chi² = 3.619; d.f. = 2
   was here. / — /   (·2 level)
   a. He arrived at 6.00 p.m.   NS = 4%; NNS = 8%
   b. He was very thirsty.   NS = 10%; NNS = 20%
   c. It was sour.   NS = 86%; NNS = 71%

9. The boy was here, and he drank the   Chi² = 5.640; d.f. = 2
   milk. / — /   (·1 level)
   a. He arrived at 6.00 p.m.   NS = 6%; NS = 19%
   b. He was very thirsty.   NS = 81%; NNS = 64%
   c. It was sour.   NS = 13%; NNS = 16%

10. The boy was here; consequently, he   Chi² = 4.366; d.f. = 2
    drank the milk. / — /   (·2 level)
    a. He arrived at 6.00 p.m.   NS = 11%; NNS = 14%
    b. He was very thirsty.   NS = 44%; NNS = 56%
    c. It was sour.   NS = 45%; NNS = 26%

11. The boy drank the milk; thus, he must   Chi² = 6.701; d.f. = 2
    have been here. / — /   (·1 level)
    a. He arrived at 6.00 p.m.   NS = 92%; NNS = 74%
    b. He was very thirsty.   NS = 6%; NNS = 18%
    c. It was sour.   NS = 2%; NNS = 8%

12. The boy was here. He drank the milk.   Chi² = 6.135; d.f. = 2
    / — /   (·2 level)
    a. He arrived at 6.00 p.m.   NS = 2%; NNS = 6%

b. He was very thirsty.   NS = 31%; NNS = 47%

c. It was sour.   NS = 67%; NNS = 46%

13. The boy drank the milk. He was here. Chi^2 = 4.164; d.f. = 2
   / — /   (·2 level)

   a. He arrived at 6.00 p.m.   NS = 92%; NNS = 79%

   b. He was very thirsty.   NS = 8%; NNS = 17%

   c. It was sour.   NS = 0%; NNS = 3%

14. Because the boy was here, he drank Chi^2 = .925; d.f. = 2
   the milk. / — /   (No significance)

   a. He arrived at 6.00 p.m.   NS = 8%; NNS = 13%

   b. He was very thirsty.   NS = 63%; NNS = 56%

   c. It was sour.   NS = 29%; NNS = 30%

15. Since the boy drank the milk, he was Chi^2 = .94; d.f. = 2
   here. / — /   (No significance)

   a. He arrived at 6.00 p.m.   NS = 83%; NNS = 77%

   b. He was very thirsty.   NS = 13%; NNS = 18%

   c. It was sour.   NS = 4%; NNS = 5%

16. Being here, the boy drank the milk. Chi^2 = 2.816; d.f. = 2
   / — /   (·3 level)

   a. He arrived at 6.00 p.m.   NS = 8%; NNS = 18%

   b. He was very thirsty.   NS = 63%; NNS = 57%

   c. It was sour.   NS = 29%; NNS = 25%

Notes

NS = Native Speaker; NNS = Non-Native Speaker. / — / = the point at which the insertion should be made.

A number of native speakers complained that the items 6-16 were boring; it is likely that some native speakers stopped trying after item 12.

Additional analysis yielded the following results:

	1	2	3	4	5	6	7	8	9	10	11	12	13	14	15	16
df=2	.001	.01	.001	.05	NONE	.001	.02	.2	.1	.2	.1	.2	.2	NONE	NONE	.3
df=8	.001	.01	.001	.01	.5	.001	.02	.7	.1	.01	.05	.05	.1	.5	.2	.5
CHANGE			#	#				#		#	#	#	#	#	#	#

10   Syntactic skill and ESL writing quality

Patrick T. Kameen

Intuition, rather than empirical evidence, has long been the basis upon which composition teachers have judged the writing skill of their ESL students. Unfortunately, the intuitions handed down through the years from rhetorician to composition teacher offer few insights into the relationship between writing quality and syntactic skill (see Hunt 1977).

The purpose of this exploratory study was to determine if there is a correlation between syntactic skill and scores assigned to compositions written by college-level ESL students.

A randomly-drawn sample of 50 compositions written by college-level ESL students (25 'good' and 25 'poor' writers) at Syracuse University was used. Fourteen different native languages were represented in the sample (see Table 1).

Table 1   Native languages

Language	'Good' writers	'Poor' writers
(1) Arabic	10	10
(2) Chinese	1	0
(3) Farsi	1	4
(4) French	1	0
(5) Hebrew	1	0
(6) Ibo	2	0
(7) Italian	1	0
(8) Japanese	0	1
(9) Lambya (Malawi)	2	0
(10) Malay	3	0
(11) Portuguese	0	1
(12) Spanish	2	7
(13) Thai	0	2
(14) Urdu	1	0

Each composition analysed was a thirty-minute timed writing on an assigned topic given as part of the *Michigan Test of English*

Language Proficiency. Because the test was administered a number of times in 1976, several different topics were used (see Table 2).

Table 2 Topics assigned

Topic	'Good' writers writing on topic	'Poor' writers writing on topic
(1) The U.N. should pass a law limiting a woman to a maximum of 3 children or 3 pregnancies (whichever comes first). Do you agree or disagree? Explain your answer.	15	14
(2) Who do you consider the most important person who has ever lived? Give a short biography of the person and explain why you have chosen him/her.	2	4
(3) Which event in history has had an important effect on your country? Describe this event and how it has changed and/or influenced the progress and development of your country.	4	3
(4) All men and women should be required to serve their country either in the army or in some other government-designated way for a minimum of 2 years. Do you agree or disagree? Present arguments to support your position.	1	1
(5) What is the value of education to the individual and to society in your country? Give examples, reasons, and supporting arguments in your composition.	2	1
(6) Do you believe that honesty is a quality that government officials should have? If so, why? If not, why not?	0	1
(7) International students who are sponsored have an obligation to return to their own countries after they have finished their training in the U.S. Do you agree or disagree? Develop your views giving reasons and supporting arguments.	1	1

Each composition had been graded holistically on a scale of 100 by two highly-qualified, independent raters with over twenty-five years of experience in grading compositions written by ESL students. This researcher did not grade any of the compositions. In no case did the raters disagree by more than 3 points, this strongly suggesting that they were applying similar standards in evaluating the compositions. Small differences in grades were averaged to arrive at a single, final grade based on the raters' general impressions of its quality. 'Good' compositions were those that had been assigned grades of 79 and above, with a mean of 80.6. 'Poor' compositions had received scores of 68–71, with a mean of 70.2.

The compositions were all of different lengths and were read in the form that the students had submitted them. Physical appearance, then, may have contributed to a 'halo' effect — the tendency to assign a score partially on the basis of the writer's more appropriate use of the conventional mechanics of writing, such as punctuation and spelling (see Braddock, Lloyd-Jones and Schoer 1963).

Non-parametric (distribution-free) procedures were used to statistically analyse the data.[1] The Wilcoxon test, one of the most powerful rank tests, was used to convert raw scores to z-scores — their respective number of standard deviation units from the mean. In general, this study analysed such things as length of various types of writing units (e.g. T-units[2], clauses, and sentences), incidence of passive voice[3], types of clauses, and types of joining devices between writing units.

A two-sided rejection region of one half the test statistic was used, and the criterial figure for significance within this level of confidence was $+1.96$. The Bonferroni inequality test, with a criterial figure of $+3.025$, was then applied to determine if 'good' writers in the sample differed from 'poor' writers in terms of simultaneous factors — factors which form a cluster and which, when taken *together*, characterize the writing of a certain group.

The Wilcoxon test revealed that 15 of the 40 factors were significant as *individual* factors differentiating between the writing of 'good' and 'poor' writers. The Bonferroni inequality test revealed that 12 of these factors were *simultaneously* significant. Twenty-five factors were non-significant, and the 12 simultaneously significant factors naturally collapsed into three larger, more general categories: (1) T-unit length, (2) clause length, and (3) incidence of passive voice. Table 3 displays the statistical results for the 40 factors considered in this study.

Table 3 Syntactic factors

Factor	'Good' writers mean	'Poor' writers mean	Z-score for 'poor' writers
A. *Simultaneously significant factors:*			
1. Number of long T-units (21+ words)	5.60	2.24	−4.71
2. Number of 'dynamic' passives	3.40	.50	−4.69
3. Number of sentences with at least one passive	3.10	.50	−4.65
4. Number of words in non-fragment sentences	294.20	203.40	−4.49
5. Passives per clause	.12	.03	−4.47
6. Words per clause	10.83	8.54	−4.45
7. Passives per T-unit	.20	.05	−4.39
8. Passives per non-fragment sentences	.24	.06	−4.38
9. Words per T-unit	18.40	14.30	−3.62
10. Number of passives in main clauses	2.16	.24	−3.50
11. Ratio of long T-units to all T-units	.36	.19	−3.41
12. Number of passives in secondary clauses	1.24	.28	−3.12
B. *Individually significant factors:*			
13. Ratio of short T-units to all T-units	.11	.26	2.77
14. Number of words per non-fragment sentences	23.00	18.30	−2.50
15. Number of short T-units (1-8 words)	1.90	5.04	2.16
C. *Non-significant factors:*			
16. Number of secondary clauses	11.00	9.10	−1.48
17. Number of words in fragments	1.30	4.20	1.39
18. Number of clauses	27.30	24.80	−1.23
19. Number of adverbial clauses	4.44	3.64	−1.21
20. Number of T-units joined by *and, but, or*	2.04	2.76	1.14
21. Number of non-fragment sentences	13.40	12.10	−1.13
22. Number of noun clauses	3.50	2.76	−1.01
23. Ratio of #20 to all T-units	.12	.16	0.87
24. Number of actives in secondary clauses	9.76	8.70	−0.82
25. Ratio of #26 to all sentences	.03	.01	−0.78
26. Number of sentences begun with *and, but, or*	.40	.20	−0.72
27. Number of T-units (= main clauses)	16.30	15.70	−0.72
28. Clauses per T-unit	1.74	1.66	−0.67
29. Ratio of secondary to all clauses	.40	.37	−0.62
30. Number of actives in main clauses	14.10	15.30	0.62
31. Ratio of adjectival to all secondary clauses	.28	.33	0.59
32. Number of fragment sentences	.04	.20	0.48
33. Ratio of nominal to all secondary clauses	.29	.27	−0.48
34. Ratio of mid-length to all T-units	.53	.55	0.47
35. Number of adjectival clauses	3.04	2.68	−0.29
36. Number of mid-length T-units (9-20 words)	8.84	8.44	0.16
37. Number of T-units joined by (;)	.72	.60	0.14
38. Ratio of adverbial to all secondary clauses	.42	.40	−0.12
39. Ratio of #37 to all T-units	.04	.04	0.09
40. Number of actives	23.90	23.90	0.03

Clearly, there is a correlation between incidence of certain syntactic factors and scores assigned to compositions written by college-level ESL students, thus supporting the alternative hypothesis and rejecting the null hypothesis. The most interesting findings involve T-unit length, clause length, sentence length, and incidence of passive voice.

T-unit length (word/T-unit), especially incidence of long T-units (21+ words), is apparently a powerful index for differentiating between the writing of 'good' and 'poor' college-level ESL writers. 'Good' writers wrote approximately 29 per cent more words in each T-unit, writing an average of 18.40 words/T-unit as opposed to 14.30 for 'poor' writers.

This finding correlates with the findings of three other researchers. Hunt (1965), in his analysis of the writing of fourth, eighth, twelfth graders and professional adults, found T-unit length to be the most reliable index of syntactic maturity through the grades. Potter (1967), who analysed the writing of 'good' and 'poor' tenth-grade writers, found that 'good' writers wrote longer T-units than did 'poor' writers. In addition, Schmeling (1969), in his analysis of college freshman writing, found that there was a significant difference in T-unit length between 'first' and 'improved' versions of quality-differentiated compositions.[4]

Mean clause length (words/clause), found by Hunt (1965) to be the second most powerful indicator of syntactic maturity, correlated significantly with rated quality of writing among the college-level ESL writers in this study, but not among the college freshman writers in Schmeling's (1969) study. Of equal importance, however, the results of this study indicate that there were no significant differences between 'good' and 'poor' college-level ESL writers either in terms of number of clauses attached to or embedded within a T-unit (clauses/T-unit) or in terms of mean incidence of various types of clauses — nominal, adjectival, or adverbial. These findings have widespread implications, pointing us in the direction of the types of exercises from which 'poor' writers may benefit, and away from those from which 'poor' writers will most likely not benefit.

First, the commonly-held intuition that 'good' writers have a superior command of the use of subordinate clauses, allowing them to embed more clauses of various types within a main clause matrix than do 'poor' writers, is in no way supported by this study, thus inviting us to question the practice of emphasizing, in the ESL composition classroom, the mastery of the techniques of subordination. Obviously, 'good' writers earned their higher quality ratings and 'poor' writers their lower quality ratings for reasons other than their ability to write subordinate clauses.

Second, since it was clearly an increase in the *number of words* in each clause, rather than an increase in the *number of clauses*, that accounted for the fact that 'good' writers wrote significantly longer T-units than did 'poor' writers, 'poor' writers may benefit from exercises in sentence combining. And with sentence-combining exercises — exercises which present the students with numerous short sentences directing them to combine them into longer, more economical units (see Kameen 1978) — we can give students practice in writing longer clauses and T-units, particularly by showing them how to reduce full *clauses* to prepositional, infinitival, and participial *phrases*. By our showing 'poor' writers the various techniques for reducing and consolidating larger and larger chunks of information into fewer (but longer) clauses, we will be leading these students in the direction of reduced redundancy and increased succinctness (see Hunt 1965), thus helping 'poor' writers write more like their 'good' writing counterparts.

A surprising result, and one which challenges one of the most commonly-held intuitions about student writing, is that sentence length may not be as powerful an index for differentiating between 'good' and 'poor' writers as has been previously thought. Of the 15 factors found to be individually significant, the sentence-length index placed just above the cut-off point for non-significance. This finding is not completely surprising, however, in light of the fact that three other investigators, Hunt, Potter, and Schmeling, found sentence length to be a very unreliable indicator of either syntactic maturity or rated quality among native English-speaking students. Thus, with the decidedly more powerful indexes of T-unit length and clause length at our disposal, it would be wise to carefully re-examine any intuitive trust we may have in the discriminating power of the sentence-length index.

Perhaps the most interesting result of this study involves incidence of passive voice. Since it has long been thought that the use of passive voice leads to ineffective writing, it is indeed surprising that there is such a high positive correlation between incidence of passive voice and scores assigned to compositions written by college-level ESL students. Specifically, 'good' writers wrote approximately 6½ times as many passives as did 'poor' writers, the former using a passive in 25 per cent of their sentences and the latter in only 6 per cent of their sentences. In addition, 'good' writers wrote 4 times as many passives per clause, 4 times as many per T-unit, 9 times as many per main clause, and approximately 4½ times as many per secondary clause. The differences, regardless of writing unit, are certainly clear cut. And while all 7 factors dealing with passive voice proved to be significant, all 3 factors involving incidence of active voice were non-significant.

It is surprising that prejudices against the passive continue to flourish, for data from other studies correlate with the findings of this study. Hunt (1965) found that mean incidence of passive voice increased through the grades, correlating at the .01 level of confidence with age. Eighth graders wrote approximately 3 times as many passives as did fourth graders, and twelfth graders wrote approximately 4 times as many passives as did fourth graders. Potter (1967) found that 'good' tenth-grade writers wrote twice as many passives as did 'poor' tenth-grade writers. Similarly, Schmeling (1969) found that among quality-differentiated papers, 'improved' versions of papers contained approximately twice as many passives as did 'first' versions. Finally, Wolk (1969), in his analysis of the writing of ten professional authors, found that nearly one verb in six was in the passive and that nearly one sentence in three contained at least one passive.

In short, many different types of writers of different ages and language backgrounds use the passive voice quite frequently, with 'good' and older writers using more passives than do 'poor' and younger writers. Mean incidence of passive voice, then, seems to be a reliable indicator of both syntactic maturity and rated quality of writing, all this suggesting that we should thoroughly re-examine our present attitude toward teaching the passive, for there is simply no apparent justification for our so completely discouraging its use.

It is clear that the results of this study have a number of specific and general implications for the ESL composition curriculum.[5] First, in terms of length of writing units, T-unit length and clause length appear to be much more reliable indexes of rated quality than is the time-honoured index of sentence length. Statistical counts of these syntactic factors, then, may be used as one part of the overall procedure for properly placing ESL composition students, using these indexes for the same purposes as other objective measures are used in education: 'prediction, . . . exemption, growth measurement, (and) programme evaluation' (Cooper 1977, p. 16).

Second, the much-maligned passive voice, long considered one of the primary ingredients in the recipe for dull, ineffective writing, apparently does not greatly detract from writing quality, at least in the dialect of formal, expository prose — the type of prose which the assigned topics were designed to elicit, and exactly the type of prose that we are instructing our students to write in when they come to our composition classes. The final answer to the question of *why* quality of writing correlated so highly with incidence of passive cannot be definitively answered here, but perhaps it is that higher incidence of passive voice indicates a greater control over the syntactic structures of the language, in some general sense leaving the reader with the impression that the writer has a higher level of proficiency in the written language. Whatever the answer to this question may be, it is clear that we need to teach our students that, in the dialect of formal, expository prose, the passive is not simply an unattractive transform of the active, but rather a valuable tool in the arsenal of 'good' writers.

Third, by our knowing more about what 'good' writers put into their writing, and what 'poor' writers do not, we will be better able to design exercises to guide 'poor' writers in the appropriate direction. Sentence-combining exercises would appear to be particularly useful in accomplishing this goal, while exercises that teach the techniques of clause subordination do not appear to be useful.

Finally, it is a solid body of empirical data, not vague intuitions, that will more clearly reveal the nature of the relationship between syntactic skill and ESL writing quality. When we have accumulated this body of experimental data, our job of teaching writing to ESL students, and the students' job of learning to write, may become a great deal less difficult, and perhaps more enjoyable.

Notes

1. I am indebted to Arthur Roth and Kenneth Kaminsky, Syracuse University statisticians, for their help with the statistical analysis.
2. A T-unit is 'one main clause plus all the subordinate clauses attached to or embedded within it' (Hunt 1965, p. 49). Thus, *The men are standing on the corner, and they are laughing* is considered two T-units, with the first T-unit containing 7 words, ending at the comma, and the second containing 4 words, beginning with and including the conjunction *and*. However, in *The men who are standing on the corner are laughing*, there is only one T-unit consisting of 10 words.

3. Passive voice is defined here as the true or 'dynamic' passive as opposed to the 'stative' passive. Examples, such as the following, were counted: *They were given the notice* and *He had been told to sit down*. The presence or absence of a *by*-phrase had no bearing on those passive constructions chosen for use in this study. 'Stative' passive examples, such as the following, were not counted: *I am interested in the results* and *My coat is torn*. Such distinctions were made in other studies to which this study is compared.

4. These were compositions that were first corrected by a rater, returned to the student, and then re-submitted in revised form. Schmeling then analysed syntactic differences between the first writing and second writing of only those compositions that had been rated as 'improved'.

5. The limited nature of this study does not imply that syntax is the whole of writing, for such things as content, development, organization, naturalness of expression and audience effectiveness all play a role in determining the quality of a composition.

11 The reliability of mean T-unit length: some questions for research in written composition

Stephen P. Witte

There can be no doubt that Kellogg Hunt's (1965, 1970, 1977) identification and use of the T-unit — an independent clause plus all of its subordinate elements — as an index of 'syntactic maturity' has greatly influenced the direction and quantity of normative and experimental research in written composition. As Hunt used the expression, *syntactic maturity* refers to the ability to use embedding and deletion transformations to say more in fewer words. In short, it is an ability to manipulate the syntax of the language, an ability which manifests itself in the texts people write. According to Hunt, this ability is measurable with such indices as mean T-unit length. However, regardless of the major role that mean T-unit length as a measure of syntactic manipulation has played in recent research in composition, a number of issues regarding its use remain — among them, questions pertaining to the procedures used for counting T-units, the relationship of T-unit length and writing quality, the validity of mean T-unit length as a measure of syntactic features, and the reliability of mean T-unit length across discourse samples. The purpose of the present essay is to survey briefly some of the research which has relied heavily on mean T-unit length and to explore one of these issues. This issue centres on the reliability of mean T-unit length as an index of writers' abilities to manipulate syntax in the discourse they write.

In research in written composition, mean T-unit length has been used principally in three ways. First, it has been used as a normative measure, allowing researchers to quantify gross syntactic differences among the texts produced by writers of different age and ability levels. From these normative studies, researchers have concluded that the older the individual the longer his/her T-units are likely to be. Among the researchers who have employed mean T-unit length as an index of the chronological development of syntactic ability are Hunt (1965, 1970); O'Donnell, Griffin, and Norris (1967); Stewart (1978a); and Witte and Sodowsky (Witte and Sodowsky 1978; Sodowsky and Witte 1978). Mean T-unit length has also been used in experimental research as a gauge of the effects of writing instruction and writing curricula on writing performance. This body of research suggests that writing T-units significantly longer than those 'normally' associated with one's age group can be taught and learned systematically. Typically, such curricular and instructional research has sought to measure the effects of a particular type of composition course on the syntax of student writers. Mellon (1969); O'Hare (1973); Combs (1976); Mulder, Braun, and Holliday (1978); the Miami University team (Daiker, Kerek and Morenberg 1978; Morenberg, Daiker and Kerek 1978), and Stewart (1978b) have, for example, concluded that the use of sentence-combining exercises can greatly increase the mean T-unit lengths of writers from the seventh grade to the college level, including writers enrolled in adult education courses. Other researchers — most notably Faigley (1979a, 1979b, 1979c) and Witte and Faigley (1980) — have shown that mean T-unit lengths can be increased through the use of sentence-embedding exercises such as those advocated by Christensen (1967). Third, mean T-unit length has been used — albeit to a lesser extent — to distinguish among texts said to represent different 'modes' of discourse. This research strongly suggests that different types of texts tend to elicit different mean T-unit lengths. Particularly important here is the research of Perron (1976a, 1976b, 1976c, 1977) and Crowhurst (Crowhurst 1978; Crowhurst and Piché 1979). The findings of Perron and Crowhurst that syntactic differences obtain across written discourse of different types tends to confirm the findings of other researchers working both before and after Hunt's identification of the T-unit (e.g. Frogner 1933; Seegars 1933; Kincaid 1953; Marckworth and Bell 1967; Johnson 1967; Bortz 1969; Veal and Tillman 1971; and San Jose 1972).

In virtually all of the research which has used mean T-unit length as a measure of syntax in written texts, one assumption prevails — whether the research is normative, pedagogical, or textual in nature. This assumption has to do with the reliability of mean T-unit length as a measure of the syntactic features of written texts of different writers. In practice, this assumption appears in two circumstances: (1) when mean T-unit length is calculated from a single writing sample and (2) when mean T-unit length is based on an average of mean T-unit lengths in several texts. In both cases, the same assumption operates: mean T-unit length for a particular individual or for a particular group does not fluctuate markedly over the time separating two writing samples, whether the samples are of the same or different types of texts, texts which differ according to either purpose or method of development.

Until recently, this assumption had gone untested, even though O'Donnell (1976, p. 33) had pointed out that 'there are no data to show how consistently these indices [such as the T-unit] measure the structural complexity of an individual student's writing in various situations'. In response to O'Donnell's statement, Anne S. Davis and I tested the assumption underlying so much empirical research in written composition. In the first of two studies (Witte and Davis 1980), we tested the assumption that mean T-unit length is a stable *individual* trait in what Kinneavy would call informative texts of college freshmen (Kinneavy 1971; Kinneavy, Cope and Campbell 1976a). Two of the informative texts were descriptions and one was a narrative. All three texts were collected under controlled conditions. With our research design and our analytic paradigm we sought to determine whether mean T-unit length was a stable *individual* trait within description and whether it was stable across description and narration. Our analyses indicated that for the particular students we studied, mean T-unit length was a stable *individual* trait neither within description nor across description and narration. The variability in mean T-unit length across the writing samples of a single student was greater than the variability in mean T-unit length within the group of students. That is to say, the students whose writing we examined appeared to use T-unit lengths in one description which differed significantly from the T-unit lengths used in a second description. That the students whose writing we examined employed T-units in one text which differed significantly in length from the T-units used in a second text of the same type led us to conclude that mean T-unit length was not a stable *individual* trait for the writers we studied. In that study, we argued that if mean T-unit could not be shown to be a stable *individual* trait across texts of the same type, then mean T-unit length could not be a reliable index of 'syntactic maturity'. Unless writers write T-units which do not differ significantly across texts of the same type, then one can question the reliability of studies which report significant differences between writers of different age or ability levels when the reported differences in mean T-unit length between the groups are based on single writing samples. Our finding that mean T-unit length was not a stable *individual* trait for the students whose writing we examined also has implications for experimental research as well as for normative research. If mean T-unit length is not a stable *individual* characteristic, then studies which urge the efficacy of a particular instructional method — such as sentence combining — on the basis of reported gains reflected in a single writing sample collected at the end of the instructional period may also be unreliable. Such studies assume that a single writing sample gives an accurate indication of the writing performances of the students from whom the discourse sample was elicited. In our first study of T-unit length stability, Davis and I also confirmed the findings of much previous research which suggests considerable syntactic variation among different types of texts. Although we looked only at the differences between descriptive and narrative texts whose purpose was to inform, our findings — as well as those of previous researchers — suggest that discourse variables must be controlled in all research in written composition. We also argued in our first study of T-unit length stability that unless T-unit length is a stable *individual* trait, then research studies — whether normative or experimental in nature — which pool several discourse samples of the same writer or groups of writers to determine the level of 'syntactic maturity' for the individual or the group may be similarly unreliable. If for individual writers mean T-unit length is not a stable characteristic within texts of the same type and if mean T-unit lengths differ across texts of different types, then analyses of pooled writing samples must accommodate differences across texts of the same type and across texts of different types if the findings are to be viewed as reliable indicators of 'syntactic maturity'. In no studies employing Hunt's index have these differences been accommodated in the respective analytic paradigms.

In our second study, Davis and I (1979) investigated both *individual* and *group* stability of T-unit length. In that second study, we collected four discourse samples from each of twenty-six students enrolled in a freshman composition class. These students, unlike the students in our first study, had undergone approximately ten weeks of intensive instruction in writing. They had written nearly every day for the ten-week period preceding the collection of the four discourse samples. Each of the discourse samples was elicited by a controlled writing topic which asked the students to produce a piece of informative discourse. Two of the controlled writing topics asked students to inform an audience through classification, and two of the topics asked them to inform through comparison. The four samples — which were on the average thirty-two T-units long — were collected during a period of approximately five weeks at the end of the fall semester. The two informative essays developed through classification were collected, and then the two informative essays developed through comparison were collected following three class meetings devoted to the use of comparison in informative discourse.

In our second study, Davis and I sought answers to two major questions: Is mean T-unit length a stable *individual* trait within informative texts developed in two different ways? and Is mean T-unit length a stable *group* trait across informative texts developed in different ways? Again using analysis of variance procedures, we determined that for the particular writing samples and students we examined mean T-unit length was a stable *individual* characteristic across informative texts developed through classification and across informative texts developed through comparison. Once we had determined that for our discourse samples mean T-unit length was a stable *individual* trait, we sought to determine whether it was a stable *group* trait across informative essays developed in different ways. To make that determination, we pooled the fifty-two informative essays developed through classification to form one data set and the fifty-two informative essays developed through comparison to form a second data set. Our analyses indicated that for the particular students and writing samples examined, mean T-unit length was a stable *group* characteristic, in addition to being a stable *individual* characteristic.

These two studies investigating the assumption that mean T-unit length is a stable *individual* and a stable *group* characteristic or trait suggest some important implications both for composition teaching and composition research. The importance of these implications derives from the ever-increasing and influential use of mean T-unit length as a measure of writing abilities in pedagogical and developmental research. The question O'Donnell raised and the one Davis and I investigated asks for what purposes mean T-unit length can be regarded as a reliable index of syntactic ability of different writers. Previous research suggests that it is probably to some extent reliable for differentiating among writers of different age levels. But it is reliable in such normative studies only to the extent that the findings are regarded as approximations of actual T-unit lengths that the writers studied use. The finding of Witte and Davis (1980) that mean T-unit length was not a stable *individual* trait across descriptions written by beginning college freshmen strongly suggests that for writers who are either inexperienced or who have not regularly engaged in the act of writing, variation in mean T-unit length across repeated measures may be so great that one discourse sample will not yield an accurate indication of such writers' abilities to manipulate syntax in the texts they write. Thus teachers and researchers should not make or recommend curricular and instructional changes for students of any age because a particular group of students happened to write shorter T-units on a given writing assignment than did the students whose writing was examined in a developmental or normative study of syntax in written discourse. The findings regarding the stability of T-unit length should also caution teachers to view sceptically the results of, for example, sentence-combining research. The two studies completed by Witte and Davis (1980, 1979) suggest that as an *individual* trait, mean T-unit length may stabilize only after writers have gained writing experience through repeated practice of their writing skills. In every sentence-combining experiment that I know of, pretest writing samples were collected under the assumption that the students' mean T-unit lengths would not vary significantly from one writing sample to another. If mean T-unit length were not a stable *individual* characteristic both at the beginning of the experiment and at the end of the experiment, then the resultant gains across time could be extremely misleading, encouraging teachers to make instructional decisions on the basis of inaccurate or inadequate information. *Group* stability of mean T-unit length is also an important issue relating to reliability. It is important for many of the same reasons that *individual* stability is important. Unless it can be demonstrated that the mean T-unit lengths of groups used in developmental or normative and experimental research are shown not to differ significantly across discourse samples of the same kind, then generalizing from those samples must, indeed, be a tenuous business.

The question of *individual* and of *group* stability of mean T-unit length has not, of course, been completely answered. Much remains to be done before we can know 'how consistently' mean

T-unit length measures the 'structural complexity' of discourse written in 'various situations'. But the two studies of Witte and Davis do suggest some ways in which that research should develop. Those two studies suggest that what may be needed is a study which attempts to determine at what age level mean T-unit length stabilizes in which types of writing. Such research should attempt to investigate the question of stability with reference to different writing purposes (e.g. to persuade, to prove a thesis, to inform, to entertain) and with reference to different ways of realizing discourse purposes (e.g. through description, through narration, through classification, through comparison, through definition). Such research should investigate the effects of interactions of discourse purposes and methods of development on T-unit length stability for different age and ability levels. Questions such as the following also could be usefully addressed. What effect does the subject matter of the discourse samples have on *individual* and *group* stability of T-unit length? What are the effects of audience considerations on T-unit length stability? What are the effects of oral or visual stimuli, as opposed to written stimuli, on the stability of T-unit length for individuals and for groups? These are all questions and issues which have been ignored in experimental and normative research depending on mean T-unit length as a measure of writing ability. And it is because these questions have been ignored that the reliability of such studies can be challenged.

Part Four
Implications for teaching

Needless to say, many teachers of writing have long been dissatisfied with the tattered remnants of the current-traditional paradigm and its implications for classroom practice. The kind of investigation of writing that we have seen in the preceding sections
of this book — the new emphasis on the analysis of the writing
process, the intensive and comprehensive studies of the development of writing abilities, the slowly growing interest in discourse
and text in relation to written production — all this points to the
need for an equally new pedagogy of writing. And indeed, such
research has almost from the beginning been turned to pedagogical purposes: a direction which promises as much revolutionary
change in the teaching of writing as the field has already seen in
the study of writing.

Current approaches to the study of the nature of writing and to
the teaching of writing in English as a first language may be
loosely divided into four schools. First there is the 'current-
traditional paradigm'. The outstanding feature of this approach is
that it starts from a traditional view of the properties of the
finished piece of writing, and makes that the basis of a pedagogy
which specifies stages that are supposed to effect the creation of
such a product. The other views, by contrast, start from the process by which a piece of writing is created. That, however, is all
that they have in common. One approach focusses on the first
and previously neglected part of the writing process — what is
sometimes called 'prewriting' and in classical times 'invention'.
Rhetoricians of this school have formulated various strategies designed to enable writers to define their tasks more precisely, and
to explore their data and generate relevant responses more pro-
ductively. The third school stresses pedagogical techniques which
address specific skills that are, or are taken to be, part of the
whole process. Characteristically, therefore, writers in this school
see the teaching of writing as the attempt to influence writing be-

haviours by means of carefully controlled tasks. In this, their pedagogy is more like what has been normal in second-language teaching. The fourth school tends to rely much more heavily on inherent linguistic abilities, and concentrates on providing occasions for those abilities to be as productive as possible. In this approach the view of the writing process is much more comprehensive, and writing tends to be situated much more explicitly in the personal, sociological and linguistic contexts in which the act of writing takes place.

The current-traditional view of writing is the one in which most people now teaching were immersed in their own education. Its prevailing assumption is that the creative aspects of the composing process are mysterious and hence unteachable; consequently, as Richard Young explains, the study and teaching of rhetoric was traditionally 'limited to the conventions and mechanics of discourse — for example, to the modes and structures of discourse, the characteristics of various genres, the norms of style and usage, a knowledge which is valuable primarily in organizing, editing, and judging what has already been produced by more mysterious powers' (1980, p. 54).

For these reasons, the teaching of composition involved any one, or any combination of, the following three strands. First, the teaching of grammar, believed against all research evidence to the contrary to be fundamental to the acquisition of writing abilities. Since editing skills had, by default, become paramount in the composition curriculum, increasingly student compositions were judged primarily (if not exclusively) by their success in avoiding grammatical errors. The teaching of grammar was believed to be the most effective pedagogic means to that end. Such teaching frequently involved the whole paraphernalia of 'traditional grammar' — defining parts of speech, parsing, and so on. Sometimes, however, the teaching of grammar meant only drilling in correct usage or, more likely, incorrect usage, since a characteristic pedagogic technique favoured by certain of the best-selling textbooks was to list all possible student errors and to provide practice in correcting them on the basis of extraordinarily contrived sets of exercises.

A second strand in the teaching of composition involved the analysis of models of successful prose, an analysis focussed primarily on organizational patterns and general stylistic characteristics — the famous unity, coherence, and emphasis. The distance between the models, however, and the student compositions remained a yawning chasm. Not only were the models written by extraordinarily gifted adults with extensive literary experience, but — more significantly — the aims, audiences, and modes of the models were radically different from those of the student assignments. The direct translation that was expected was simply not possible.

The third strand involved the explicit formulaic directions for writing enshrined in most composition handbooks: the step by step breakdown of the writing process derived entirely from an analysis of the products. First you must choose your topic, restrict that topic, then write your thesis sentence. With that single restricted thesis clearly in mind (one text suggests pinning it onto your bulletin board), write a sentence (not a point-form) outline, with Roman and Arabic numerals, capital and lower-case letters, all neatly in place. The rest follows easily. Write your essay — from introduction to conclusion — according to the outline, revise it carefully, i.e. check to see that you have avoided all possible usage and mechanical errors, and your assignment is complete. What could be easier?

The great weakness of the current-traditional approach from a pedagogical point of view is that it does not pay sufficient attention to the earlier, creative stages of the writing process. In his article 'Paradigms and Problems: Needed Research in Rhetorical Invention', Richard Young (1978) describes the increasing dissatisfaction of contemporary teachers and theorists with this view of writing, and in recent years rhetoricians have begun to redress the balance so that 'invention', which represents both the first stages and the creative aspects of the composing process, has become the central concern of contemporary theory and research (for an elaboration of this argument, see Freedman and Pringle 1980a). Arguing that creativity can be, if not taught, at least prepared for, many contemporary theorists have developed various heuristic strategies which provide the writer with a framework for information, and for preparing the mind for the insight which — with luck — will follow. Such strategies include Young, Becker and Pike's (1970) tagmemic heuristics which provides the theoretic underpinning for an important new college text by Lauer *et al.* (1981), Kenneth Burke's dramatistic method which has been presented as a pedagogic tool in Irmscher (1976), Larson's questions (1975), various versions of the classical topoi (Wallace 1975; Corbett 1965), and Flower and Hayes' problem-solving techniques (1977).

What these writers have in common in addition to their interest in invention is an Aristotelian view of writing as a craft and consequently as something that is, at least in part, subject to deliberate conscious control. As Young (1980) writes, 'certain aspects of the creative process can be taught. We cannot teach direct control of the imaginative act or the unanticipated outcome. But we can teach the heuristics themselves and the appropriate occasions for their use. And this is important, for heuristic procedures can guide inquiry and stimulate memory and intuition. The imaginative act is not absolutely beyond the writer's control; it can be nourished and encouraged' (p. 57).

As to the approaches to writing which address particular skills, one stands out at the moment both for the strength of the empirical research examining its effects and for its relatively widespread use especially in North America: the technique known as sentence combining. In its simplest form, sentence combining provides student writers with sets of very simple sentences and instructs them to combine them according to particular patterns which may either be specified or modelled. In other forms, the instruction or modelling is not provided, and students are left to find their own ways of combining the simpler sentences into more complex wholes. In advanced forms, the attention can shift to combining sentences to form paragraphs and even longer pieces of discourse, and simultaneously the attention to the rhetorical effects of different possibilities may be brought to the fore.

Historically, sentence combining has its origins in the attempts to assess the effects of teaching transformational grammar on writing abilities (Mellon 1967), but the distinction of demonstrating that the effects demonstrated by Mellon were actually due to practice in sentence combining rather than to instruction in grammar belongs to Frank O'Hare (1973). All in all, the research evidence for the effectiveness of sentence combining is now very clear; headed by O'Hare's work, it is the subject of a vast literature which is surveyed, catalogued and extended in Daiker, Kerek and Morenberg 1979. At the present time, there are a large number of sets of text materials available for the teaching of sentence combining at various levels, including O'Hare (1975); Strong (1973, 1980); Daiker, Kerek and Morenberg (1979b) and Memering and O'Hare (1980).

Similar to sentence combining is the technique of sentence expansion known as generative rhetoric, which is associated above all with Francis Christensen. Like sentence combining, generative rhetoric focusses on syntactic operations at the sentence level, and indeed it strongly favours particular kinds of sentence structures characterized by what are known in the literature in this area as free modifiers. Again like sentence combining, it has been extended to the level of the paragraph. However, whereas sentence-combining exercises provide the content of the sentences and challenge the students to explore the effects or at least the possibility of different kinds of syntactic manipulation, Christensen's generative rhetoric typically invites them to generate their own content as well as to explore the possibilities of syntactic manipulation. The theoretical justification for this approach is presented in Christensen (1967) and there is a fairly extensive literature reporting on the effectiveness of Christensen's techniques, although the empirical support is by no means as extensive as is the case with sentence combining. The major teaching work is *The Christensen Rhetoric Program* (Christensen and Munson 1968).

The fourth approach is even more radically opposed to the assumptions and methodologies of current-traditional rhetoric. The very extensive literature relating to it from the U.K. includes the work of the Schools Council project on the *Development of Writing Abilities 11–18* (Britton *et al.* 1975), the antecedent work of the London Association of Teachers of English (represented for example by Barnes *et al.* 1969), the whole 'Language Across the Curriculum' movement (e.g. Barnes 1973, 1976; Marland 1977) and the special development of that movement in such works as Martin *et al.*, *Writing and Learning across the Curriculum 11–16* (1976). Much of the current theoretical work in North America also relates explicitly to this same approach, especially that of James Moffett, Donald Murray and the research of the Writing Process Laboratory of the University of New Hampshire directed by Donald Graves.

As we have seen in the introduction to Part One, the nature of this approach is such that it does not lend itself to simply specified practical techniques which can easily be passed on to practising teachers. Rather, it requires a totally new orientation on the part of teachers, and a willingness to jettison teaching habits that may have been built up in the course of much of a professional lifetime in favour of techniques which are not only radically different, but may also seem at first sight to be naively romantic. Nonetheless, the accumulated evidence shows that this kind of approach to the teaching of writing is strikingly successful, not only in terms of the quality of the product, but also (and to most of those working in the field this is still more important) in the quality of the intellectual and emotional engagement during the writing process and, as a result, in the quality of the learning that takes place because of and through the experience of writing.

The most influential and far-reaching work has been that of the British group of researchers and teachers which includes James Britton, Nancy Martin, and John Dixon. Implicitly recognizing that what is required to change teaching techniques is a re-analysis of first principles, an important part of their published work involves such redefinitions. As we have seen in Britton's discussion of the composing process in this volume, the conviction that man is a symbol-making animal and that language is primarily symbol is fundamental to their arguments.

Consequently they emphasize what they call 'expressive' writing. This term derives from Britton's classification of all writing on a continuum which has 'transactional' at one end, 'poetic' at the other, and 'expressive' at the centre. Transactional is writing by which we get things done in the world: we report, communicate, inform, persuade. Poetic is writing where the focus is on the literary text, on the work as autonomous object. In the middle, and as the matrix of both, stands 'expressive' writing, which is writing for the self — exploratory, tentative, sometimes fragmented, as close as possible to the writer's thinking processes and experiences. It is by the use of expressive language especially that we explore and discover and learn what we mean.

In this section, Bennett's (Chapter 12) comprehensive ecological study of the place of writing in the Western Australian schools his team investigated points up the scope of the changes implied by this new orientation, whilst both Nancy Martin and John Dixon (Chapters 13 and 14) epitomize the British approach to the teaching of writing in their arguments for the primacy and necessity of expressive writing. What they recommend is a massive educational reform, well beyond decisions to employ new texts or new sets of exercises, beyond surface changes in syllabus, even beyond broad reforms of curriculum. They argue first and foremost for a change in the authority structure of the school, a shift in the relationship of learner to teacher and consequently of writer to reader. Teachers and students are to be partners in a joint exploration, and the expressive writing in their journals is to be a record of their dialogues. Learning comes about as a result of the active reconstruction by the would-be learner of the material, ideas, concepts, events, with which he is confronted, in terms of the representation of reality he has already constructed in past encounters with the world. A primary means for such active reconstruction is language, and especially exploratory talk and expressive writing. To foster learning, schools must elicit a great deal of language use in these two modes on the part of their students.

What is being recommended is thus a radical re-orientation of the traditional classroom. Some of these ideas have already taken root — in Britain and Australia, and increasingly in Canada and the United States. The New Hampshire writing experiment that Donald Graves refers to in this volume (Chapter 4), for example, involves a kind of teaching that is consistent with these goals. Children are encouraged to write from their first year; their writing is respected; and the teacher responds to the student as fellow-learner and fellow-craftsman. Similarly the kind of writing programme Donald Murray argues for at the secondary and college levels, in his writing, in his workshops, and in his own teaching, involves a close collaboration between teacher and student over the student's work in progress (Murray 1968, 1978, 1980). The assumption is that the student has something to say, that he will gain by saying it, and that the teacher is to be midwife to the creation. It should be noted, however, that this is not the wide-eyed Romanticism associated with the excesses of Deweyism. Although these educators share the Romantic and radically democratic belief in the potential of each individual to make meaning of his experience, there is no naivety concerning the need for discipline and dedication in realizing the potential.

The compatability of the new British approach with a certain amount of more structured teaching is clear from the two American papers on first-language pedagogy. Both Winterowd and Squire (Chapters 16 and 15), in their discussions of writing programmes respond in part to what they see as specifically American educational phenomena: first the standardized testing that American students are subjected to at regular intervals, especially before admission to college; and second, the increasing public pressure for accountability on the part of teachers. As Stibbs's recent book (1979) and the paper presented by Adams at the conference (Adams 1981) both show, neither of these phenomena is uniquely American. Their implication is that students must display visible and measurable progress at crucial points throughout their careers, and since (as the papers in Part Two show) writing development is notoriously difficult to measure, test-makers (and the public) tend to focus on those skills associated with writing that are statistically manageable. Proofreading and editing skills continue, then, to loom in importance.

Winterowd and Squire both provide similar solutions to the writing teacher's dilemma; they acknowledge the need to teach editing skills as well as to develop writing abilities, but they treat the two as distinct. Winterowd does so by distinguishing between the lab, which focusses on 'learnable' skills, and the workshop where the more complex and basic skills are 'acquired', using Krashen's definition of those terms. Similarly, Squire insists that educators must separate those skills associated with writing that can be taught through mastery-learning techniques from the composing process, which must be nurtured in a very different way. Implicitly in the case of Squire and explicitly with Winterowd, the kind of environment recommended for developing writing abilities is similar to that suggested by Britton, Martin, and the school they represent.

Learning to write in English when it is not your first, but a second or third language poses its own problems. It presents difficulties (of a peculiar nature) to the teaching profession as well, and until recent years has been the neglected child in the family of the 'four skills': listening, speaking, reading and writing. Furthermore, approaches to what we wanted to accomplish in developing writing skills have varied both according to the 'method' used and with the age of the learners.

During the very long period in second-language teaching in which the study of traditional grammar was equated with the notion of a language-teaching method, writing was viewed as one of a number of ways in which the student might fix in his memory linguistic forms and corresponding rules of 'correct' usage. 'Writing' meant copying words and sentences, or dictation, or translation. The aim was correctness in putting the pieces of the language together — pieces which had been learned pretty much as if they were isolates. There was no intention to teach the learner to express anything of himself through his new language; he was not really expected ever to have to do so. Writing was therefore not seen as being to any degree independent of the study of grammar; on the contrary, writing was its servant. This view corresponds most closely to the 'current-traditional' approach in teaching English as a first language, insofar as it is much more concerned with product than with process. Furthermore, in those rare instances in which the individual could hope to strive toward 'expressive' or even 'poetic' aims in a second language, the methodology employed to assist him was very much the same as in first-language education. Starting with an outline based upon a suitable model, the student would attend to various rhetorical patterns in his composition of a piece of prose.

When newer methodologies arrived in the post-war period, the emphasis was shifted to oral English. The audio-lingual and audio-visual approaches both emphasized the basic patterns of spoken language. The teaching of writing remained the same as before, however. Drills for developing writing skills were now 'structural' ones instead of being translation exercises, but the principle behind them was unchanged: writing was to be used to reinforce knowledge of orthography, of morphology and of sentence patterns. Superficial features of the language continued to have pride of place.

These approaches were used in teaching adolescents and adults. When English as a second language has been taught to very young children, it has generally been the case, at least in North America, that a first-language classroom setting obtained and that the children had to get along somehow without special language training. There seemed to be no special requirement to develop a methodology at all. Non-English-speaking children were to learn English as though in fact they already spoke the language and merely had to become literate.

This attitude to writing has something in common with past attitudes toward teaching adults to write in a second language, when one comes to think of it: it takes a great deal for granted. For adults, writing tasks have generally been assigned which reflected a tacit assumption that the learner would carry out in a second language operations he was already familiar with in his first. Any imperfections in language were attributed to a lack of knowledge of syntax and vocabulary, and it has been traditional to prescribe further study in these areas to overcome any infelicities of expression.

Changes in the kind of ESL teaching demanded, in the characteristics of its learners and in their purposes in learning English have all contributed to a growing feeling of dissatisfaction about the place of writing in second-language teaching programmes. From the standpoint of methodology, disillusionment with audio-lingual teaching is considerable and there is growing recognition that there is more to improving second-language skills than either translation or rote repetition will provide. The rise of interest in the functional-notional approach and the development of a wide range of techniques for communicative language teaching have provided a badly needed catalyst. As signalled above, the identification of the needs of the student is increasingly becoming the point of departure in planning a second-language course. Once it is accepted that these needs must be taken into account, a series of hitherto unasked — or at any rate unanswered — questions emerge.

Why do non-English-speaking adults learn to write English? If we ask this question, we come up with a variety of objectives or purposes, generally related to occupation. In fact not many adults learn to write more than enough for the most simple tasks. Those who need more require skill in the preparation of expository or persuasive prose, rather than anything else, and they are very often in a great hurry to reach their goal. Expressive writing thus is likely to have a place only in the early stages of an ESL programme, if it is not omitted altogether in the rush to get on with writing tasks which appear to be more directly related to students' final purposes. In the academic or professional work of such students, however, writing may come to assume important proportions, and there is no more reason to assume that all literate adult non-native speakers can write in this way than to assume that all native speakers can do so. Certainly what is needed is something far more than exercises in spelling and syntax.

Raimes' (Chapter 18) contribution to this volume exemplifies the concerns of a number of writers with process rather than product. Her paper thus provides an important link between the teaching of writing in first-language settings and in second-language settings. She argues that for the non-native speaker it is just as much a creative activity to try to form ideas in English as it is for the native speaker of English, and she therefore provides tasks which she believes will assist the student to this end.

The demand for programmes or courses in English for Specific Purposes (ESP) has made it necessary to teach certain types of discourse fairly directly. Work in discourse analysis and in the examination of text types is yielding pedagogical exercises in writing which also differ radically from the traditional ones in what they require the learner to do. They tie in with similar needs-oriented work in the teaching of reading and study skills, in the case of university students, or in reading and job-related skills, in the case of professional and managerial staff. Johnson's paper (Chapter 17), representing such work, reflects the fourth type of approach to programmes in teaching writing skills: the reliance on inherent linguistic abilities with personal and sociological contexts taken into consideration. Working within the general framework of communicative language teaching, he states that holistic practice must be provided throughout the writing programme, rather than being reserved for a final stage occurring after the student has mastered what he refers to as 'sub-skills': that is, after linguistic form is mastered.

Johnson accordingly suggests that the student needs to explore relationships of the sort Widdowson discusses in his paper in Part One, that is, relationships between the utterances occurring in a particular type of discourse and their contexts and intents. His concern, like Widdowson's, is for sociolinguistic aspects of language as communication, and in the relationship of the writer to his audience.

If Raimes shows something of how work in ESL may stand to gain from the work going on in the first-language field, Johnson's paper points once again to the area in which first-language research needs to be more conversant with the concerns of ESL pedagogy. The tentative explorations throughout this book of the relationships between these two fields are still at a very early stage. The differences between the two remain more striking than their similarities, just as they are more pervasive throughout the book. Clearly they are conditioned firstly by the different levels at which first and second-language learning of writing typically occurs, and thus, secondly, by the different scope of the teaching. First-language specialists to a much greater extent see the task of the teacher as that of an enabler, responsible for providing an environment in which writing can take place, so that overall development can ensue. Second-language specialists, because of the different exigencies of the second-language situation, are more likely to see the responsibility of the teacher as the task of causing development to take place in specific aspects of writing ability. Paramount among the concerns they share, however, is a recognition of the continuing importance of writing as a human activity; from this follows their recognition of the great importance of learning to write as an educational activity.

12   Writers and their writing, 15 to 17

Bruce Bennett

The research project which I am about to describe was rather grandly called 'An investigation into the process of writing and the development of writing abilities, 15 to 17'. In fact, it was a small-scale pilot project involving students and their teachers in four Western Australian high schools between 1977 and 1979. Analysis of the data is still continuing. The investigators were a director (myself), a full-time research officer (Adrienne Walker) and five other members of a team comprising university and high school teachers.[1] The objectives of the project were to describe the kinds of writing done in the senior years of these schools (years 10 to 12)[2]; describe the attitudes of students, parents and teachers towards writing; investigate changes in students' writing over the three year period; and relate such changes to personal or situational factors. An underlying and more general aim was to contribute to evidence and knowledge of the writing process.

Some assumptions

Underlying the design and operation of this project were a set of assumptions which relate closely to what Rex Gibson has called a 'counter-tradition' in educational research (Gibson 1978). This counter-tradition accepts subjective meaning as central to the research enterprise and insists that human behaviour be located socially and historically. According to Gibson, 'self-understanding, the intentions of the human actor, must . . . take precedence over causal explanations which lie outside the individual' (Gibson 1978, p. 24). Hence our insistence on the centrality of extensive (and expensive) discussions and interviews with a small number of students, whose perceptions of their writing were recorded, transcribed and analysed. It was paramount that their voices, the voices of the prime actors in the drama of writing, should be heard clearly. Similarly, though to a lesser extent, we were concerned to hear the voices of teachers, parents and the investigators themselves, which would contribute jointly to that 'composite picture' of writing which we wished to construct.

That picture required more components than the individual voices however, if it were not to seem impossibly surrealist: the individuals whose voices we wished to present and whose writing we wished to investigate should be seen against the fabric of their group and their society. We were therefore required to carry out some of the more traditional empirical and descriptive tasks of educational research including surveys, questionnaires and interventions in the school programme. In regard to the development of the research, we accepted some premises of what has been called the 'anthropological' approach (Stubbs and Delamont 1976): that a broadly based situation be accepted and its often bewildering array of variables not wilfully eliminated to prove a point (the 'if it moves, shoot it' approach); but, recognizing that not all aspects of the total scene can be analysed, we decided to carry out a species of 'progressive focussing' — periodic reductions in the breadth of the inquiry to give closer attention to emerging issues. The chief advantage of this approach is that it is flexible, in that its results are less likely than those of most research to be circumscribed in advance; its chief disadvantage is 'messiness', time wasted on false leads or hunches, information spilling over the categories provided for it — like life, perhaps. Nevertheless, we felt justified in this approach in a pilot project which set out to generate rather than stifle hypotheses.

The sample

Case studies, surveys, questionnaires and interventions involved the senior years (years 10, 11 and 12) of four Western Australian high schools. The first was a small (enrolment 320) government high school in a wheatbelt country town; the second a middle-sized (enrolment 706) government high school in a recently developed, affluent coastal suburb; the third a large (enrolment 1,090) government school described as 'disadvantaged' in a government report (its retention rate of students into the senior years was lower than the other schools and it contained a high proportion of students with migrant and working class parents); the fourth an independent boarding school for boys (enrolment 610) in a long-settled suburb, where retention into the senior years was very high and parents were generally members of the business or professional classes. The senior students sampled in these schools for larger scale survey purposes numbered 584 in the first year of the project. 60 of these were initially selected for case study analysis. Our initial expectations of how many case studies could be completed were excessive: to date, case studies of 11 of these students have been published.[3] Data is available for many more.

Over the three year period, there was a continual interplay between different elements of the project: for instance, insights from the case studies influenced the design of surveys and questionnaires, and vice versa. However, since we gave high priority to individual experience in this research, I will describe some aspects of the case study work first.

Case studies

Initially, students were selected for close analysis in case studies according to criteria such as general ability (high, medium and low as perceived by at least four teachers), attitudes to reading and writing (positive and negative) and disparities between speaking and writing abilities.

Most of the case study data came from interviews with students (about six per student), regular collections of written work, visits to schools, discussions with teachers and, in some cases, parents. The interviews were conducted as informally as tape-recorded situations allow, usually in a room in the student's school. While general areas of questioning were agreed upon by participating members of the team, such as the physical contexts of writing, the effect of teacher/student relationships, the process of writing (including prewriting phases), home influences, and reading and television habits, in practice the interviews were generally unstructured and were allowed to develop in directions which followed students' interests. In this way, many valuable insights were gained which would have been lost in a more rigorously selective interview situation.

As interviews and discussions proceeded, the initial categories assumed much less significance and different features of students and their writing emerged as important. The exercise became increasingly subtle as we attempted to explicate the sub-texts of our transcribed interviews. For instance, what lay behind the label 'non-writer' which had been applied to the following student?

INTERVIEWER:	What is the point of writing? For you? Is there any purpose or point in it?
STUDENT:	Er . . . I just do it because the teacher tells me to do it.
INTERVIEWER:	Yeah.
STUDENT:	(*indistinct*) I really don't want to do it.
INTERVIEWER:	Yeah. Well, that's a very honest response I think. Do you think that it's — there is any other — point apart from that for you?
STUDENT:	No, not really.

The student, 'Michael', was a sixteen-year-old Aboriginal boy living in depressed circumstances in a country town. His low sense of self worth, expressed in his general attitude to and performance in writing, appeared to relate to antagonistic community attitudes towards him and his people. But to be able to show the same student speaking fluently and enthusiastically about one writing task that *did* succeed for him was a dramatic contrast to the above. We were able to show, by talking with Michael about the conditions and circumstances of the writing of his successful script that, for instance, prewriting discussion of a certain kind and the teacher's ability to connect the topic and certain events in the boy's previous experience gave him the necessary impetus to write relatively well, and to enjoy it. From discussion of this and other case study material, members of the team developed a sense of the importance of situation, motive and audience which carried through to other aspects of the investigation.

A number of students have stunned us with their insights into the relationship between thinking and writing. Here is one:

'If you just think, um, all these ideas will just rush through your brain and there's all these different ideas and they're just rushing through your brain and you're trying to figure out something, trying to think of something concrete — all flashing — you can, but as soon as you write a word on paper you've written that down and it's materialized it — that idea has materialized and it can't disappear. You can look at it and you can watch it and all your ideas can sort of focus on and continue on, instead of just flowing, um, all over your mind.'

This sixteen-year-old son of Greek parents in an Australian suburb has expressed one of the great universal commonplaces: the ability of the human mind to construct meaning out of chaos; but what makes his statement exciting is the freshness and immediacy of his discovery, the drama of its process.

As we discussed the case studies in weekly meetings or more informally, some areas of common interest and concern emerged. We were struck by the prevalence of students' initial definitions of writing as finished products; to talk in terms of process was in itself a breakthrough. The yardstick of success was generally performance in examinations or teachers' assessments in terms of spelling, grammatical correctness and neatness of presentation; seldom was a more personal self-assessment forthcoming from the students. When the process of writing was probed further a number of students stressed the importance of discussion in the prewriting phase to clarify interests and objectives and to give a sense of purpose to the task (many complained of the difficulties of 'writing cold'); getting started' with a title or an opening sentence was often perceived as a great barrier. We were struck by different approaches to backtracking and thinking ahead in writing and by the ignorance or neglect of editing or re-writing skills. Among weak writers there were some who had not 'automated' their handwriting movements to the point where they could forget the task of forming letters and concentrate on spelling, syntax and the general flow of ideas. An observation made by weak as well as able writers was that the narrowing range of writing options in the senior high school years prevented them from writing 'creatively' in their own voices. It became clear that for most students some degree of imaginative engagement was a prerequisite to successful sustained writing. Instead of attempting to draw a profile of the ideal writer, we returned to separate drawing boards to write up our individual case studies.

Very few models exist for the composition of case studies in educational research, but we were guided by Donald Graves's strong advocacy of this approach (Graves 1975), by Janet Emig's use of 'writing autobiographies' (Emig 1971), and by the helpful advice of MacDonald and Walker (1977), who suggested that a fusion of the styles of artist and scientist might not be inappropriate to this kind of educational research — something closer than most traditional research to traditions in journalism, documentary film-making and the novel. These approaches were bound to appeal to members of a team who had all experienced a literary education (supplemented in two cases by degrees in linguistics); the notion of personal histories as dramatizations of general issues had fallen on fertile ground.

Surveys

The broader picture has been easier to assemble than the case studies, though it is not yet complete. It has involved in the first place an analysis of two surveys conducted in 1977 and 1978. In the first of these, all writing done by 584 students in years 10, 11 and 12 over ten school days was sampled; in the second, all writing done in schools and at home in one week (including a weekend) was sampled. In addition, the latter survey included a sampling of the amounts and kinds of talk that occurred in classrooms during the week in which amounts and kinds of writing were recorded. The first generalization to emerge from these surveys was that a high proportion of class time in the last three years of high school was spent in writing activities of one kind or another, as the following table shows:

Table 1 Proportions of class time spent writing in one school week

	Year 10	Year 11	Year 12
1977	44%	40%	40%
1978	49%	40%	33%

Although a slight diminution may be observed across years 10 to 12, writing (defined here as any writing activity lasting more than five minutes) was clearly a major part of classroom activities at each level and in all four subject areas — English, Social Studies, Mathematics and Science.

What kinds of writing occurred? Those students who had complained of a narrow range were vindicated by two kinds of analysis. In the first, all scripts were sorted into the three 'function' categories defined by Britton and his London University colleagues as transactional, expressive and poetic (Britton *et al.* 1975, Chapters 6 and 7).

Table 2 Comparison in 1977 and 1978 surveys according to function categories

	Transactional	Expressive	Poetic
1977	86.9%	2.9%	9.2%
1978	97.0%	1.9%	1.0%

The differences between 1977 and 1978 may be explained partly at least by different sampling techniques (we had relied on teachers' submission of 'typical' scripts in 1977 but had collected all writing by students in 1978). The dominance of transactional writing reflects tendencies elsewhere in Australia and in Britain and North America. It highlights the relative neglect, especially in the 'serious' years towards the end of secondary schooling, of writing in the expressive or poetic modes.

In an attempt to describe in finer detail the types of writing done in these years, we devised six categories which could be applied to all subjects of the curriculum and be easily interpreted by students as well as teachers and parents (see Table 3 below). Student recorders (two per class) noted the amounts of time spent in each school period on each of these types of writing. The results were as follows:

Table 3   Types of writing, expressed as percentage of total writing time in class

	1	2	3	4	5	6	7
1977	47%	35%	8%	4%	3%	2%	1%
1978	33%	42%	14%	6%	2%	3%	–

Types of writing categories:
1. copied notes from book, board or teacher;
2. short answers (a sentence or less) to comprehension exercises or tests;
3. more fully written report or summary in own words;
4. essay based on facts;
5. essay based on personal views;
6. personal writing — own experience, attitudes, feelings, imagination, e.g. diary, story, poem, play;
7. other.

Underlying these types of writing categories was the assumption that they represented a continuum from perfunctoriness to engagement with the writing task, or impersonal/regurgitative to personal/creative. (Although not strictly comparable, categories 1 –4 include writing that might be called 'transactional' in the London team's categories and 5–6 would probably correspond and overlap significantly with the 'expressive/poetic' functions). The most striking feature of Table 3 is the enormous scope given in the senior years of high school to the copying of notes from book, board or teacher and the writing of short answers of a sentence or less to comprehension exercises or tests. Reports or summaries

(Category 3) were the next most prevalent type of writing, typi-cally occurring in Social Studies or Science subject areas and accounting for similar proportions of the total time spent writing in years 10, 11 and 12. The more extended types of writing, such as essays or narratives, were given much less scope in the class-room. There was a diminution in the proportion of class time spent in personal writing between year 10 and years 11 and 12, but the proportion of time spent in that type of writing was very small in all three years. Where differences occurred among schools in the time given to personal writing this appeared to be the result of a particular teacher's enthusiasm. Differences among the four schools in the amounts and kinds of writing that went on in their senior classes appeared not to be significant.

The value of note taking and the ways in which students make sense (or nonsense) of it deserves further investigation along lines suggested by Howard Gannaway (in Stubbs and Delamont 1976, p. 62). Moreover, the intensity of thought that occurs prior to the writing of short answers to comprehension tests should not be underestimated. But the *prima facie* evidence of the above sur-veys suggests that a high proportion of the time spent on writing in these schools was confined to a restrictive range of 'regurgita-tive' writing activities — the kinds of writing that may be used by teachers as a means of disciplining classes or 'keeping them under control'. These activities appear not to contribute much to *learn-ing to write*, which could be more confidently expected to occur in extended writing activities where writers are encouraged to con-sider their own intentions and directions.[4]

Although the type of school attended did not appear to be a major factor in the time spent writing or the type of writing done by students, some differences among the subject areas were note-worthy. The proportion of class time spent in writing activities was generally highest in Mathematics and lowest in English. En-glish provided, as might be expected, the widest spread of types of writing; indeed, it was the only subject in which each of the six types of writing was represented — a fact which sceptics about the value of the subject English might ponder alongside the relatively narrow range of writing activities provided in other subject areas.

Although we had expected that writing at home would com-pensate for the minimal attention that was given to sustained writing tasks at school, this was generally not the case. Certainly, an increase in the amounts of home writing through years 10, 11 and 12 was apparent: 1.5 pages per student per week in year 10 increased to 4.8 pages in year 11 and 7.3 pages in year 12. But transactional writing (including copied notes) was the overwhelmingly dominant category again, with very little writing in the expressive or poetic modes. In keeping with this picture, and in spite of the efforts of some teachers to encourage the use of journals, voluntary or 'private' writing appeared to be a minority activity, carried out by only one in nine students in the survey group, and then often only of a cursory kind. Such voluntary writing as we saw in the pads used by students for all writing in the survey week included drafts of letters, diary entries, poems, songs, lists and slogans, sometimes accompanied by doodling or other illustrations. However, it is unlikely that much genuinely private writing would be submitted in this way and this area was explored in greater depth in one of our case study booklets.[5]

Talk and writing

The importance of discussion in the prewriting phase has been widely documented and was reinforced by a number of our case histories. We were concerned to draw the outlines of a picture rather than make a close analysis of verbal interaction in classroom talk such as Douglas Barnes and others have made (Barnes *et al*. 1971. See also Martin *et al*. 1976). As in the previous survey, student recorders provided the data. In general, talk represented a lesser percentage of class time than writing, as Table 4 shows:

Table 4   Percentage of total class time spent in talk and writing

	Year 10	Year 11	Year 12
Talk	28%	25%	36%
Writing	49%	40%	33%

The table shows that classroom talk increased in year 12 and slightly overshadowed writing, but this was accompanied, as mentioned earlier, by an increase in the amount of writing done at home. A number of students commented on being treated, 'at last', as adults in year 12. The relatively high proportion of time given to writing compared to talk in year 10 may reflect a conscious decision by teachers at that level to provide practice in composition, but since most of the writing was note taking and

hort answers, this is a less likely explanation than the one provided by some students, and teachers themselves, that writing is
often used to maintain discipline and a quiet classroom.

Changes in the relative prominence of different kinds of classroom talk are expressed in Table 5. Our attempt to compose a
broad picture of classroom talk drew on the student recorders'
noting of all occasions on which talk occurred for a period of five
minutes or more.

Table 5 Three major kinds of talk represented as percentage of
all classroom talk

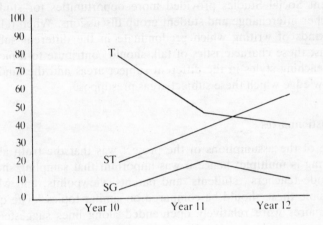

T   Teacher to pupils
ST Interchange between students and teacher
SG Student group discussion

As Table 5 shows, there was a tendency for teacher-dominated
talk to decrease considerably from a very high rate in year 10 to a
good deal less in year 11 and to decrease again, though to a lesser
extent, in year 12. However, teacher-dominated talk still represented about one third of all classroom talk in year 12. The
second category, where students and teacher talk, but the students
do most of the talking (ST) showed a steady increase from year
10 through years 11 and 12. A remarkable increase of student
group discussion occurred between years 10 and 11 but dropped
sharply between years 11 and 12; this kind of discussion remaining even in year 11 less than 20 per cent of all classroom talk. The
great majority of talk, then, was teacher talk, but the increasing
scope given to student-teacher interchanges reflects what some

case histories revealed, that a more mutually respectful relationship is achieved in the last two years of high school; and this
seems to result partly from smaller classes comprising students
who have chosen to stay at school beyond the statutory minimum
leaving age. While there was a remarkable increase in the time
spent in small group discussion between years 10 and 11, this did
not continue into year 12, perhaps in response to examination
pressures, which allowed less time for 'leisure' activities.

When the above categories of classroom talk were broken
down into subject areas, we found that teacher talk predominated
in Mathematics and Science; English and to a somewhat lesser
extent Social Studies provided more opportunities for student-
teacher interchange and student group discussions. When related
to kinds of writing which predominate in the different subject
areas, these characteristics of talk should contribute to a picture
of teaching styles in the different subject areas and the kinds of
knowledge which these subject areas presuppose.

Questionnaires

One of the assumptions of the project was that the truth about
writing is multiple: hence it was important that sampling should
include teachers', students' and parents' viewpoints; and where
possible these should be compared on similar topics.[6] The questionnaires were relatively open-ended along lines suggested by
Barnes and Shemilt (1962) and Bussis, Chittenden and Amarel
(1976). The 85 per cent of teachers who responded to the questionnaires (47 teachers) represented all subject areas except
Mathematics in the four project schools. 359 students responded
to the questionnaires as did 96 parents.

A meeting was held between members of the team and a group
of teachers from outside the sample schools in order to discuss
areas of concern in the teaching and learning of writing and to
outline some broad areas of questioning. Categories were constructed so that comparisons would be possible between teachers'
and students' perceptions of writing. The categories were:

(a) Kinds of writing done in school and kinds of writing that ideally
     should be done.
(b) Aims of writing.
(c) Contexts provided for writing to take place.
(d) Changes or developments which have occurred in writing.

The results are too complex to report in detail here. However, one observation seems inescapable: that the discrepancies between students' and teachers' attitudes to writing indicate a breakdown in communication on the purposes, functions and value of writing. Some of the most revealing discrepancies occurred when 'actual' and 'ideal' writing tasks were discussed: for instance, whereas only 17 per cent of teachers would have encouraged more 'creative' writing in the upper school years, 28 per cent of year 11 and 43 per cent of year 12 students would have liked this. (As case studies had also indicated, students seemed more aware than teachers of the narrowing range of writing tasks in the upper school along with an increasing emphasis on transactional writing.) Most teachers were satisfied with the writing tasks they set; of those who weren't almost all blamed external constraints (end-of-school examinations, 'the system', students' lack of motivation or ability). Only a few teachers (all English teachers) attributed responsibility to the teacher for widening the range of types of writing. In short, it would seem that most of these teachers set writing tasks, their students 'did' them and there was very little discussion about the value or significance of what was being done or of students' views on what might be done. The students were not without ideas: frequently they were quite specific about the kinds of writing tasks they would have liked to attempt and their suggestions ranged widely over different modes and tasks.

Perhaps the attitudes outlined above explain why there was such a small proportion of teachers (12 per cent) who perceived self development, 'growth' or the extension of thought as important aims in writing. Similarly, virtually no students referred to personal growth through writing; on the other hand, a high proportion of students (40 per cent of year 10 and 34 per cent of years 11 and 12) considered 'developing skills' a major aim. Whereas no teacher considered his or her aim to be to 'punish' students with writing, one in six year 10 students and one in twenty year 11 and 12 students thought it was. Most teachers agreed that writing enabled them primarily to find out what students knew; students in their turn perceived the teachers' main use of their writing to be a means of assessing and grading them.

One barrier to more open and flexible approaches to the teaching and learning of writing in these schools appeared to be the overwhelmingly negative attitudes which teachers brought to students' writing: 80 per cent of responses to year 10 writing were predominantly negative ('unoriginal', 'slapdash', 'poorly presented', 'superficial', etc.). Teachers' responses to the writing of final year students were more favourable (56 per cent positive, 33 per cent negative, 11 per cent neutral), but comments of a desperate or dismissive kind still occurred, indicating a sense of powerlessness among these teachers to 'improve' the kinds of writing which they found unsatisfactory.

Analysis of the parents' questionnaire is still at an early stage, but several observations are possible. Many respondents admitted ignorance about their children's writing; yet most agreed on its importance, for reasons ranging from utility ('You cannot get a good job without being able to write') to facilitating learning ('I think it helps them to understand/learn/remember things better'). Others wrote of writing as an expression of personality, and as a means of broadening knowledge and extending imagination. The non English-speaking migrant's special uses of writing were also mentioned: 'A person will understand something better if it is written first'; and 'Writing helps you communicate with people you can't see often'. Asked to observe what changes or developments had occurred in their child's writing over the past few years, many parents concentrated on its appearance (the demise of the copybook was lamented by several) or on spelling, grammar and punctuation. Others probed deeper and some interesting attitudes emerged, as in the following comment by the mother of a seventeen-year-old girl: 'Her writing has matured. Become concise. Less and less imaginative'. Does 'maturity' involve a diminution of imaginative exploration and an increase in conciseness and analytical ability? Some parents and teachers clearly thought so. Yet several parents stressed the continuing importance of writing for 'interpersonal communication' in the face of what one parent called 'direct, media-orientated electric-powered communication'. According to one father of a sixteen-year-old boy at a country high school: 'Loss of the written word might well mean the loss of the art of analysis and reflection for the sake of immediacy and efficiency'. The mother of a seventeen-year-old girl at the same school expressed concern for humane values and their expression through writing:

> 'It is through the written method that a vital part of creative expression and identity is developed — it is communication — and people who cannot do this are usually rather stilted both in human relationships, as well as appreciation of life and of their world.'

uch values were more noticeable among country than city arents.

Further investigations are clearly required also to analyse and valuate the generation gap that appears to fortify parental crit-cisms such as the following:

'A Lot of children write to small. The Children Try to write too Fast and too untidy through Lack of interest . . . They wouldn't get Far without it (writing) for the Children Taking on Book Work or any Office work.'

he prevalence of such notions among parents (whose writing is ften less proficient than that of their children) indicates a utili-arian view of writing which diminishes its importance as an agent f learning.

nterventions

)ne of our few interventions into the normal school programme vas the setting of similar writing tasks for the same group of stu-lents as they progressed through the last three years of secondary chool. The interventions occurred at three stages.[7]

In 1977 a large sample of students (596) in years 10, 11 and 12 vrote in response to a newspaper photograph. In 1978, those stu-lents in the sample who had remained at school (382 students in ears 11 and 12) wrote in response to another photograph. Then, n 1979, the remainder of the sample group (169 students in year 2) completed the final stage by responding to a third photo-raph. This design allowed for a synchronic analysis across the ears 10, 11 and 12 in the 1977 intervention and a diachronic nalysis of those students who stayed from 1977 (year 10) to 1979 year 12).

The stimuli were copies of photographs from the local news-aper. The first was of a small boy holding a school bag; the econd was a man, back to viewer with hand on hip, surveying a arge burning object; the third was a group of people crossing a ity road in the rain. On each occasion students were given a hotograph and the written instruction: 'Please write about the hotograph in any way you like'. Our first interest was in the forms of writing that would be chosen by students. Over the whole sample, story was by far the largest category, but over the whole sample and in each school, except the country school, the percentage of stories decreased with increasing age, and the percentage of essays increased. Other categories, such as descriptive prose and verse, were much less frequently attempted. The expectation that the more expository and analytical essay form would increase at the expense of the more expressive story form was confirmed. The extent to which such choices can be related to students' maturation or to the expectations of teachers and parents deserves further investigation, as does the possibility that particular stimuli may encourage particular forms of writing.

Another tentative form of analysis involved the application of a rating scale (0–3) to features of writing in a sample of 96 papers by fifteen-, sixteen- and seventeen-year-olds. These features, which members of the team derived from reading and discussing the sample papers were: engagment with the task; fluency; presentational skills; humour; feeling for the whole; appropriateness and control of style; originality; reader interest; vocabulary; figurative language; speculation. The definition of these features (or categories) was difficult; and as they were trialled we gained valuable insights into the problems and possibilities of their application. A major difficulty in this exercise was deciding the writer's intention; when we disagreed on this we found that it affected our judgment of most features of the script.

Although the preliminary and tentative nature of this synchronic study must be admitted (diachronic analysis of sets of the same students' writing will follow), we were interested to find increases according to age in the following categories: fluency, figurative language and generalization. These categories deserve closer definition and further testing. Feeling for the whole showed a marked increase between years 11 and 12, as did vocabulary between years 10 and 11: these areas, together with presentational skills and style also seem worthy of further attention. Speculation and humour were most notable for their absence: further investigations might ask why, in a period of life that is notable for its zany humour and speculative intensity, these qualities are so seldom transferred to writing in school.

Conclusion

We entered this project without grand theoretical preconceptions and have tried to retain the naivety of novitiates in spite of wide exposure to various theories.[8] We have tried to focus progressively on issues that arose from a wide view of writing in schools, informed by a close and continuing acquaintance with the experience of a small number of students: from such work, we believed, grounded theories might be developed; and we still believe that the most pressing need of research on writing is in the accumulation of a rich bank of data arising from direct observation and experience; where possible, of a longitudinal kind. The idea of an international bank of case studies is appealing; in practice, it might stimulate more 'action research' among teachers and lead to the kind of close observation out of which the best discoveries are made.

No research, however, is value-free and certain emphases are inevitable if an investigation is to be brought into focus at all. Ours was a stress on the *writer in the writing*, an emphasis which led us away from the admirable and well documented work of Loban (1976) and Harpin (1976), where development in writing was demonstrated primarily in terms of linguistic variables such as sentence length, clause length and 'elaboration' and towards the use of terms such as intention, motive and situation. Somewhat closer to our desired emphasis on 'the whole child' were Wilkinson's scales of development (see Chapter 5 of this volume) which we encountered mid-way through this project.

We remain sceptical about discovering discrete 'stages of growth' in writers and writing between the ages of 15 and 17. Not only does the literature on adolescence (and our memories of it) warn us against over-simplifying the many complexities of these years; but Bruner (1966, pp. 5–6), even accepting Piaget's biological evolutionary notion of growth, has indicated important *discontinuities* in a person's problem-solving capacity. How much more must such discontinuities occur outside the strictly cognitive realm in those kinds of writing where feelings and moral judgment become part of the process? Furthermore, what is the 'mature' state towards which such learning behaviour is claimed to lead our students? Cazden (1972, Chapter 5) has prudently warned against perceiving the stages through which a child passes on his way to 'mature knowledge' as mere partial versions of 'adult knowledge'. We should question further the initiation rites via writing into 'adulthood' in our 'advanced', technologically oriented societies.

These investigations in four Australian schools have led to a sense of the central importance in writing of the child's evolving self concept as a writer: confidence, independence, motivation, knowledge and understanding of the uses and purposes of writing, combined with situation, all contribute to this self concept.

Major obstacles preventing senior students achieving a satisfactory concept of themselves, and of their potential as writers, appeared to be a knowledge gap among parents and a crisis of confidence among teachers.

Notes

1. Other members of the team were: Don Bowes, Christopher Jeffery Simon McPhail, Andrew Sooby and Julie Stone. Many others have contributed, especially Nancy Martin, David Tripp and Bob Hodge. The project was funded by the Australian Government's Education Research and Development Committee. See Bruce Bennett *et al.*, *An Investigation of the Process of Writing and the Development of Writing Abilities 15 to 17*. Report to E.R.D.C., University of Western Australia, 1980.

2. Western Australian schooling is based on a seven years primary and five years secondary pattern. Year 10 is the third year of secondary schooling, traditionally perceived as the final year of the middle school and the year in which about one-third of fifteen-year-olds conclude their schooling. (The average retention rate for government schools into year 11 is about 55 per cent and for non-government schools about 75 per cent.)

3. The case studies of eleven students are contained in booklets published by the English Department, University of Western Australia. Their authors, titles and dates of publication are as follows: Bruce Bennett, *Michael*, August 1979 and *Marion*, January 1980; Don Bowes, *Victor*, March 1980; Andrew Sooby, *Adrian*, August 1979; Julie Stone, *Gina*, August 1979; Adrienne Walker, *Andrew, Karen and Tracy: Three Private Writers*, November 1979; *Janet*, April 1979; *Simon*, November 1979; *Stephen*, August 1979.

4. See, for instance, James Britton *et al.*, *The Development of Writing Abilities (11-18)*, Ch. 2; James Britton, *Language and Learning*, Allen Lane, the Penguin Press, London, 1970. Ch. 6. This observation was strengthened by an impressionistic survey of 'voluntary' writing by senior students at a drama camp and the same students' writing under examination conditions.

5. Adrienne Walker, *Andrew, Karen and Tracy: Three Private Writers*. See also Bruce Bennett's *Marion* and Adrienne Walker's *Janet*.

6. Christopher Jeffery took responsibility for this aspect of the research. 'Teachers' and Students' Perceptions of the Writing Process', *Research in the Teaching of English*, **15/3**, October 1981.

7. For a fuller report on this aspect, see Adrienne Walker, 'Changes in Writing', in *An Investigation of the Process of Writing and the Development of Writing Abilities*, op. cit., Ch. 9.

8. Early and obvious theoretical influences on this project were James Britton and his colleagues, *The Development of Writing Abilities (11-18)*, op. cit., and James Moffett, *Teaching the Universe of Discourse*, Houghton Mifflin, Boston, 1968.

13 Scope for intentions

Contexts for writing with special reference to unassessed
journals written for the teacher.

Nancy Martin

This paper is about the contexts for writing in school, and looks
particularly at unassessed journals written, in part, for the
teacher. It is based on work I did in Western Australia in 1978,
though it takes some of its direction from some discoveries we
made in 1976 when I was directing the British Schools Council
Project, *Writing across the Curriculum*. Neither of these projects
was a research study though both combined a practical brief with
certain elements of research.

In some learning situations writing can be (and is) regarded as
a different and separate aspect of English from reading and talking. We chose to study their inter-relationships. So in this paper I
worked on the assumption that things that affect English will also
affect writing as a part of English.

Writing across the curriculum

In the *Writing across the Curriculum* project in 1976 a particular
problem was to find good transactional writing in any quantity in
any one class; where we did find it, it seemed to be related to
'scope for intentions' — student intentions in particular — using
the term as Bruner uses it in his work with infants (Bruner
1975), as a gatherer of tacit powers. Scope for intentions, in turn,
seemed to us to be related to particular features in the learning
environment — the context of the school. Our limited study suggested that such scope was provided by the following circumstances:
- the writing was associated with ongoing, fairly long studies representing something like two terms' work;

- the topics were self-chosen in consultation with a teacher;
- they all contained field-study work based on personal first-hand experience;
- they allowed for variation in the kind of resources that were drawn on. (Some drew on books, others made more use of interviews or written or spoken accounts by people contacted.);
- all the students had received good instruction in the presentation skills for such studies.

Our tentative conclusions were:

1. that the first-hand experience was the means by which they made sense of the secondary information;
2. that the option of choosing their own topic (together with the field studies) caused the writing to be a genuine communication of a learning experience;
3. that the role of the teachers was deliberately more advisory than directive: intentions were relatively mutual;
4. that for students' commitment to learning (and writing) to happen on a wide scale there might be a need for enough teachers with a shared view of learning and its circumstances to create a different set of possibilities in the school.

Contexts for English in some West Australian high schools.

In 1978 I was invited to lead a team conducting a survey of English in the government high schools of Western Australia. In addition to relating the study to some of the current research on evaluation we set out to study particularly the contexts for English – to attempt to identify the constraints and liberating features for students and teachers and to see how the intentions of each fared in different circumstances. We supposed that we should find groups of interacting influences, not single ones.

At one end of the scale we tried to tap the quality of what went on in classrooms. We assumed that understandings, beliefs and values are major determinants of the environments that people create, and are more influential than sets of instructional materials, packaged programmes and the like (Bussis *et al.* 1976).

At the other end is what Parlett and Hamilton (1976) call the 'management framework'; that is the wider set of arrangements belonging to the organization of the school and its part in the system. The life of classrooms is, to a greater or lesser degree, embedded in these institutional matters — such things as assessment procedures, timetabling, length of lessons, availability of library and copying facilities, secretarial assistance, etc.

In the middle, in schools large enough to have one, is the English department and the senior English master. Here, hierarchy may or may not be powerful; consultation may or may not take place; decisions may or may not be shared; the department may be pretty well autonomous or may contribute to a general school ethos. Working on what we thought we knew about the wider scale of possibilities arising from groups of teachers with shared intentions, we paid special attention to the way English departments worked.

We based our survey on eight case-study schools chosen to be representative of some obvious differences which we thought might affect the teaching and learning of English; such differences as size, physical features, country or metropolitan, organization, sources of curricula (school-based or externally mandated), etc. We later added two schools where special innovations (not confined to English) were being carried out.

But one of the problems in looking at schools is that there is always a gap between intent and practice. A teacher provides all sorts of activities and encounters, the *perceptible* form of the curriculum, but behind them are the learning priorities and concerns that a teacher holds for students — what he wants them to know, do, and care about. In short, his intentions in teaching. We thought that the connections that were made (or not made) between the classroom activities and the teachers' learning priorities might turn out to be a powerful influence on English.

For this paper I have taken the written work from one school and have tried to set it throughout in its context of particular teachers, the English department, the special project, and a particular class or year group. I have focussed on the form of writing which gives most scope for intention (journals), though I have given a brief mention of all the writing the students do in order not to distort the picture.

'Intention' is a difficult word to use in so broad a context. I use it to cover a wide spectrum. At one end are those concerns which cause students to write about this rather than that in free-choice situations — which concerns are often unrecognized until expressed; and, on the part of teachers the fostering of students', attempts to find their own directions, in the belief that this is where powers of language and thought are most easily gathered.

At the other end are all the manifold deliberate intentions, such as practising comprehension tests for an exam, or writing a journal three times a week or any other decision to do this or that. We were interested in the significance of intention as an aspect of commitment to learning and writing. It is this aspect that is dealt with in this paper.

The school

West Coast High School is an old established school in a flourishing town of some 20,000 inhabitants. Because of the great distances and scattered population the town is the educational centre for the area and contains three high schools and seven primary schools. There are about 1,000 students in West Coast High and they come from a cross-section of the community. There is an English department of six teachers. We studied the work of two classes in years 11 and 12 (aged sixteen and seventeen). All were entering for the Tertiary Admissions Examination (TAE) — in practice the upper school leaving exam. Students must all take English or English Literature. I am reporting only on the writing done by students taking English. No set syllabus exists. Teachers are expected to make their own curriculum, but since the exam papers have certain regular features — an essay on a set topic and a comprehension paper — in some schools the writing is dominated by practice in these two techniques. West Coast High School's exam results over a long period have been very satisfactory, and in some years above average.

The special project and its relation to writing

The Schools Commission (Federal project funding agency) funded the Senior English master to develop talk and personal writing as a means of assisting learning in all subjects. It also funded an Education Centre with equipment, books and a full time Warden to run it. The Senior English master set about creating a team of teachers from any of the schools in the town from any subject, and primary or secondary schools who were interested in the role of language in learning. Though one of their chief aims was to document small group talk, they also aimed at developing personal reflective writing as the link between talk and writing on the one hand, and between talk and thinking on the other. With this aim the keeping of personal journals written for the teacher but unassessed were made part of the regular programme at West Coast High, and also in years 6 and 7 (ages eleven and twelve) in some of the primary schools.

Mutual understanding: a shared view.

I have indicated in general terms the kinds of influences we expected to find affecting English, and writing in particular. In West Coast High we could see the Senior English master deliberately attempting to counteract the negative influences and organize for the positive ones. As a foundation he worked on a principle of cooperation and discussion with English staff and students. For example, the year 12 students were asked to discuss in small groups what they thought were the aims of upper school English and then to write up individual statements. One student wrote:

> I think the first and foremost aim is to ensure we all pass the TRUMPET (TAE).
> I know the teachers try to convince us and themselves that this isn't the main aim but when it all boils down, the only reason we are at school is to receive our TAE certificate.
> I think other than this the teachers aim to:
> – allow us to be able to formulate our ideas and express them with confidence within a group;
> – give us a wide diversity of reading so we can learn to appreciate all kinds of literature;
> – help us to develop our sense of creativity and learn the joys of writing things for ourselves;
> – help us to discover and nurture what literary talents we possess;
> – let us develop our own unique style of expression.

Another wrote (among other things):

> Certainly English is a curriculum where a student can learn about himself. ... The English lesson should also be enjoyable, an oasis from the rest of school drudgery. Unlike other subjects, English is an avenue for developing and putting to use creativity and imagination.

These examples are typical.

Perhaps the most surprising thing about these statements is that 'passing the Trumpet' is seen as distinct from all other aims. The students do not see them as connected in any way. Yet, if the first writer's aims were fulfilled by the by the students, they would pass their TAE in their stride, which apparently they did.

Part of the management framework of a big school, or department, is the circulation of written notices. In this school the

Senior master's circulars are for information *and* discussion; some are just for discussion. They are brief and the sense of orders coming from above is counteracted by their tone and sometimes an eccentric heading. One was headed: 'How I learnt to stop worrying, love the English department and let it run itself: some notes on administration'. His discussion sheets are personal in tone. In one about the assessment of written work he prefaced his practical suggestions by writing:

> I explained to my class that I believed they write best when they write for a real purpose and a real audience. . . . and that they learn to write by writing. I suggested that as I believed assessment could affect the quality of their written response negatively, I would only assess five pieces of writing during the term. . . . My original intention was to tell the class which five pieces would be assessed. They asked instead that they hand up their best five pieces at the end of term. . . . .

Similarly, he explains things to parents. In a homework policy statement to them he wrote:

> . . . we believe that students learn to write by writing — perhaps in much the same way that they learn to talk by talking. . . . They are generally expected to complete one piece of extended writing each week. In addition most teachers provide opportunities for students to write regularly — perhaps in a less formal way. One such opportunity involves writing in a journal. In this students are encouraged to write informally about things that are important to them. It is their personal view of the world. We would hope that students would write in their journal daily, or at least three times a week for from ten to fifteen minutes. . . . Although the benefits of reading, writing and talking are always obvious, we believe that these do contribute to students' language development.

And for students — in his sheet for them he introduced the assignments for writing by the following:

> I believe the best assignments are those which evolve as a result of reading combined with the personal experience of the writer. So you are asked to do some background reading. . . . You could also include the viewing of television films or listening to radio as part of this background work.
> We expect you to become involved in a personal way in the assignment. Try interviews — but don't just report what was said; describe your reaction to what was said. . . .

About journals he wrote:

> It should consist of your own personal expressive writing. You may write in any form you like, or a variety of forms, including poetry,

prose, drama or art work. You should write about things that are important to you. It can be written for a private, restricted audience. Over a period of six weeks, or longer if you wish, it should show your view of your life and of the world in which you live.

There are other documents which space does not permit me to quote, but they all carry significant implicit messages. They assert a belief in relationships based on face-to-face talk irrespective of status within the school hierarchy — and this goes for students as well as staff. Because they share this view the English staff have created an environment in which discussion and reading and writing is the *modus vivendi*. The English staff room is itself a continuing seminar for ideas about literature, about writing, about education and about the place of language in learning.

Options for writing: years 11 and 12

The programme for written work falls clearly into two parts — the development of general writing ability, and specific preparation for the TAE examination. Each is treated with similar thoroughness and understanding of its value. I deal briefly with the latter because the focus of this paper is on the former. It is too often assumed that these two aims are mutually exclusive. The written work in this school demonstrates that they are not. In a circular to the staff the Senior English master deals with all the practical and administrative details of the written exam: information about the availability of test materials and past papers, assessment requirements, warnings that concentration on test material is not the best way to help students pass their exams, advice about the need to put some pressure on — and also the need to take it off — and a reminder that literature is always at the back of good writing. It's all here. I now turn to the long assignments that the English teachers regard as being of great importance in the development of the students' general ability. Students in year 11 undertake one long assignment; in year 12 they do two. Options in both years include:
– a six weeks' journal;
– any topic of their own choosing;
– a major creative work — a play, a radio play, a book of poems, two or more short stories.
In addition, the 1978 topics suggested by the teachers were: Un-

employment, Old age, Your future career, Immigration, Primary or special education.

One might be tempted to say that the suggested topics are limited by their sociological slant, but the emphasis that these teachers place on first-hand experience needs remembering; this itself places a limit on the topics. Furthermore, in every assignment one of the options is 'a topic of your own choosing'. This together with the option to write poems, stories or a play gives scope for more imaginative directions. And there is the journal. It is clear, I think, that all the options except the suggested topics give scope for the students' own directions, and the topics only include those where first-hand experience is possible. The connection between the perceptible form of the writing curriculum and the learning priorities of the teachers is clear. They know what they are doing, and why. We thought this was a contextual feature of importance.

Journals in the upper school

Anything written is potentially matter for reflection in that it exists, out there, as an object for contemplation, but in the world of school it very seldom is one. All the West Coast journals have this element of reflection. At the end of their course they write about what value they have found in the various things they have been doing in English. I quote some excerpts about journals:

Student A
> Because I was so apprehensive and inhibited my first few pieces were very blunt and somewhat similar to a history book. . . . reading back over what I've written my change from formal impersonal English to a flowing and natural style is evident, and by ambiguous, self critical and half conversational types of writing I amused myself making the hassel of writing every night pleasurable. . . . The most outstanding value gained for me was that I became more aware of the outside world. . . .

Student B
> I found that with writing regularly, my ability to write improved enormously, not only in the quality of the result but in the ease of actually doing the writing. . . .
> I often used my writing as a thought-formulating process. . . . The journal also helped me to understand myself and my place in life. . . .
> In a very indirect way this better understanding of myself helped me to develop an identity and gain confidence in myself as an individual. I wrote what I really thought and felt — just what I wanted to write and what was 'me'.

Student C

When I started writing it I hoped to make my journal more interesting by making it more for public consumption. I suppose I am a person who likes other people knowing what I think about things. . . .

Student D

I dislike others reading what I write because I fear they may think it dribble (so to speak). I know that I cam improve my writing by writing something which only you (teacher) and myself can read. To tell you the truth I have lost some of my inhibitions as the year goes on through writing a journal at home.

(Different students reflecting on changes in themselves and in their writing.)

In reading the journals (with permission) one is struck both by their diversity and some similarity. Perhaps the similarities are aspects of adolescence and of their shared school lives; the diversities are more unexpected. Some students take on a persona and a style to match and obviously enjoy the game; many include poems and others present a whole range of experimental forms and lay-out; even the least able write direct and thoughtful pieces.

Student E

(This journal is characterized by the way the writer uses language in any way he wants and obviously enjoys doing so. It is much taken up with reflections about school work, about breaking his leg, and about poetry.)

I think I went fairly well (in a maths exam) after such a disasterous start, and this is probably because I enjoy maths so much this year. You would too if you had Captain Brown for a teacher. With a unique combination of nautical terminology and mathematical theory delivered at great volume through the smoke haze of the occasional Marlborough, one cannot help but pay attention. . . .

(After breaking his leg)

It is my considered opinion that old Davies (doctor) is at the centre of a sordid little conspiracy to rip off the ignorant and unhealthy of this town. . . . The old Gremlin was hunched over a pile of papers writing furiously. He was unimpressed by the drama which surrounded my entry. . . .

(An incident from the Anzac Day parade)

The parade was long since over and the accompanying festivities were drawing to a close. . . . A hundred yards from the door of a rusting iron roofed hotel, an old man had managed to prop himself into a sitting position against a nearby lamp post. The bottle he had been drinking from rolled from infirm hands. . . . A row of medals pinned in random precision to the lapel of his suit was mute testimony to his part in the dawn parade. He was an original Anzac. (The story concludes) The men in the white car who came to take him away seemed to agree that he had been asphyxiated in his own vomit. . . . I thought it strange that a man who had braved so much and been a distinguished soldier should have suffered the indignity of being slain by such an enemy.

I haven't been so goddam bored as this ever, even. I can't go to school because I can't walk without crutches. . . . Chronic boredom like this calls for desperate remedies. I now resort to poetry writing whether you like it or not. It is called 'Sheep on the River' and was written under the influence of suntan oil fumes and sunshine. It is also about a dream I had last night.

(Unlike his other poems, this is a mocking one)

Student F

(An excerpt and a poem from an extremely varied and decorated journal.)

ADDRESS UNKNOWN

Where I am now is through no influence of my own. An old man made me and an old lady helped. Old, that is, in relation to my youngness. They have been there. Not only by them was I made. I was made through circumstances, instances, feelings, moods, times, places: by people. I was made by impressions because I am an impressionable person. I was created by an old man, a stranger whom I met on the wharf, and a foreign lady with a very strong will. Indeed, not solely by my parents . . .

OUR KITCHEN TABLE.

Many years it has withstood bangings, cuttings, jolting and cluttering
Long has it stood unheeded, quiet, unobtrusive
Now in the corner, now along the wall
I remember Mama making scones on it at shearing time
and how Janice (who came to help) spilt some water
and nearly electrocuted herself . . .
It was still there when we came back after two years.
Ruth made bread on that table, and afterwards
We all sat round and ate it hot.
I have often sat there, head in my arms, bewildered,
Or talking over a cup of tea with Barb.
Plain table top, smooth with age, at each leg a convenient toe hold
And under each leg, — a folded piece of paper.
   For balance you know.

Student G

(More at the level of day dream than reflection but captures the ebb and flow of feeling more than some.)

Since sitting here for ten minutes many strange thoughts have come over me; this is the first time I have deliberately sat and thought back

over the days, people I have known, experiences and what's in store. . . .
I'm just filling in five minutes before Paul comes. I havn't been out
for so long and I just love going out. . . . I'm getting nervous what I'm
going to talk about. . . . I havn't done anything exciting. . . .

I'm just loving this exploring and research topic in Geography (a field
study) so much that I intend to write to the Career Centre to see if
they can advise me on a career that is based on such work. . . . I think
I might join the Historical society also; it's about time I had a hobby.

It's good being sick, lazing in bed, radio, drinks and imagination going
wild. One minute I want to go on the dole, travel the beaches and rage
continuously — then next I want to be a teacher, have a nice flat, a
dog and live a conservative, simple life like the rest of us. . . . I'm sure
people in this world don't do what they want to do, but just what
others would like them to. . . .

I have some exciting news — Donna and I came second in the State-
wide open Geography competition: that was for our assignment (field
study). . . . It's great to know that all that hard work is rewarded —
$50.00. I feel rather proud actually and it's the first time I have ever
won a prize at anything.

Doubts are often expressed about the value of this kind of writing
which is so near speech. It is possible that the benefits are indirect; however, the fact that this student won a prize for a
Geography study suggests that she had a more formal mode available to her.

Two of the English teachers in written statements said:

Mrs K: Perhaps the journal could be said to combine speaking and
writing. They speak to their journals certainly, in a different, more
cultivated language than that of spoken conversation, but infinitely
more expressive than the kind of writing on which so much emphasis
is placed in many classrooms.

Mr G: Writing of this sustained, informal kind 'frees the hand'.
Rather than fighting every word, willing it on to the page, it gradually becomes a fully natural response, i.e. the writer is not alienated
from his writing.

I can't here report on the development of open or personal
writing among the younger children or in the other schools, but
through the Education Centre self-initiated teacher education
continues. This is itself a significant element in the context of
English in the participating schools.

In conclusion I want to suggest that school writing gives few
opportunities for students to reflect about their own learning —
to think about thinking, and to begin to know themselves. Jour-

nals offer such opportunities, and the ones studied are convincing evidence of their value.

But the journals written in West Coast High School were effective as genuine communications in the context of English in this school; they were appropriate in its climate of talk and mutuality of intentions. In less favourable circumstances where the contexts for English were different, and where journals might be set as just another type of written exercise, they would be unlikely to be effective.

I think it worth noting too that the contexts for writing in English in West Coast High School were similar in many ways to the contexts for writing in Social Studies in the British comprehensive school described earlier in this paper. New possibilities were created in both schools by the shared learning priorities of a number of teachers, and resources for writing released by the scope given to intentions.

14 Writing in response to literature

John Dixon

I want to propose a major review of current practice, and of the theoretical assumptions that underlly much writing based on response to literature. Necessarily I am going to be schematic. There is limited scope to invite you to look closely with me at the evidence to support such a proposal. Indeed, as you will be aware, if I am to bring out the main points in a short space there will inevitably have to be some polarization in the evidence selected. So let us begin by warning ourselves about these things, and take advantage of the discussion both to challenge and to build out from the introductory framework I shall offer.

The problem

After four years' work on my current project, working with teachers drawn from many different parts of the U.K., I have learnt that we must ask again: What counts as evidence of literary response? In current conditions the danger is that — apart from a gifted few — students of sixteen to nineteen are inhibited in their written tasks from drawing on what actually went on as they read a text, listened to a presentation, or watched a play. Often, it seems, they are learning to substitute intellectual sophistry for the effort to give authentic articulation to their literary response.

If this is true — and if you suspect it may apply to some degree in your own country — we must look again at the supposed benefits when students and teachers read literature together. The expectations of my own generation have always been high, I think, and we owe that in part to a critical tradition widely shared among our leading university teachers. Let me try to sum up in their words what I have learnt to expect of reading literature:[1]

> 'Works of art... exist always through their moment-by-moment experiencing by one or several perceivers.' 'The primary centre of the

whole activity of reading is some state of our feelings that we call, for lack of a better word, enjoyment. How enjoyment comes about is never very clear, but it seems to depend in some fashion on various kinds of activity that lead to understanding. It may also be supported by those typical though maybe not essential activities that form a kind of intelligent comment (perhaps pre-verbal) on the work as it is being experienced.' In *King Lear*, for instance 'we not only respond with delight to the ever-changing local realizations . . ., we bring together the varying and even contradictory meanings of "need", "justice", "folly", and so on, as imagery and action enforce them. In this way routine notions and attitudes are broken down, and a new direction of consciousness emerges from the interplay of meanings: not meanings, so to speak, "out there", as though we were trying to understand a legal document, but meanings in which the reader or spectator is involved as a person, simply because moments of sympathy or antipathy, of assent and dissent — in short of judgement from a personal centre — are a necessary part of them.'

'Analysis . . . is a more deliberate following through of that process of creation in response to a poet's words than reading is.' 'A critic can certainly give some account of what he believes to be his response to a particular text. But this is far from rehearsing all that is available to an interested reader . . . Moreover, a critic is (often) limited by the medium in which he writes; that of conceptual prose . . . The critic cannot do more, in fact, than semaphore what he perceives and hope that this will make his readers perceive it too.' 'Today one senses danger from the over-anxiety of some teachers to train their pupils in close reading.' 'What we seem to be in need of is an understanding of criticism which, while remaining faithful to the principles of analysis and judgement, will make us more sharply aware of our personal responsiveness.'

I realize, naturally, that some may come from a different critical tradition; nevertheless, I hope we can find pointers to common concerns in that summary account of reading and a creative critical response. The interplay between enjoyment and understanding, for example. The personal encounter with meanings through imagery and in action. The inherent limitations to any account (let alone a student's early attempts) of what it has meant to be involved as a person in reading. The possibility — indeed the demand? — that writing 'criticism' should make us more sharply aware of our personal responsiveness as readers. Certainly it is ideas such as these that will become important criteria as we consider what students are doing as they write in response to literature.

Negative evidence

I want to start with some of the traps that currently betray the unwary teacher and student. To get at them, I believe we must begin with some extracts — however brief for the moment — from student writers and, giving their language the careful attention we would to literature, ask ourselves what exactly is going on. These extracts,[2] as it happens, come from essays that have gained their writers credit in school or in the specialist Literature exams current in England for students of seventeen or eighteen plus. The first is the opening paragraph of an essay based on *Lear*.

> In *King Lear* the influence of evil on all the characters is very apparent, the whole play is full of evil which destroys both the good and evil characters: because there is so much evil in the play, much of it is set at night-time and during bad weather.
>
> 5   There are two groups of people in *King Lear*, the good and the evil, and both recognize that man's nature is essentially evil but the good, Edgar, Cordelia, Kent, Albany, try to overcome this evil, whereas Edmund, Cornwall, Regan and Goneril are quite content to live a life of evil and to use it to gain their own ends. The two
> 10   different attitudes may be seen in the contrasting philosophies of Edgar and Edmund, Edgar believes that man can rise above evil and live a good moral life; Edmund bases his philosophy on self-interest and rejects the conventional morality, he is one for his own gain no matter whom he hurts in doing so.

When this paragraph was put to panels of readers drawn from schools and universities in the U.K., they saw in the main a foreground filled with generalizations lacking the weight of any residual contact with imaginative poetry and action. The counterpoint of 'content to live a life of evil' and 'rise above . . . and live a good moral life' offered an extremely simplified view of *Lear*. Only the occasional phrase hinted (awkwardly) that impressions of the play might be still alive — the darkness, the vigour of a man set on 'his own gain'. Rightly, I believe, they suspected that here was a student too engaged in grappling with the terms of a set question to be able to draw on or control any reference to his actual response — for the moment at least.

The second extract represents a later stage in the same essay.

> The 'evil' group do not try to live up to any standards. Edmund uses other people's weaknesses to his advantage, he uses Gloucester's credulity to turn him against Edgar.
>   'A credulous father. A brother noble'

5   He considers which sister will be most use to him before he can de-
        cide which to marry, he says
                'Which shall I take
                Both? One? Neither?'
        Goneril must kill Albany herself, for Edmund will not take the
10   risk.
                'Let her who would be rid of him
                Devise his speedy taking off'
        He uses his illegitimacy as an excuse for his evil deeds but he him-
        self does not actually believe this. He only shows a better side to
15   his nature when he is dying, saying,
                'I pant for life, some good I mean to do'
        and he explains that he has ordered Cordelia to be hanged, making
        it look as though 'she fordid herself'.

Again, in the panels' view, the student is preoccupied with the
demands of conducting an argument — integrating quotations at
this stage into a developing pattern. There is a kind of rhetorical
competence, but the language of his commentary diminishes the
richness of the text, rather than sparks off a new creation of it.
There is little to suggest the recall of an imaginative encounter,
no time to be worried for instance by Edmund's strange final
statement.

And yet . . . *King Lear* is surely a play in which routine notions
of 'evil' might be broken down, through the reader's involvement
as a person. As teachers we must ask, then, what features in the
context for this piece of writing — and for many others like it
currently passing as creditable work — may have prevented the
student from getting as far as square one in such an enterprise.

Constraints on the student writer

Most of us are familiar I expect with the constraints still regarded
as 'normal' in the examining of Literature courses in England.
There the student is still expected to produce an essay answer to
an unseen question in 45–60 minutes and without having the text
available. This seems such a travesty of the appropriate conditions for *anyone* to try to express what they have gained from the
kind of reading described earlier — let alone a beginner in the art
— that I must reject it for the moment as indefensible.

However, in looking closely at writing during the course, well
before those exams loom up, one realizes that there are more
fundamental problems. It is true that writing is then being done
with the imaginative experience fresh in mind, with the text avail-

able, on topics negotiated with the teacher or suggested by the student, and without time pressure. Nevertheless, even given these enabling conditions for the writer, the teacher's model of writing may be inadequate in two vital respects.

The first of these concerns social relations. There is evidence that, in writing, we dimly or sharply feel a relationship between ourselves and imaginary 'other(s)', a relationship which allows or constrains our potential sense of self, on the one side, and our sense of what might be invited, expected or demanded, on the other. When a student writes for teacher and others I assume that he or she projects a social relationship on the basis of past encounters. Writing is seen, then, as part of a broader process of interaction. What I want to know, therefore, is who the actual readers turn out to be and what kinds of roles they are expected to play (interested collaborators? consultants? oracles? judges?).

This relates directly to a second factor, the stage of formulation the student has reached, and the choice of an appropriate form for the further articulation of thoughts and feelings. Hughlings Jackson offered the valuable polarity between 'new-now-organizing' speech and 'old organized': this has obvious relevance to student writers. To some degree each move from the inarticulate to the fuller and more interwoven articulation of understanding and enjoyment stands in need of provisional 'now-organizing' forms whose shape is amenable to emerging pressures during the act of writing, rather than the 'organized' forms one might reasonably expect the present paper to have reached, for instance!

And this question of appropriate form raises a further and — I guess — more controversial matter. What poetry has to offer may be sensuous and passionate; the effect of drama on our feelings and person may be like a purging ... you all know the traditional descriptions of the power of imaginative literature. In that case, within the range of appropriate forms there must be some, I assume, that are able to convey the power of what went on as we read or watched. (I am disagreeing, I'm afraid, with my mentor who earlier thought criticism was limited to the medium of 'conceptual prose', a fairly vague expression come to think of it.) So as a teacher I am now looking to see what sense of freedom or constraint the proposed form offers, both for articulation in general, and for the expression of that complex unity of thought and feeling which our encounter with an imaginative vision of life often invites.

Roads to a solution?

To the best of my knowledge, in England we are just at the beginning of this road, and there may be more than one of course. Some schools I know are experimenting with more fragmented forms (annotations, jottings, journals . . .) suited to early impressions. Others are trying to broaden the expressive range of the language of criticism, and to allow for complementary forms. In one or two schools the two strands seem to be interwoven. Both of them propose new roles for the teacher, as reader of students' writing.

We have room for just a few fragments. They come from a 16+ student of Richard Gill,[3] one of a group of Leicestershire teachers who invited our project to work with them on this problem. The class had been reading and discussing some of *The Songs of Innocence and Experience* and Richard suggested they should make notes on some of the poems they felt interested in. The following paragraphs are extracted (separately) from a point roughly halfway through one student's notes on *The Poison Tree*:

> There is nothing profound about the first two lines — but there is something lively and strangely attractive about the rest of the poem — it is very insidious. The foe is avaricious, comes into the garden at night with the intention of taking what is not his — the apple. The motive for the deed is that the apple is bright. In fact there is an ironic contrast between the apple being so bright, a product of something as murky and underhand as stored anger.
>
> As the poem progresses, we notice a separation between the man and his anger which becomes a tangible object — a tree which bears fruit. This perhaps explains the apparent aloofness the person feels when recounting that 'I see my foe out-stretched beneath the tree' when he awakes in the morning. It is a terribly chilling tone as though the death is nothing to do with him.

Members of our panels noted the ambivalent feelings (here and later), an interesting state in relation to the poem. The writer was reformulating *and* responding, his mind thinking its way along, with shifts over time — for example, from 'insidious' to 'terribly chilling'. But the second response wasn't necessarily better. And some thoughts seemed to be shoved aside.

The second extract is the end of the notes:

> There is a sense of discovery about the poem. It is not just the killing but it is the state of mind he is left with at the close; his whole life has been taken up with this. Thus he is relieved when he can *see* the result of his 'labours' — the use of 'glad' (1.15) shows this — 'In the morning glad I see'. There is something wholesome and innocent about the

word 'glad' even though it is strange that he should feel glad — but then he has done something — it is his work which he has slaved at with his 'tears', his 'smiles' and his 'soft deceitful wiles'.

The relief is shown in the last two lines which are much more re-posed and calm. There is an uneasy confidence about these lines, the way they are spoken — one gets the feeling that he might even let it happen again.

To go back a line, if I may:

'When the night had veil'd the pole', the 'pole' being either the pole star or the tree trunk, there is a feeling that the night becomes an active agent in the dead. After 'pole' there is an assured break before the frighteningly revealing final two lines.

He puzzles away about the last two lines, the panels comment. Thus he is not at ease with his own interpretation of 'glad'. It is a struggle with complexity of feeling, and gets better as he goes on brooding over them. He is writing and discovering what he does feel.

I would add that he is facing, here and elsewhere in the notes, his own feelings about evil (as you might call it!), and what strikes me repeatedly is his daring openness to that experience. Something lively and strangely attractive... very insidious... terribly chilling... frighteningly revealing, finally. These explicit personal responses — judgements from a personal centre — suggest to me the central value of joining Blake in contemplating the experience of *The Poison Tree*.

This is one road, then. The understanding that these were 'notes' has left the student free to follow pressures in his own active, developing response. Equally, I think we could assemble evidence from these extracts to characterize the social relation he projects with the reader, the kinds of freedom offered him, on the one hand, by this dialogue with his teacher, and on the other, the expectations it sets up in him.

Both for this student and for others much less drawn than he is to intellectual explicitness, there are still many expressive possibilities to explore in notes and other provisional forms (such as free verse). I can only hint at these for the moment.

Further work: My main thesis is that we teachers have thought too little about the effects of constraining conditions on the student writer. Our university education — in the U.K. at least — has left us with naive models of writing. In the classroom this leads inevitably, I believe, to an impoverishment of what the student has to offer. At its best, however, the tradition of close reading equips us to perceive in fine detail the positive and negative effects of changes in those conditions. I hope that the 1979 CCTE conference and its outcomes will, among other things, stimulate an international exchange among teachers concerned to preserve and extend the vitality of written response to literature.

Notes

1. The quotations come from Barbara Hardy, W.W. Robson, L.C. Knights, F.R. Leavis and Ian Gregor.
2. The two essay extracts come from Stevens, F. *English and Examinations*, Hutchinson, 1970.
3. The two extracts are from Gill, R. 'Initial Work at A Level' in *Students Articulating their Response to Literature*, Schools Council English 16–19 Project, Bretton Hall College, Wakefield (1979).

15 Instructional focus and the teaching of writing

James R. Squire

The range of topics considered and the variety of contributions made at the International Conference on Learning to Write were not only a tribute to the vision and ingenuity of leaders in the Canadian Council of Teachers of English but a recognition that two decades of research in writing and composition is now reaching fruition in the teaching and learning in schools:

- research in language acquisition and language development;
- studies of the processes of composing;
- discourse analysis and research into prose learning;
- studies of the impact of learning outcomes on the quality of instruction;
- new rhetorical analyses of English prose;
- applications of research in instructional effectiveness and instructional design;
- competency testing and competency-based education.

All of these developments — whether publicly funded or privately sponsored — combine to bring more excitement to the teaching of writing and comprehension than we have seen in almost two decades. Indeed not since the academic reform movement which followed the launching of Sputnik in 1958 has the teaching of writing received such widespread attention and even then the emphasis was largely placed on the secondary school years. With today's new insights into early learning and the foundational experience of the elementary school years, a cohesive developmental and consequential programme in composing now seems capable of attainment. Recognizing that others at the conference would focus on rhetorical and linguistic dimensions involved in learning to write, I plan to concentrate on five principles of basic instruction which, if applied consistently and with good common sense, can make the learning of language more efficient, the teaching of language more effective, and the experience of schooling more focussed and more enjoyable. Not all of these principles are new but all are far from being applied in the more than forty American school districts in which I have studied the teaching of writing during the past two years.

1 Productive language and receptive language have unique requirements which must be accommodated through planned curricular experience

To achieve proficiency in writing and speaking — the productive language skills, or in reading and listening — the receptive language skills, a child requires carefully-planned instruction and instructional experience. Clearly delineated learning outcomes must be achieved in each language skill area, outcomes so specific that they sometimes require a careful structuring of classroom language activities. For this reason, teachers must be wary of so interrelating all language activities that the requirements of specific skills do not receive attention. Certainly the teaching of reading cannot drive the primary language arts curriculum if children are to progress in writing and speaking. Nor can writing or literature serve as the only focus of activity in upper grade or secondary school classrooms. Witness, for example, the lack of attention to reading, speaking, and to varieties of written experience in traditional high school classrooms where only *belle lettres* and a single genre of expository writing receive attention.

Balanced attention to all language arts is especially critical during the primary years. Significant differences in conciseness, abstractness, and the skills of visual communication differentiate oral language from the language used in print.

Important, too, is providing writing experience as early in schooling as possible — a provision sometimes forgotten when writing is so 'interrelated' with reading that it is neglected as a basic instructional thrust. Graves has demonstrated that the average first grader is capable of two to three pieces of independent writing per week (Graves 1973). Carol Chomsky and her students, working in experimental classrooms, report arresting results when they encourage a kind of 'rebus writing' by kindergarten children even before they begin formal reading instruction.[1] The important understanding is recognizing that the urge to write and communicate is a more natural inclination than the urge to read and that it needs to be nourished and cultivated from the time children are in school.

Some kinds of integrated language arts activities especially need to be avoided. Spelling, for example, is a writing and manuscript skill, not a reading skill. Any major attempt to relate spelling and reading beyond using encoding as a check on decoding will ultimately impair the early development of skill in reading since by the end of grade 1 and thereafter, a child's reading vocabulary far outstrips his spelling vocabulary. Each of us can read many more words than we can spell. (Try, for example, writing from dictation the familiar sentence 'The city of Pittsburgh is located at the confluence of the Allegheny and Monogahela Rivers'.) Spelling and writing, these need to be related, not spelling and reading.

Yet there are specific kinds of interrelationships that need to be planned more carefully. Writing activities which encourage children to reconstruct the ideas and vocabulary presented through reading clearly advance comprehension (Wittrock *et al.* 1975). So does directed listening practice in listening comprehension provide close support for skill development in reading comprehension. Beyond such specific relationships, much of value can also result by organizing instruction in topical or thematic units so that children repeatedly use a similar core of concepts and vocabulary terms in reading, writing, and speaking over a period of several weeks. In so approaching instructional planning, the basic thematic ideas serve in effect as advance organizers for the instructional activity that is to follow.

The essential point then is clear. Integrate the language arts when integration supports desirable growth. But recognize, also, the need for planning independent and discrete learning experiences in each skill area to help children achieve particular learning outcomes.

2 Providing learning time on appropriate tasks is critical to improving pupil performance in writing

During the past ten years, American schools have improved the tested competence of primary-level children in beginning reading by doubling the amount of instructional time devoted to teaching reading. The average primary classroom now spends close to 120 minutes per day on reading compared with 55 to 60 minutes at the intermediate level.[2] And whatever was right in how we were spending our classroom time a decade ago, we can assume that we have doubled what is right in our efforts today.

Clearly, time on task has been rediscovered as a critical variable in influencing the quality of children's learning. Yet along with the discovery comes recognition of the enormous variation in the amount of time children are permitted to devote to critical academic tasks. The Beginning Teacher Study in California, for example, found the variation in practice in computation ranging from 12 minutes to 220 minutes per week for fifth-grade children in the same school.[3]

Time on the writing task is important if children are to learn to write. Think of the accumulated experience of the child who begins writing two or three times per week in the first grade, as Graves recommends, and continues for twelve years — 100 pieces of writing per year, perhaps 1200 or more through total schooling. Contrast this with the cumulative experience of a child who is encouraged to write only four or five times a year and the need for engaging children in writing is manifest.

But gross writing activity alone is not sufficient to guarantee reasonable growth. Some class time must be spent on direct instruction in how to write, some on practising writing, some on evaluating, and some on learning the supportive skills associated with excellence in writing. Not only is the overall time provided for writing limited, but care must be taken to provide balanced attention to all dimensions of the composing process. Durkin, after all, recently demonstrated that less than one per cent of the time spent on reading in intermediate classrooms is devoted to teaching comprehension (Durkin 1978–9)! Can we be sure our approaches to teaching writing are more balanced?

There is no problem, for example, in improving the competence of children on the discrete language skills often assessed by competency tests. Such separate skills are inevitably identified. By focussing instruction and practice on the particular skills for six or eight weeks prior to testing, teachers can improve tested performance by 15 to 20 per cent. Even more important is that by limiting the concentration of these tested skills to a six or eight week period, teachers have the opportunity both to assure mastery and to free the remainder of the school year for more basic instruction and practice in composing.

The real problem then is to find ways of increasing the amount of writing and composing that can occur within the experience of schooling. For almost two decades we have seen school purchases of lined handwriting paper or booklets decline in inverse proportion to the increase in use of plain copying paper, those sheets needed for short answer exercises and for multiple choice drills. Most publishers know that teachers resist questions in textbooks and workbooks which require written answers. Indeed Jeanne Chall found little actual writing required in either elementary school or secondary school textbooks in reading, literature, history, or even books on grammar and composition (Chall 1977).

One barrier to increasing substantially the time spent by children in writing is the conscientiousness of teachers who feel they must personally read and annotate each paper written by each student. Techniques must be developed to save teacher time in responding to papers, whether through use of group conferences, peer assessment, primary trait scoring, parent involvement, or other methods (Klaus *et al.* 1979). What is important is that teachers come to recognize that if they limit children's writing to only those papers that the teacher can fully annotate, they will limit the child's writing experience and thus limit each child's capacity for growth.

3 Schooling must offer children planned experience with a variety of functions and uses of language and provide time on task with each

Much of the research in language development during the past decade has focussed on the need to expand the traditionally restrictive schoolroom language activities to embrace other modes and functions of language. Too often our elementary curriculum has focussed only on a particular kind of 'creative' writing: our secondary schools, one variety of expository. Beginning especially with the studies of Michael Halliday and the attempts of the British Schools Council to develop school programmes which provide for direct experience in a wide variety of uses (Doughty *et al.* 1971), specialists have been concerned about achieving variety in writing, reading, and speaking activities. How can high school students, for example, be expected to develop skill and competence in writing the expository essay if they seldom have the opportunity to read and analyse any but literary works? How can a seventh grader be expected to write a research report if he has never read one? Can a fifth-grade child write an interview, a business letter, or a diary if he is not sufficiently familiar with the particular genre to understand the particular ways in which it requires language to be used. And if the teacher cannot find business letters, research reports, or interviews appropriate for student reading at any developmental level, one wonders whether the writing task can be an appropriate one.

The ways of classifying the uses of language into a variety of modes or functions vary. Traditional rhetorical concerns with exposition, narration, description and the like have yielded to more complex analyses such as those advanced by Britton *et al.* (1975) (expressive, poetic, transactional), by Courtney Cazden *et al.* (1972), or Frank Smith (1977). Less important than any particular schema seems to be the attempt to identify varieties of language experience and to insure that children have instructional and practice time on each.

Of all of the classifications of language activity, one that strikes me as particularly appropriate in designing school curricula is the division into basic operational categories — ways of thinking, feeling, and valuing — that emerged from a study group at the York International Conference. Eight modes of thinking and feeling through language form the basis of this approach — communicating, analysing, reporting, persuading, imagining, inventing, interpreting, and reflecting. By considering the need to provide planned experiences in each of these linguistic areas, the teacher has a framework for planning a balanced classroom approach.

But providing a rich variety of experiences in using language must extend to all subject matter areas. One of our current problems is that so little writing occurs in the content areas that children only infrequently find opportunity to learn the vocabulary of the subject disciplines and the unique ways in which language is utilized in each. One modest study of the amount of writing in Science, Social Studies, and Mathematics beyond the fifth grade suggest that more than 40 per cent of all science classes may provide writing experiences contrasted with around 22 per cent of Social Studies and substantially less than 5 per cent in Maths.[4] Small wonder that with so little opportunity to use the vocabulary of these disciplines, many children experience difficulty with the reading of high school titles.

4 Basic processes in writing and reading must be distinguished from 'basic skills'

In many ways our school programmes in language development

have confused the acquisition of discrete skills, basic to reading and writing, with the fundamental processes of communication.

Most specific skills — decoding skills; applications of grammatical understandings; principles of punctuation, capitalization, and manuscript form; the forms of English usage — can be taught through modes of mastery learning with children provided with appropriate instruction and intensive practice sufficient to ensure the achievement of mastery (Bloom 1976). Indeed for most children the mastery mode of teaching is extremely effective for acquisition of specific skills, provided that priorities are sufficiently well established to permit focus on a limited number of skill objectives and that a long range programme of skill maintenances is developed.

But most basic processes cannot be taught through mastery learning which focusses on initial instruction, concentrated practice, and criterion-level achievement. One simply does not learn to write an effective paragraph as the result of six weeks of practice and then maintain the skill thereafter. Rather, competence in writing paragraphs grows slowly over a period of years, as does skill in inferential comprehension and in applying most of the higher thought processes to reading and writing. For these processes, a growth model of learning, rather than a mastery model seems to be required.

But teachers of English must deal with both basic skills and basic processes, and recognize crucial differences in the ways in which they are taught and learned. Those supportive skills which can be easily taught at each grade level need to be clearly identified, priorities carefully assigned, and programmes instituted to ensure maintenance of proficiency once the skill is acquired. Given the fact that at least five days of class time will be required for every skill to be emphasized (one for instruction, three for practice, one for assessment and needed additional help), not more than 30 to 35 skills should be designated for attention during any one school year. This is a small number, to be sure, given the total number often introduced, but if 30 are mastered each year and then maintained, school programmes would be far more efficient than today's programmes which 'expose' children to a hundred or more different skills and never really teach any.

By distinguishing basic skills from basic processes and developing classroom approaches appropriate to both, teachers today can develop far more effective developmental programmes than in the past.

5 Analysis of the processes of composing helps to identify the most teachable moments for providing instruction in basic skills

Recent studies of the composing process help to clarify the time when instruction can be most effectively planned. Although the ways of analysing the processes of composing are legion, viewing the process in three phases tends to be particularly helpful: *The prewriting phase* — what occurs before writing occurs; *The composing phase* — that which occurs during the actual process of writing; and *The post-writing* or *editing phase* — that which occurs after writing has taken place (Cooper and Odell 1977).

The prewriting phase is the period of planning, the period of invention, the period when children acquire and organize ideas. It is during this phase of writing that the teacher is most effective in helping children acquire ideas, in stimulating them to ask appropriate questions about their own experience (who? when? why? and the other *wh* questions).

This is the time, too, for providing needed instruction with aids to organizing — the topic sentence, various methods of organizing outlining. Such aids for planning are most effectively taught prior to writing so that the child can actually apply them as he plans. But taught, too, in a sense as crutches or aids to organizing since not every paragraph requires them nor does every writer use them. Look, for example, at the limited use of topic sentences in the professional work of Jessamyn West or James Reston. Consider the small number of writers who actually outline their ideas in advance (Emig 1971). Such limitations should remind all of us of the need to exercise restraint in introducing such concepts to children.

The composing phase, the period when children actually create a piece of writing, should to the greatest extent possible occur during the classroom period when the teacher can identify boys and girls with problems and provide assistance at the time when they will most need it. A teacher who assesses the writing of his pupils only through final papers is working with product, not process, and to a considerable degree, it is the process that must be improved. Graves reports that even as early as grade 1, the effective writer can be distinguished from the ineffective by his ability to predict what he will write from four to ten sentences ahead (Graves 1973, 1975). By identifying those children who cannot predict, those who are having difficulty, the teacher can provide additional help at the time when it can be most effectively used.

The post-writing or *editing phase* of the composing process is the period for sharing, for assessing, for editing and revising. All pupils need 'feedback' on their papers whether from parents, teachers, or fellow students.

The editing phase provides the moment when instruction in functional grammar, in manuscript form, in the mechanics and usage of English are most effectively integrated into classroom activity. Who can after all unlock an ineffective sentence unless he can identify the predicate and then the subject? Instruction in the grammar and mechanics of English, albeit unimportant in helping children compose, is essential to helping them revise. But to do so it must be taught as a part of the revision process, not independently or as part of actual writing.

The National Assessment of Educational Progress has effectively demonstrated the lack of proficiency of school students in editing (National Assessment 1977). Indeed until recently little help on editing has been available to students or teachers beyond lists of proofreading symbols. Such an approach deals with superficial form, not the essence of the problem. Through a developmental programme which introduces children to basic structures in their language and relates these understandings to actual uses, much progress can be made in strengthening proficiencies in editing.

The five principles that I have discussed can give the teaching of composition a more effective instructional focus and result in improved schooling:

- recognizing the unique requirements of learning to write and relating curriculum and instruction to reading and literature only when results can be clearly mutually supportive;
- strengthening the amount of time spent on the writing task;
- organizing curricular experiences to provide planned attention to a variety of uses of language;
- developing learning models for basic processes diverse from those used to teach basic skills;
- finding the most teachable moments within the overall composing process for introducing instruction effectively.

These five principles, applied in appropriate ways, can revolutionize the teaching of writing in our various countries. They offer a perspective that focusses on the learning outcome of our pupils without neglecting the requirements of the teacher.

Notes

1. Reported at a conference on beginning reading at Learning Research and Development Center, University of Pittsburgh, 1976. A report on this conference edited by Lauren Resnick and Phyllis Weaver is in preparation.
2. Annual Reports on Language Arts, Institutional Tracking Service, White Plains, New York, June 1979 and earlier.
3. *Beginning Teacher Preparation Study*, Report VII-1; Technical Report Series, Far West Regional Laboratory, 1979.
4. Reported by Donald Graves. See the discussion in his monograph *Balance The Basics; Let Them Write*. N.Y.: The Ford Foundation, 1977.

16 From classroom practice into psycholinguistic theory

W. Ross Winterowd

In 1975, one of my students (now Dr Dorothy Augustine of the University of Houston) and I set out to design a composition programme for the Huntington Beach (California) Union High School District. This programme, now in its fourth year, has been successful as judged by most criteria: District evaluations have indicated that we are getting more than satisfactory results, teachers have become increasingly enthusiastic, and from 1975 to 1978, the District leaped from the 73rd to the 86th percentile on the verbal portion of the California Assessment.[1]

Going into the project, Dr Augustine and I had some fairly clearcut notions or theories, in mind.

1 In-service preparation: understanding

Teachers need a conceptual-theoretical background in which to work, or else all of their pedagogy is *ad hoc*. Further, this background must be shared knowledge, i.e. teachers in a school or a district need to know the rationale behind the 'official' policy, but the policy itself is not a set of laws, merely a conceptual framework that gives coherence to what goes on within and among individual classrooms. It is important to stress that I am *not* talking about a syllabus mandated by the District. Furthermore, this framework should square with what we know about how language actually works, i.e. should take account of linguistic, psycholinguistic, learning, and rhetorical theory.

An example: we felt that work in syntactic fluency would be a crucial part of the programme, as indeed it has demonstrated itself to be, but we chose not to mandate that teachers should devote X amount of time to fluency exercises with Y students.

Rather, we hoped that teachers would grasp the linguistic and psycholinguistic underpinnings of sentence combining and use it when appropriate. (More about appropriateness and syntactic fluency later.)

In setting forth concept and theory, we were not demanding or even asking that teachers abandon their own practices — only that they understand the what and the why of the programme that we were setting forth.

Therefore, it was essential that we organize and conduct extensive in-service preparation, for, as I have argued elsewhere, very few composition teachers have any preservice preparation, though the situation is gradually changing.

2 In-service preparation: knowhow

Composition teachers need techniques for intervening in the *process* of writing, and many 'old hands' have an array of effective methodology, but many teachers, old and new, concentrate on the written product, 'correcting' and grading without paying attention to how the present text can be reformulated or how the next one might be more successfully written. We adopted the following maxim: when you levy a criticism against a student paper, you must always add, 'And I'll show you at least one way to do it better'.

Again, an example: it is futile to admonish students to reformulate (revise) and leave them to it. We demonstrate to them in general and specifically that reformulation involves the *addition*, the *deletion*, the *rearrangement*, and the *substitution* of words, phases, sentences, paragraphs. . . .

We have made an arbitrary division of the composing process into *prewriting, writing, rewriting*, and *editing*, and teachers need the knowhow to intervene in every stage of the process. (We realize that our segmenting of the composing process is artificial, but it is strategic.)

3 Scenes: workshop and laboratory

Following a hint by Mellon (1969), we felt that the kinds of learning necessary for successful writing could be roughly divided into two categories, the rhetorical and the arhetorical. Rhetorical skills would be learned in the workshop and arhetorical in the laboratory. (In fact, the theories of both Kenneth Burke and Roman Jakobson were very much in our minds.)

In 'Developing a Composition Programme' (in Freedman and Pringle 1980a), I give the following characterization of the workshop and the lab:

> To characterize the workshop and how it interacts with the lab could best be accomplished with a video tape that would demonstrate, not tell about. However, a picture of the workshop can be presented.
>
> Here is a montage of the kinds of things that go on there:
> 1. Discussion of and practice with prewriting techniques by the whole class.
> 2. Small group activities of two or three students, e.g. two students reacting to and making suggestions regarding a paper (perhaps a rough draft) produced by a third student.
> 3. Composing-on-the-board, with volunteers making attempts to solve a given writing problem, e.g. getting a paper by one member of the class under way effectively.
> 4. Whole class discussions of one, two, or three dittoed papers produced by class members.
> 5. Conferencing, the teacher circulating about the class to help individual students with writing problems while the other members of the class work on their papers.
> 6. Some editing lessons for the whole class, dealing with a limited problem that all have in common.
> 7. Reformulation exercises, in which all of the class members make suggestions for improving one of their fellows' papers.
> 8. Class discussion of audience, the adjustment of a given paper for a certain audience.
> 9. Free-writing.
> 10. Journal writing.
> 11. Language games, such as the round-robin sentence, in which students successively add modifiers to a base. . . .
> 12. Publishing activities. . . .
> 13. Class development of writing assignments. . . .
>
> The workshop is a messy place, highly charged, purposive in terms of writing something for someone for some reason.
>
> (pp. 168–9)

> The laboratory should be the best scene for producing optimum users [of editing skills], and, in fact, that has been our experience. . . . The laboratory, as we stress again and again, is not a place, but a concept. It is a given kind of instruction for certain goals.
>
> (p. 167)

The laboratory, then, teaches primarily the skills of editing: punctuation, verb agreement, pronoun reference, and so on'.

Our conception of the programme — which I have outlined in

its barest bones — was soon given a sharper definition by the work of my colleague Stephen Krashen. In August of 1976, Professor Krashen issued his important paper 'Second Language Acquisition' (Krashen 1977), the explanation of his 'monitor theory' of language learning. Subsequently, he published 'On the Acquisition of Planned Discourse: Written English as Second Dialect.' (Krashen 1978). In the following pages, I would like to outline Krashen's monitor model, to show how it influenced our practice, and to demonstrate how our practice leads to an enriched version of the monitor model — from practice into theory. I quote from 'Developing a Composition Program':

> The term 'learning' is inadequate when one dicusses the acquisition of a second language (and we view learning to compose as, in many ways, like learning a second language), for in that acquisition, two quite different processes go on (in the case of most learners, at least). On the one hand, the learner listens and reads and begins to talk and write; *input* provides the basis for *output*. Whether in a classroom or on the street of a foreign city, this kind of learning is necessarily rhetorically charged and value-laden. Often there is an audience and a controlling scene to which the learner must try to adjust his or her purpose. In other words, we have all the elements of natural language learning. . . .
>
> But, of course, we can also turn to paradigms and rule systems which we consciously master. Thus, we memorize the system of German definite articles and, at times, consciously use that knowledge to produce the correct forms in written or spoken German.
>
> In second-language learning, then, there are two related processes: the 'naturalistic' one which often takes place in (results from) a rhetorical situation; and the 'artificial' one which results from the desire to learn certain skills of language. The first sort of learning is called by Krashen *acquisition*, and the second he terms *learning*. . . . The result of learning is the construction of a *monitor* which allows the user consciously to regularize or correct output. Thus:

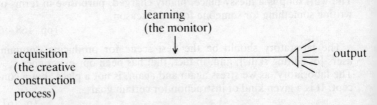

> In a sense, the monitor is a low-level device; one cannot consciously learn extremely complex rules of language, but internalizes them through acquisition. (Indeed, not all the 'rules' of language can be stated, for example, those concerning audience and scene.) One can, however, learn such rules and paradigms as those which make up the

system of articles in German or which constitute standard punctuation in English. . . .

Now we can redefine workshop as a place where compositional skills (prewriting, writing, rewriting) are acquired and the laboratory as a place where editing skills are learned [if they have not already been acquired]

(pp. 166–7)

When we learned of monitor theory, we were able to schematize simply and usefully thus:

PROCESS	*Prewriting*	*Writing*	*Rewriting*	*Editing*
'LEARNING' SCENES		Acquisition Workshop		Learning Laboratory

We often say, not totally in jest, that the line between acquisition workshop and learning laboratory is the most important line in the profession.

In spite of this neat formulation, however, important questions have arisen. (Or because of this neat formulation!) (1) What can be learned? (2) What *must* be acquired?

Krashen and I are at odds in regard to learning, but the evidence, I think, is on my side. I believe that editing skills — the skills necessary to make the surface of a text conform to the features of what we call Edited Standard English — are learnable, and I base this conclusion on extensive reports by teachers, on the results of the California Assessment, on the basis of gains on the District's own *Test of English Writing Skills* (which is almost exclusively editing), and on our observation of the pre- and post-tests of writing which we administer each year.[2] Admittedly I am on shaky ground here, for no compelling evidence indicates that students have not *acquired* these skills in the general process of their educational maturation, but we can demonstrate that virtually all students show gains in the pre- and post-tests of laboratory skills. What we cannot demonstrate — and this is the rub — is that the laboratory learning has carry-over into the writing situation, though we feel strongly that it does.

Of more theoretical interest than editing is the learning of global skills such as paragraph development. If students can *learn* such skills, then it must be the case that the elements of these skills are precisely specifiable. That is, we must be able to present algorithms — and I use that term somewhat loosely — the application of which will result in the desired written product. The infamous five-paragraph essay is just such an algorithm, as is the tagmemic concept of the paragraph (Becker 1966), which we are using with remedial students. In its barest form, this algorithm asks students to supply a 'topic' sentence and to illustrate it two or more times, thus:

Topic	Living near the beach has many advantages.
Illustration	You can go surfing every weekend.
Illustration	The air is not smoggy on the coast.
Illustration	Beach cities are cooler than downtown.

The enriched monitor theory, then, would include not only the learning of specific rules ('capitalize the first letter in a sentence'), but also of paradigms (such as a chart of the forms of the present tense of *be*), and of algorithms that apply to paragraphs and whole essays.

The greatest potential for development of the monitor theory lies in the concept of acquisition. In our continual fascinating and friendly go-arounds, Krashen and I meet head-on at one point. He implies in his published work and states flatly in his conversations that acquisition of the ability to write is through 'input', i.e. reading. I believe that position to be untenable. Sticking to the communication jargon, I believe that *feedback* is as essential as input.

'In 'On the Acquisition of Planned Discourse', Krashen states:

It is useful to posit that the well-educated adult native speaker of English has several 'dialects' available to him: an *unplanned* style, which is used primarily in spontaneous conversation, a *planned* dialect (Pl_1), used for certain kinds of writing (such as narratives and descriptions), and a third code, *well-planned* discourse (Pl_2), used for written essays of the expository kind. . . .'

The freshman English situation is exactly what the [monitor] model predicts. There seem to be at least two kinds of students in freshman English. There is the mature writer at one extreme, the student who has done some reading and has at least acquired Pl_1. Instructions from the teacher on how to write, rules on the use of topic sentences, transitions, etc. are in a sense old information for such students, as they have already acquired them subconsciously. This student, at best, may gain learning where acquisition was already present, a kind of composition appreciation. More commonly, he will wonder why the teacher is explaining the obvious. At the other extreme is what Shaughnessy . . . calls the 'severely unprepared freshman', the student who has not acquired Pl_1. . . . For these cases, such instructions are new information, and rules are to be taken as definite orders as to how to perform. When such students do carry out these instructions, the result is often a wooden, awkward paper, a product of the fact that instructions given in the writing class represent only a small portion of the rules for planned discourse. Discovering and teaching all the rules for Pl_1 and Pl_2 in the classroom are not the answer. The work of Keenan, Loban, Crystal and Davy, and others shows that many of these rules (lexical, structural, pragmatic, semantic, etc.) are extremely complex; their conscious control is beyond the capacity of even our best students.

Krashen does not characteristically become muddled; in fact, he is one of the clearest thinkers I know. But in this instance, he has tripped himself up and in so doing has partially eviscerated his own monitor theory. To explain what I am getting at, I would like to outline some work that is now being undertaken by myself, Krashen and our colleague Betty Bamberg. We might term this 'The Bamberg-Krashen-Winterowd Theory of Freshman Populations'.

The data is not yet in, but we posit that at the University of Southern California, as at other colleges and universities, freshman composition students will fall into three groups upon entry: (1) those who test out of the course, or would be able to test out if given the opportunity; (2) those who can produce Pl_1 and halting versions of Pl_2; (3) 'basic writers', 'target students', 'remedial students', or whatever term seems least scarifying. The second group can be subdivided into two populations: those who have done extensive pleasure reading during the ages ten to fifteen and those who have not. (Members of group (1) will invariably have been readers, and members of group (3) almost invariably will not have been.) For economy, we will refer to the subcategories of group (2) as R (readers) and NR (non-readers), but it is important to realize that the NR students can read well enough to matriculate and are not 'hardcore' cases. The NR students are not typically admitted to the university under special dispensations, as are members of the third category, nor is their lack of experience in reading apparent to their instructors in most of their courses.

We predict that the R students will very quickly — perhaps in as little as one semester — begin to produce Pl_2, and we also predict that follow-up studies will reveal that they did not have extensive writing instruction in high school, if any at all.[3] What they brought with them to the university was 'input', what they had never attempted was 'output', and what they had never received was 'feedback'. To be sure, the R students do not need to 'learn' rules, for they have acquired these through their reading. What they need to do, however, is to activate this acquired knowledge in a rhetorical situation, in a workshop.

With a certain amount of impish glee, then, I take Krashen to task for his failure to differentiate between the kind of acquisition provided by a writing workshop and the kind of learning that some writing classes try to set forth. In fact, the NR students need more learning than do the R students, but as Krashen points out, most of what must be 'learned' about composition is far too complex to be stated specifically as a set of rules.

One might say that the R students are primed for the acquisition of rhetorical skills while the NR are not. What, then, are these rhetorical skills that must be acquired — not necessarily in a writing workshop, but through some kind of intense feedback? I would enrich monitor theory by bringing rhetorical theory to bear upon it.

The modification of Krashen's work through rhetorical theory is, I think, necessary, but it would be the subject of a much longer paper than this one, which is already extending itself pages beyond what I had originally envisioned. One microcosmic example (drawn from work that I am doing with Dr Dorothy Augustine) must suffice.

From the standpoint of my enriched monitor theory, we would say that a student who has not *acquired* the ability to produce a sentence like the following may *learn* to do so, perhaps through exercises in syntactic fluency or pattern practice.

(1)   I claim that the fuel shortage is a capitalist conspiracy.

From the standpoint of rhetoric, however, we might say that the sentence (in context) might involve problems of *ethos, pathos*, and *logos*. If Hearer (H) does not accept the authority of Speaker (S), an argument *ad hominem* may ensue:

(2)   H: You've always been a lousy communist.
       s: I have not! I'm just a socialist.

The problem here regards *ethos*, the character of the speaker. If it turns out that S misjudges the nature of H, nothing will result from the opening statement:

(3)   H: So what are you telling me for? I've been making that same claim to you for six months.
       s: Yeh, I guess I wasn't thinking.

The opening statement has misfired on the basis of *pathos*. The argument *ad rem* — the only real argument — comes about when there is the *possibility* of negating a proposition (*pace* Kenneth Burke), that is, when the focus is on *logos*. Thus,

(4)   s: I claim that the fuel shortage is a capitalist conspiracy.
      h: It is not a capitalist conspiracy, for Atlantic-Richfield is spend-
           ing millions of dollars to promote fuel economy.

And the dialectic has begun.

The rhetorical force of the performative verb is also worth considering, for rhetorical force — as opposed to intention — seems to constitute what Kenneth Burke calls 'attitude'[4] and certainly contributes to the hearer's sense of rhetorical stance and tone. A 'claim' is stronger than a 'statement' and not so strong as an 'avowal'.

Though *ethos, pathos*, and *logos* (with all that they imply, which is a very great deal) are 'messy' concepts, not amenable to tidy formulation, they are nonetheless real. The skills that could be characterized as 'ethical', 'pathetic', and 'logical' can only be *acquired* — which means attempt and response, in other words, a writing workshop or its equivalent.

Finally, a concern which for some time I called Sentence Combining (SC); growing tired of that term (and of the whole subject, for that matter), I changed to Syntactic Fluency (SF). Being bored to death at this point, I have chosen the term Sentence Manipulation (SM). Though SC/SF/SM is not a conceptually rich aspect of our field, it is enormously important, and from our practice with it in Huntington Beach, we have developed one further modification of the monitor model.

In our original plans for the Huntington Beach composition programme, Dr Augustine and I firmly planted sentence combining in the laboratory. It was programmatic and arhetorical, we thought; it was a skill to be learned by those students with a deficit. Very soon, we discovered that in practice, our best teachers were bringing sentence combining into the workshops, in the form of language games, the writing of parodies, and so on. What we began to realize is that with some students (perhaps those whom we would characterize as readers), the fluency exercises very quickly activated a competence which must have been there all along, for the rapidity with which these youngsters increased their stylistic options and hence sophistication could not be attributed to the painfully slow processes that learning such complexities must entail.

On the other hand, we find that some students need extensive, carefully planned work in sentence combining in the laboratory. We propose that these students are learning — not via rules or any kind of descriptive statements, but by doing, though not in the 'natural', 'holistic', 'unconscious' way that characterizes Krashen's acquisition. There seems to be a middle ground between acquisition and learning and between workshop and laboratory, and sentence combining, we have discovered, is one bridge.

A revised monitor theory — the result of experience and rhetorical theory — might, in brief, look like this:

Acquisition: the 'learning' of the skills of *ethos, pathos*, and *logos* through input and feedback.

Learning: the 'learning' of arhetorical skills through rules, algorithms, paradigms, and programmed exercises.

Put more simply, acquisition takes place rhetorically, and learning takes place arhetorically. That, I think, is a significant contribution to the work that Krashen began so ably and that has been so valuable to me and my colleagues.

Notes

1. The programme was not designed specifically to raise scores on grammar-usage tests; hence our gains on the California Assessment were a bonus of sorts — but very impressive to the District's administration and board. The following quotation from the *1978–79 Ninth-Grade Writing Programme* evaluation report shows something of the results of in-house monitoring:

   The data presented in this report show that, on the average, post-test writing scores were substantially higher than pre-test writing scores. The gains were much higher among the students showing low pre-test performance. This may, in part, be accounted for by normal regression effects. However, the 1978–79 gains for this group are considerably higher than those for 1976–77 comparable group, suggesting a greater programme impact. The same conclusion holds for the total ninth-grade population.

2. The writing tests are holistically scored essays, in general like those administered by the California State University and Colleges system. Scoring is guided by a rubric, and each paper is read at least twice.

3. Our predictions have been partially verified by a study that a graduate student, Ronald Kimberling, carried out.

4. In a discussion with graduate students at the University of Southern California, Burke says that attitude — with which he would now expand his Pentad into a hexad — encompasses illocutionary force.

17   Communicative writing practice and Aristotelian rhetoric

Keith Johnson

1 Introduction

The starting point for this paper is the concept of a communicative language teaching; one which, in the most general terms, aims to teach communicative competence in a second language along the lines described in Hymes (1970). It is not automatically assumed that such a language teaching need necessarily involve a semantic (notional/functional) syllabus, and when the question of syllabus design is touched on at the end of this paper, it is in the context of whether such a syllabus is the most appropriate vehicle of achieving communicative aims.

The tendency in European applied linguistics has been to consider communication from the point of view of *what* the student will want to communicate; indeed the term 'communicative language teaching' often refers simply to one which derives teaching content (specified in notional/functional terms) from a specification of student communicative needs. This paper is more concerned with *how* the student communicates; with, that is, the communicative skill. It will argue that communicative events, as responses to relatively 'unique' combinations of stimuli, are in themselves non-stereotyped (though of course derived from sets of rules which are discoverable). It will claim that notional/functional approaches which identify discrete semantic areas and simply present a set of exponents for each, are therefore severely inadequate as overall teaching strategies. It will attempt to outline an approach which takes into account the non-stereotyped nature of communicative events.[1]

The specific 'universe of discourse' for this paper is the teaching of academic writing, and what is said stems from experience in producing and piloting a set of academic writing materials.[2] Throughout, the term 'semantic syllabus' is used as an umbrella term for any syllabus specified in notional and/or functional categories; the word 'utterance' is used for any stretch of discourse, in written or spoken medium; 'context' is used to describe the complex set of linguistic and non-linguistic features within which an utterance takes place.

2 Communicative events

An area of study possessing a rich literature as yet comparatively untapped by the applied linguist is that of skills psychology. Welford (1958) describes the skilled performer (or 'receptor') as:

> . . . a kind of calculating machine capable of receiving several different inputs and producing an output which is derived from the various input parameters acting in concert. Such a system results in a response which is unique on each occasion, although it is determinate and based on constraints which are, at least in principle, discoverable.
>
> (pp. 32–33)

Applied to a skill like playing tennis the various input parameters leading to the response of playing a single stroke would include speed of the ball, position of the receiving player, position of his opponent, etc. Since the response would be to a unique combination of input parameters, it would itself be a 'unique' event.

Applied to a skill like language the input might be characterized in terms of the various parameters to which the utterance (as output) must conform. In Hymes's (1970) programmatic and thus inevitably general terms these parameters are four: the appropriate, the possible, the feasible, the performed. Subdividing his 'appropriate' into 'appropriateness to intent' and 'appropriateness to context' we arrive at the following diagram to exemplify the aspect of skilled behaviour Welford speaks of.[3]

In this diagram, the number of boxes appearing under 'intents' and 'context' is arbitrary, but more than one in each case to express the fact that an utterance will have more than one intent, and must conform to very many more than one parameter of context.

The diagram indicates a number of things. Among them:

1. that an utterance is a complex event which must conform along many parameters at the same time. It is the product, in Halliday's (1970) term, of 'simultaneous planning'. One pedagogic implication of this, already realized and acted

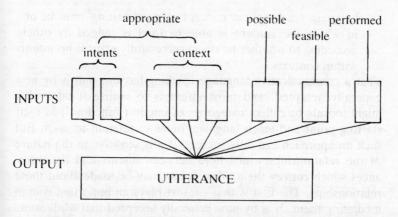

upon by many teachers, is an emphasis on holistic practice involving the combination of the various sub-skills (being structurally correct, being appropriate, etc.) together to form actual pieces of discourse. Our realization of the complexity of communicative skill has contributed to our suspicion of a ('synthetic') strategy based on the isolation of the various sub-skills and practising them in isolation.

2. that any language teaching which, like much past language teaching, places predominant emphasis on conforming to the linguistic system (the 'possible' box) gives scant preparation for communication, not merely because it produces students who make mistakes along other parameters, but also because it fails to represent the complexity of communicating, to simulate the quality of 'doing more than one thing at the same time'.

3. that a large part of any communicative language teaching must be concerned with the expression of intents within contexts. In terms of the teaching of writing this seems to lead towards an Aristotelian view of rhetoric, defined by Grierson (1945)[4] as 'the study of how to express oneself correctly and effectively, bearing in mind the nature of the language we use, the subject we are speaking or writing about, the kind of audience we have in view ... and the purpose, which last is the main determinant'. The quotation relates well to the diagram given earlier — the 'nature of the language' falling within the 'possible' box; the 'subject' (topic) and 'audience' being parameters of context; and 'purpose' being 'intent'. Within such an Aristotelian rhetoric (and communicative

language teaching) our concept of 'good writing' must be one
in which the student is able to (and is judged by others
according to whether he does) successfully express his intents
within contexts.

That a communicative language teaching has this aim is by now
generally accepted, and most attempts to realize it take what
might loosely be called 'categories of intent' ('functions') as their
starting point and teach language items in relation to each. But
such an approach can only succeed if it is sensitive to the nature
of the relationships which hold between intents and the utterances which convey them. Two points may be made about these
relationships. The first is that context plays an important role in
mediating them. It is by now generally accepted that while some
utterances obligingly proclaim their communicative intent (*prom-
ising* sentences which begin 'I promise . . .', *defining* sentences
which include the structure ' . . .may be defined as . . .', for example), most utterances are not of this type. We rely on context
(and the set of presuppositions, felicity conditions, etc. it carries)
for the interpretation of communicative value. Thus we will interpret utterances like 'the adder is a poisonous snake' variously as
classification, descriptive statement, warning according to context. This has clear implications for the teaching of reading, but
no less for writing. The way we express intents depends crucially
on the contexts we are to express them in; our ability to express
intents depends crucially on our ability to perceive how we will be
interpreted in context.

The second point is that these sets of relationships — intent/
utterance, context/utterance are both delicate and complex. They
are delicate because a slight change in intent will necessitate a
change in utterance — the 'marks on the page' will have to
change. Similarly, a slight change in context (perhaps involving a
change in the set of presuppositions) will render inappropriate an
utterance previously appropriate. The relationships are complex
because they are realized, not by rules involving binary correct/
incorrect decisions, but by ones relating to felicity conditions, topic-
comment relationships, distribution of information, and so on.

These two points are important because they indicate that communicative events are non-stereotyped not merely because of the
number of parameters which derive them (which is, in essence,
Welford's point); but also because of the complex and delicate
way in which those parameters which are crucial exert their
control.

3 General implications for the teaching of writing

There are two general implications of this view of communication, one negative and one positive. The negative implication is that any approach (and most 'notional' approaches have been of this type) which identifies specific areas of use, presents several forms associated with each, perhaps differentiating the forms crudely in terms of some scale such as formality-informality, has severe inadequacies.[5] The kind of problems such an approach meets may be exemplified within the area of *defining*. It may be that a needs analysis isolates (1) and (2), exemplified in (3) and (4) as profitable exponents to teach for this function:

(1)   An X $\begin{matrix} \text{who} \\ \text{which} \end{matrix}$ —————— is known as Y.

(2)   A Y is an X $\begin{matrix} \text{who} \\ \text{which} \end{matrix}$ —————— .

(3)   A person who does not live in one fixed place is known as a vagrant.

(4)   A vagrant is a person who does not live in one fixed place.

As soon as the materials producer attempts to present and set up practice for these forms he is made aware of their non-equivalence on various levels. On one level is the fact that a cat is an animal which has four legs, but an animal which has four legs is not known as a cat. Failure to realize the non-equivalence of these exponents on this level leads students to produce both (5) and (6):

(5)   Zoology is a science which studies living things.

(6)   A science which studies living things is known as zoology.

And one is left to explain why the indefinite article, appropriate in (3), is inappropriate in (6) — though it could be replaced by 'one', as in (7):

(7)   One science which studies living things is known as zoology.

The two exponents are also non-equivalent as regards contextual appropriateness. Thus (because of the rules governing the distribution of 'old' and 'new' information in discourse, with 'old' information usually opening a sentence) both (3) and (4) would be appropriate to only one of the following contexts:

(8)   The vagrant population of American is large. —————— .

(9)   A large number of people in America do not live in one fixed place. —————.

(10)   —————————. There are many vagrants in America.

Examples like this, and of course part of the point is the frequency with which the materials producer will meet them, indicate the healthy distrust for generalization which the non-stereotyped nature of communicative events should breed. They argue against a strategy which provides a set of exponents and which implicitly or explicitly makes a statement like 'this is how we define (classify, exemplify, etc.) in English'. They argue instead for (the second, positive, implication) an approach which begins with pieces of discourse exemplifying a specific set of writer intentions and a specific set of contextual features for the exponent to be taught; which makes statements like 'this is how the writer has defined in this set of circumstances', and explores why he has done so in that particular way.

4 Aspects of the second approach

What does this second approach imply in terms of pedagogic procedures? Two related implications will be considered here. The first is that any communicative writing course would have a large 'analytic component'. This component would present examples of discourse and would lead the student to explore the complex, delicate and crucial relationships holding between its constituent utterances, their contexts and intents. The component would be large for the reasons discussed above — because the relationships are complex and delicate and can only be elucidated by considerable exploration; because many of the language points we wish to make can only be explained by careful consideration of contextual features; because high exposure to stretches of discourse seems the only valid strategy for approaching their constituent, non-stereotyped events.

Much of this 'analytic component' would consist of what is traditionally called reading comprehension, and might cover the following types of activity:

(a) *Exploring intent/utterance relationships*
e.g. – asking the student to identify the writer's main point in a paragraph (or larger/smaller unit);
   – true/false exercises in which the student must identify points made by the writer in a passage.

(b) *Exploring context/utterance relationships*

e.g. – cloze procedures in which the student must supply (or choose from a multiple-choice selection) missing words or sentences, i.e. he must decide what is appropriate to the given context;

– page-covering exercises. The student looks at the first paragraph of the passage, covering the rest of the passage with a piece of blank paper. He is asked to speculate on how the passage might continue. He then looks at the second paragraph and compares his speculation with what is actually written. He continues in this way through the passage.

(c) *Exploring organization*

e.g. – asking a student to add given sentences (or larger/smaller units) to the passage. With a judicious choice of sentences to add, this can lead the student to lengthy consideration of how the passage is organized;

– functional ordering. The student is given a set of randomly ordered 'functional labels' (e.g. 'comparing', 'defining', 'classifying') which describe what the writer says in the passage. The student must order these.

This can be the first stage in a *parallel writing* exercise which continues as follows:

(ii) The student does the same for a second passage. This passage includes the same functions as passage 1, but expounded in a different order.

(iii) The student rewrites passage 2 to expound the functions as they are ordered in passage 1, i.e. he rewrites passage 2 to have the same organization as passage 1.

Parallel writing can be used at several levels. At its most complex it can involve highly detailed analysis of discourse and the reorganization of passages.

As several of these techniques exemplify, the 'analytic component' feeds naturally into production practice. Our initial questions may be 'What is the writer saying here?', 'Why does he say it like that?' and 'Why doesn't he say it like this?', etc. But we move naturally into questions involving an element of production — such as 'How would the writer have put it if he had wanted to say something slightly different?' and 'How would the writer have put it in a slightly different context?'. In exercises like these (which might be dubbed '*if*' exercises) we suggest a change in intent or context and ask how it would affect the utterance. '*If*' *exercises* represent a highly productive technique and may result in the complete reorganization of a passage. Examples are given later.

These observations lead to a second implication, related to the first, that a highly fruitful approach to communicative writing is 'discourse based'. In such an approach, the starting point for production exercises is pieces of discourse which the student is asked to do operations on. The appeal of this approach is its specificity. We are providing a specific set of utterance-intent-context relationships embodying a specific set of presuppositions and felicity conditions; we explore these in the 'analytic component'; we then require specific tasks to be done on them.

The following techniques exemplify the types of operations the student can be asked to perform:

(a) *Inserting information*
  (i) The technique of giving sentences (or larger/smaller units) to be added to a passage has already been mentioned.
  (ii) As a (more demanding) alternative, pieces of information in the form of a 'list of points' can be given. The student must not only decide *where* to make these points, but *how* to make them also.
  With ingenuity it is possible to ask the student to add a number of points to a passage using a discrete number of language forms, e.g. the student can be asked to add five 'concession points' to a passage, using *although* (and/or other chosen exponents).

(b) *Subtracting information*
  As with the insertion of information, asking the student to take a piece of information out of a passage can lead to substantial reorganization of its content.

Both these types of task are 'natural' ones, i.e. they are the types of operation which every writer of academic prose is constantly undertaking.

(c) *Reorganizing a passage*
  In order to make the same points in a different order, it is often sufficient simply to give a new introductory or concluding sentence to provide the stimulus for reorganization.

In this form the exercise may provide useful practice in cohesion and coherence, but it remains a mechanical one unless the student is given a reason for reorganization. An Aristotelian rhetoric would presumably require, where possible, the differentiation of alternative organizations in terms of intent and effect. The techniques mentioned below are less mechanical in this respect.

(d) *'Rhetorical transformations'*
This type of exercise, discussed in Widdowson (1973) involves rewriting a stretch of discourse to change its communicative value, e.g. rewriting a set of instructions as a description. (e) and (f) below elaborate this technique.

(e) *Changing standpoint/point of emphasis*
Rewriting a passage to convey the same information but to argue a different point or to change degrees of emphasis.

(f) *Changing 'style'*
e.g. changing a lecture transcript into a piece of academic prose. This may involve considerable replanning if (as many are) the lecture is loosely organized and repetitive.

To conclude this section by viewing the issues from a slightly different angle: a central tenet of communicative language teaching is that it should provide practice at expressing intents within contexts. One widespread (and fruitful) response to this has been a partial shift of role on the part of materials producer and teacher. They have tended to become initiators of language behaviour, following the principle that 'we set up a situation in which we provide the student with something to say; we let him say it, then we examine what he has said in relation to what he wanted to say'. A pedagogic problem this approach poses is to set up initial situations in a way which is specific enough to lead to fruitful discussion and use of language by the students. A central feature of the approach expounded here is that it provides initial 'situations' in the form of pieces of discourse written for specific audiences to achieve specific purposes.

5 Observations on syllabus design

What are the implications of such an approach for syllabus design? Three observations will be made:
1.   The approach leads towards that followed in the teaching of

receptive skills where we begin with a piece of discourse (a taped dialogue or a reading passage) which we exploit in a number of probably unconnected ways, e.g. we might use a dialogue to explore questions of pronunciation, vocabulary, grammar, appropriacy. We would certainly consider it cost-ineffective to exploit a long dialogue in only one way, and the approach thus involves a 'cluster of activities around a stretch of discourse'. A similar approach for the teaching of production skills would move away from the reasonably entrenched practice of covering one discrete (functional, structural) area per teaching unit. It moves towards an approach touching on many (probably unconnected) areas per unit.

2.   A second, connected, observation concerns the status of the syllabus. In such an approach it tends to lose its status as pre-determiner of ordering. Traditionally it is at the syllabus design stage that the sequence of presentation of language items is established. In the suggested approach the selected pieces of discourse would to some extent determine unit content and hence overall sequence. The syllabus would then become largely an inventory of items to be covered on the course as a whole; it would function as a 'check list' against which we 'tick off' points covered, rather than as an 'algorithm' which imposes a predetermined ordering.

3.   The third observation concerns syllabus content. It is perhaps today relatively uncontroversial to remark that the procedure (largely followed in semantic syllabus design) whereby we select semantic categories and specify a set of surface structures associated with each, is fundamentally behaviourist. The procedure certainly seems open to the kind of criticism that Chomsky made of Skinner — that it postulates a simplistic S-R relationship for language behaviour. Indeed, the central argument of this paper is that such a procedure dangerously oversimplifies.

We seem to need for language use what Chomsky attempted to provide for syntax — 'deeper' rules, in the case of use relating intents through contexts to utterances. Some of these rules will certainly be specific to discrete semantic areas (i.e. they will help to specify such things as 'how we define/classify/exemplify, etc. in English'.) But many (because they are 'deep') will embody generalizations which will cut across notional/functional boundaries. When we have such rules we may therefore find that the arrangement of teaching materials under notional/functional headings is not the most cost-effective solution. According to such a view, present day semantic syllabuses might be seen as a temporary solution to the problem of teaching language use.

Notes

1. It is not, of course, only certain notional/functional approaches which prescribe 'stereotypes' for language use. Many textbooks of rhetoric (for example, within the American freshman English tradition) set up models for different types of writing, which the students are expected to follow. To the extent to which this paper is polemical it is questioning the validity of such approaches as overall strategies. It is certainly my experience that most students quickly master conventions within their particular area of writing (they learn, for example, how an 'English laboratory report' is usually structured). But this takes them a very short way towards being able to express their particular intents within the particular context of a piece of writing they are undertaking.

2. These are entitled *Communicate in Writing*, published by Longman in 1981.

3. This diagram is *not* intended as a performance model. It merely exemplifies the aspect of communication under consideration.

4. The quotation, and indeed the link between communicative language teaching and Aristotelian rhetoric are taken from Curry (1975).

5. It will, of course, be argued that in some teaching situations an approach of this sort is all that is possible. It is the 'phrasebook' approach, and its application can be particularly strongly argued for two types of situation — with low-level students, and where there are severe time restrictions. In the former situation, the validity of a semantic approach can be questioned (cf. Johnson 1978) and one might wish to argue that at the point in the teaching operation where focussing on aspects of use becomes both feasible and desirable, such an approach provides poor fare. In the latter situation (where the validity of a semantic approach can also be questioned — cf. Johnson 1978) all kinds of issues concerning cost effectiveness arise. Is it better to provide a phrasebook covering a large number of semantic areas in a superficial way, or (as the second approach discussed in this paper might provide in a situation with severe time restrictions) detailed consideration of a few instances of language use?

6. The taxonomies given in the latter part of this paper are intended only to exemplify. They are based on exercise types found in *Communicate in Writing*.

18 Anguish as a second language?
Remedies for composition teachers

Ann Raimes

When I first started composing this paper, I felt some anguish myself. I knew I was dealing with the general topic of the problems of ESL composition, but I couldn't decide what to narrow it down to. I felt overwhelmed and went off to Macy's to buy my kids some underwear while my family played havoc with my title: luggage as a second baggage, penguin as a second bandage, and sausage as a second sandwich.

Then I decided to begin, at least, in the way that I advise my own ESL students to begin: to observe and describe. So I watched my students and examined their written work. In both I saw the signs of anguish. Student writers chew their pencils, they shuffle their feet, they sigh, groan and stretch, they ask, 'How much do we have to write?' They thumb through their little dictionaries. They write a sentence, read back over it, cross out a word and substitute another — often a wrong one — and then attack the next sentence. They produce dry, flat, mechanical prose, full of unsupported generalizations, repeated concepts, and errors. When asked what they find difficult about composition they invariably reply, 'I don't know the right words', 'I don't know how to organize', 'I worry about grammar', or 'I can't think of anything to write'. Their anguish becomes our anguish as we read more and more pieces of writing not only filled with grammatical errors but empty of life and content.

Native speakers suffer in the same way, those whom Mina Shaughnessy calls 'basic writing students' (1977). She first talked of their 'written anguish' (1976, p. 235). I am using and extending her term to explore what makes composing even more agonizing in a second language and what we can do to relieve the pain a little.

Teaching and learning ESL composition spreads over two huge

fields: composing and second-language acquisition, separate fields of research and pedagogy. These fields do not meet often in professional conferences or publications — this one is an exception — but they *must* merge in the classroom for teachers and students.

Composition theory and research are almost exclusively devoted to examining the products and processes of native-speaker writers, skilled and unskilled. When unskilled native speakers write, they do, however, have to learn what amounts to a new language for them: the language of standard edited English or academic English. Many of these student writers are, as Janet Emig points out in her study of composing processes, 'enervated by worries over peripherals' such as spelling, punctuation, and length (1971, p. 99). ESL student writers have all of the worries of the native speaker and many more besides, for all of them have to acquire or consciously learn the phonology, grammar, syntactic structure, vocabulary, rhetorical structure, and idiom of a new language in addition to learning the mechanics of prose. With so much to be done, it is hardly surprising that many of our ESL composition courses have stressed the acquisition of the rule-governed forms of the second language. We accept and strive for compositions that show mastery over grammar, syntax and mechanics. And this job is so vast that there is often little time left over for attention to the ideas and the meaning of a piece of writing. Yet we all know how we welcome the composition that says something to the reader, even if it has some incorrect verb forms. For then communication of ideas becomes primary and the rest is truly peripheral.

So why do we emphasize the acquisition of grammar and syntax first in our sequence of learning and our hierarchy of priorities? Peter Elbow explains why when he says, 'It's no accident that so much attention is paid to grammar in the teaching of writing. Grammar is the one part of writing that can be straightforwardly taught' (1973, p. 138). Feeling slightly uneasy about this emphasis, we disguise it by the language we use: we say we assign guided or controlled *compositions*. These, however, have more to do with control than composition. Students are copying, substituting, transforming, and manipulating prose written by someone else. They are not composing. But we like to think they are.

We keep our task straightforward when we deal with paragraphs and essays, too. We give paragraphs to be amplified, unscrambled, or written according to specific guidelines. But ESL students who are not skilled readers and writers in their first language need more than patterns, even if these are presented as a study of contrastive rhetoric. It's not a different paragraph form that is the problem so much as lack of experience with the concept of any written paragraph and with the mental processes needed to express ideas for a reader rather than a listener. The students who do read and write well in their first language also need to work on the new creative activity of forming ideas in English for English-speaking readers.

Yet most of us ESL composition teachers have emphasized structure (a good old ESL word), first syntactic and then rhetorical structure, implying as we did so: 'Here's the way to do it. Now go ahead and do it'. So after careful teaching of, for example, coordinating conjunctions, sentence connectors, and chronological order in a paragraph, we get back this:

> Louie rushed and got ready for work, but, when he went out the door, he saw the snowstorm was very heavy. Therefore, he decided not to go to work. Then, he sat down to enjoy his newspaper. However, he realized his boss might get angry because he did not go to the office. Finally, he made another decision, that he must go to work. So, he went out the door and walked to the bus stop.

Many of us, at one time or another, have praised a student for such a piece of writing. No grammatical mistakes. I have seen such flat paragraphs as this applauded as excellent and I, too, have assessed similar papers with a check mark and the comment 'very good'. Most of us have. We teach a discrete item of grammar in class and test it in a writing exercise. If the students get it right, we feel we have taught something, and we offer praise to the students who have learned. We respond to the piece of writing as item checkers, not as real readers.

Why does this happen? I think it's because we have stressed the ESL part of ESL composition at the expense of the composition part, and we have done so because we have thought that students need mastery over the sentence before proceeding to the paragraph, and mastery over the paragraph before proceeding to the essay. So we have provided controls and limits which make the task easier for us. The question is, do they make it easier for the students too? We have, I fear, trapped our students within the sentence. They worry about accuracy; they stop after each sentence and go back and check it for inflections, word order, spelling and punctuation, breathe a sigh of relief and go on to attack the looming giant of the next sentence. Research such as

Nancy Sommers's on native speaker student writers shows how their revision consists primarily of rewording (Sommers 1978). They are concerned with vocabulary and not with concepts. We don't have the same body of research on the composing process for ESL students, but I suspect that the prison of the word and the sentence has even stronger bars. And when we have tried to move beyond the sentence, our emphasis on patterns — patterns of the paragraph and of the essay — has reinforced the restraints. Students begin with a given topic sentence and thus lock themselves into a semantic and rhetorical prison. This first sentence restricts them before they have begun to develop their ideas. But they wonder why, when they have the pattern of the mould, they fill the mould, and they proofread, why isn't this an A paper? After all, they have done what was asked for!

What we need to ask for as well is the composing side of ESL composition. Grammatical accuracy and rhetorical formulae have little force if the piece of writing is not expressing the writer's ideas clearly and forcefully, with an involved imagination. Students who are asked to write an essay on 'Holidays in My Country' with no sense of purpose or audience try to guess what the teacher wants, try to find the words and the correct grammar, but have no intellectual or emotional investment in what they are writing about. They are saying something that nobody cares about in order to practise something else. Communication must surely be as important in the composition classroom as it is now becoming in the spoken English classroom.

Composing means expressing ideas, conveying meaning. Composing means thinking. Let us look at a master writer and teacher's definition of composing. For Tolstoy, the mechanism of composing consists in 'the ability to combine what follows with what precedes, all the while keeping in mind what is already written down ... in thinking and writing at the same time without having one of these acts interfere with the other' (Berthoff 1978, p. 252). Although one past U.S. President might have found it difficult to walk and chew gum at the same time, thinking and writing should be (in spite of much ESL pedagogy) inseparable when our students compose. That thinking/writing process is also a way of discovering what we know, a way of 'form-finding' (Berthoff 1978, p. 254). The very act of writing itself has a creative function. Writing helps us find out what we want to say.

How many of us pay attention to that function in our ESL classes? Don't we often assign a piece of writing, collect it, correct or indicate errors and return it, perhaps with a request for correction? We stress editing skills rather than the creative act of communicating meaning. We exhort our students to apply learned conscious rules as they edit: to turn sentences into *yes/no* questions, to check sentence boundaries, to combine sentences, to check inflections. Many of our students need that. They cry out for rules, for something concrete to monitor their writing performance with. So we give them grammatical Band-Aids and doses of paragraph models. We must then realize that we are teaching editing and imitating. We're not teaching composing.

There is, of course, no one remedy, no panacea for all teachers in all classrooms. But all of us can examine what we have been doing in our classes, we can ask 'What's going wrong?' 'Why?' and 'What can we do that is better?' It is certainly time to move away from what some ESL books for teachers say about ESL composition. We read in one the rationale that 'writing is one way of providing variety in classroom procedures' (Paulston and Bruder 1976, p. 203). We are told that free writing is useful for students to 'give vent to their feelings' (Paulston and Bruder 1976, p. 230). However, we are reminded in another that 'not all students have the gift of imagination' (Rivers and Temperley 1978, p. 317). Yet another recommends checklists to note errors in (of course) spelling, punctuation, structure and vocabulary, with the magnanimous concession: 'You may prefer, if ideas are important, to give two points for ideas', and then the addendum: 'If you think four ideas are necessary, give half a point for each' (Finocchiaro 1974, p. 88).

If ideas are important and necessary! Let's now assume they are, and let's switch focus from elimination of error to thinking and communicating ideas. I'm going to suggest some approaches we might try in place of the old one of controls before freedom, sentences before paragraphs and pattern practice and accuracy above all. I'm not offering a miracle cure by any means, but I am proposing a change in treatment. We can't cure arthritis by giving treatment for a stomach ulcer. We won't improve composing in any language if we teach only rules of grammar and models of form. I have discussed elsewhere some strategies for helping students with their difficulties in grammar, syntax and rhetoric as they compose (Raimes 1978(a)). I have also published teaching materials that include many grammatical exercises to back up each writing assignment (Raimes 1978(b)). Grammar *is* important for ESL students, but it has been well covered in the literature. Let us turn now to the neglected areas of the process of composing in a second language and the writer's generating of ideas throughout that process. I'll be discussing how we can pay attention to those areas when we do three of our composition teacher's jobs: give assignments, mark papers, and provide readings.

1 Giving assignments

A carefully chosen assignment generates its own many varied classroom activities and paper-marking procedures, so it is worth putting the work in at this early point. Giving an assignment involves more than selecting a topic for students to write on. It means giving suggestions as to how to go about writing it. At this point we can build in the chance for students to pay attention to the writing and revision process: we can give them time to work on a paper, time alone and with each other, time to deal first with content, then with organization, and only finally, at the proofreading stage, with grammar (though that will, of course, crop up in discussion of content if it is preventing clarity of expression). Researchers on composing for native speakers are pointing out that the process is not the linear one of prewriting, writing and revising. These three activities are, rather, inseparable and intertwined, all going on all the time throughout the process. When we devise assignments, we need to avoid forcing students into three separate activities. I tell my students *not* to begin with an outline, and *not* to begin with the introduction. Instead, they make a list of ideas, they write about words in that list, they observe, describe, define, and classify objects, actions, and concepts in that list. They write a paragraph and then shorten it by two sentences. They write a paragraph, then throw it away and write another. While this writing is going on it is prewriting, writing and revision all rolled into one.

Students will only see the importance of revision if the teacher expects it, too. I show students drafts, give them time and opportunity for revision, in class discussion and in conferences, so that they don't see writing as a one-shot deal, put down on paper and marked right or wrong. Five minutes spent helping a student with revision even during the class when everyone else is writing can do more good than another whole essay assignment. Praise and honest criticism of ideas can make students want to revise and, ultimately, want to proofread. And that is when proofreading is done effectively.

While we give time for the process of revision, we can also give advice on what students use to engage in the process. I ask my students to use legal notepaper with wide margins for their lists, notes and all drafts. They, their fellow students, or I can then write questions and comments in the margin. I suggest different colour pens for changes on drafts, scissors and tape for rearranging.

From the process and the tools to the topics themselves: what do we ask ESL students to write about? An ongoing ungraded and uncorrected journal in which they record their observations about objects, people and events, or write stories and poems, can help generate ideas for further writing and increase fluency. For academic purposes, however, I move away from the expressive mode to the referential, persuasive and heuristic functions of writing. A shared classroom experience gives everyone something to respond to; they make their own observations and their own connections. We look at a photograph of an accident and write an accident report. We write instructions and letters. We look at a Peanuts cartoon in which Lucy exhorts Linus to add a waterfall, a sunset, a forest and a deer to his drawing of a log cabin and lake because, as she says in her loudly charming way, 'That's art!' Students describe the cartoon, writing their own responses and questions in the wide left margin. Then we look at a Cézanne still life, a Cubist Picasso guitar and an Andy Warhol soup can. Students observe, describe, ask questions, and react, writing all the time. Only after they have many pages down on paper do they begin to devise their own topic and to work on an essay, but by now they have vocabulary, structures, and ideas to put in it.

What I try to do with assignments like this is to do what any good assignment must do: provide ' a bridge from the familiar to the unfamiliar' as Ann Berthoff so aptly puts it (1978, p. 250). Early ESL lessons at elementary and intermediate levels are rooted firmly in the familiar and the concrete: 'This is a book', 'I'm reading a magazine', 'The van is longer than the sportscar', and teachers carry bags of pictures and realia around with them to provide this familiarity. But at more advanced levels and particularly in composition classes students need to deal with causes, categories, and relationships. We must give them the opportunity to use this new language of theirs to form concepts, not just to ask for the salt. Many of us, from the worthiest of motives, have assigned topics we think will be easy enough so that our students will be able to concentrate on their ESL grammar and sentence structure. Such topics, even in freshman composition (e.g. describe a custom of your country), offer invitations to writing that *should* receive the response that Edith Wharton's Anson Warley used to decline dinner invitations: 'I decline the boredom'. We assign these because we feel that grammar and syntax are enough of a challenge: with a familiar topic the student can wrestle with them unimpeded. But when we realize that what we are really saying there is that ideas are impediments to what we call 'good' writing, it's time to re-examine what we are doing.

Some teachers try hard to establish a purpose and a specific reader for every piece of writing. I've done it, too: Write to the people in the apartment above you complaining about the noise and asking them to stop — first politely and then, three weeks later, angrily; now write to the landlord terminating your lease. Write to a magic genie in his 'Have three famous people to dinner' competition and convince him that your reasons for wanting your three are the most compelling. Students like these assignments and usually do them well. But they are aware of the artificiality. They know in their heart of hearts, as we do too, that their readers are only the teacher and perhaps their classmates, too. If a system of credit and grades is involved, then you can be sure they know all that. The teacher is the reader, and the purpose is to improve the students' written English. There's nothing wrong with that. But somehow we don't use it. We circumvent it and pretend it isn't there. Students are usually eager to improve their writing. They distinguish clearly between good and bad writing or even between good and less good. They are like the students in Robert Pirsig's *Zen and the Art of Motorcycle Maintenance* who balk at defining quality in writing but are amazed to discover they can recognize it. Pirsig, a teacher of rhetoric, writes about a student who was stuck on an assignment to write about her home town. He didn't prescribe a fictional purpose or reader. He told her to begin by looking at the upper left block of the Opera House on Main Street. Unblocked, she now wrote 5,000 words just on the front of the Opera House (Pirsig 1975, p. 185).

So our assignments should provide our students with the opportunity to 'look and see freshly' for themselves (Pirsig 1975, p. 186), to write to form their ideas, to work as long as necessary to express those ideas as clearly as possible to a real and responsive reader. Choosing topics should be the teacher's most responsible activity. Yet I've observed teachers who, in the last minute at the end of a class, say, 'Oh, yes, the assignment for next time...' flip through the book, pause, and continue, 'Try essay number 2 on page 85. Hand it in on Monday'. I've done that myself, too.

Choosing topics with care will not only nurture the development of composing abilities but will also pay attention to our ESL concerns of grammar and syntax. James Moffett sees 'cognitive stimulation' as the 'best developer of syntax' (1968, p. 180). He noticed third graders using *If*... or *When*... structures in their journals, both unusual structures for eight-year-old writers. But they were reporting on their observations of candle flames and needed the structure to express concepts like: 'If I cover the candle with a jar, then it goes out.' In ESL composition classes the teacher can predict what syntactic structures the topic is likely to generate and review these before the composing begins and stress them again in the proofreading. A recent assignment of mine asked students to comment on an excerpt from John Cheever's *Bullet Park* in which a father, annoyed by his son's addiction to TV, has a long argument with him and throws the TV set out of the back door. He then pours himself his fifth drink of the day. A week before we began discussion of this, I reviewed structures like: *should have...; shouldn't have...; could have...; rather. ..; if...* And students used them when they wrote about the moral dilemma.

The assignments chosen can make or mar a composition class. They can turn it solely into a grammar class, or an imitation class, or a 'following directions' class. Or they can unite form and content, ideas and organization, syntax and meaning, writing and revising, and, above all, writing and thinking. But here, too, as elsewhere in life, we are not free from the consequences of our actions. We assign, students write. And our chickens come home to roost. We have to mark the papers we assign.

2 Marking papers

There is no one prescription. There are as many as there are teaching styles. The way you would mark an essay would inevitably be different from the way I would mark it. We adapt our marking to fit what we teach and what we emphasize. Our topics and our marking reflect our philosophy as well as our pedagogy.

Those who see teaching composition as mainly teaching grammar look for errors, which they either correct or indicate. Some mark all the errors, while some mark only those that have been discussed in class. Some use checklists to indicate errors or to reinforce correct usage. A few use peer correction, with students working in pairs.

But correcting is not all there is to do. If we want our students to keep on writing, to take pleasure in expressing ideas, then we should always respond to the ideas expressed and not only to the number of errors in a paper. Some ESL teachers I know no longer correct or even indicate errors in grammar and syntax at least on the first two drafts. I try not to, but force of habit sometimes wins. I prefer to note what problems each individual student is having, to explain in conference or in a small group the grammatical or syntactic point and then to assign some exercises that move from recognition to production. Then, a little later, I assign another topic for which the student is likely to generate the structure in question. Understanding and producing accurate grammatical forms is a parallel activity to composing. It should not be allowed to inhibit and interfere. Paul Diederich, author of the classic work *Measuring Growth in English* believes that 'noticing and praising whatever a student does well improves writing more than any kind or amount of correction of what he does badly' (1974, p. 20). There is no reason for us to assume that ESL students should not be included. Good beginnings, felicitous phrases, pertinent word choice, smooth transitions, sound logic, humour, realistic and lively detail should all be praised so that students feel that what they have to say is of prime importance and get a sense of what they can do well.

When my students get their first draft back from me, they gasp in horror because there is writing all over it. They assume from past experience that these are all corrections. Then they look more closely and see that there is praise — 'I like this point', — a response — 'The same thing once happened to me' — or a question — 'Can you tell me more about this?' Here is one student's paragraph:

> Ever since I was a small child the magic of tricks always were mysterious to me. One person who I believed was a master of it is Harry Houdini. He was the greatest, and his magic will live on as the greatest. If I was to meet him at my magic dinner, all my mysteries would be answer. Maybe he will even teach me a trick to amaze my friends. I feel I'm the person who should find out the secrets that were buried with him.

These are the comments I made:

> What did he *do* that was so great? What mysteries do you want to
> have answered? What were the secrets that were buried with him? I'd
> like to know.

The student then revised, and really improved on her first version, even correcting the faulty subject-verb agreement without
being prompted. She included details and rearranged sentences.
That is revising — and it's a lot more than just correcting errors.
Here is the revised paragraph:

> Ever since I was a child the magic of tricks always was mysterious to
> me. One person who I believed was a master is Harry Houdini. All his
> escapes from chains and from jails shocked millions. His death in the
> water tank truly was a mystery. Some people think he did not know
> how to escape; others believe he suffered a bad cramp. I will find out
> at my dinner. I would like him to even teach me a trick to amaze my
> friends.

The student then admitted that she had just been to the library to
check her facts and had found that Houdini had died of peritoni-
tis. So she revised again.

It is not only the teacher who can respond with questions. Fellow students can too, if a student's writing is presented as a 'reading' to the class. Students in a writing class seldom view their own
writing as 'reading' for someone else (that's a lot of what is wrong
with it). Once they see it is, they look at it differently. So when
we engage in our third major activity, providing readings, the
Xerox or ditto machine is invaluable for presenting student
writing for close and critical reading.

3 Providing readings

I think I can almost hear some of you muttering, 'But why provide readings at all in a writing class?' I am not urging readings as
models for imitation (Look at this topic sentence and support and
now write one just like it) nor simply as springboards for discussion and ultimately for writing topics, nor as a base for true/false
questions and exercises on prepositions and synonyms, though
readings can of course be used for these purposes too. I am
urging examination of what a writer says, of why and how she or
he says it. Such close reading entails determining the writer's intent, extricating and paraphrasing the meaning, asking questions
like: 'How is this related to what comes next and to what has

gone before?' and examining the words and structure used to produce the meaning. In this way students see exactly what is involved in writing well, and learn more about what is expected of them when they write for a reader.

Readings can be adapted for an ESL class in a number of ways. They can be presented first as a kind of cloze test, with words omitted. When function words are omitted, this is purely an exercise in idiom and correct usage. But when content words are omitted, students try to come up with as many alternatives for the slot as possible, discussing the tone and connotations of each word choice. Then we can give them a choice of three or four words, one of which is the original author's choice. This prediction of the author's choice of words can be extended to predicting much larger chunks of form and content. Students see that they really know a lot about tone and textual and thematic development when they are asked, 'What do you think comes next?' We can do this on a large scale, giving students the first lines of ten different novels and asking: Which one would you want to read? Why? What can you say about the novel?

When students read an opening sentence like:

> The great fish moved silently through the night water propelled by short sweeps of its crescent tail.

> (Peter Benchley, *Jaws*)

they make accurate, sensitive and sensible predictions, for writers often begin as they mean to go on; we sense the voice, the movement and direction of the piece. It is important for student writers to realize this. Movement and direction are rarely mentioned in ESL composition textbooks, and not too often in ESL composition classes, either.

How ideas are linked logically in shorter passages of prose can be examined by prediction also. If you were given the following section of text, what would you predict for the subsequent two or three sentences?

Music in Other People's Clock Radios
There are times when I find myself spending the night in the home of another. Frequently the other is in a more reasonable line of work than I and must arise at a specific hour. Ofttimes the other, unbeknownst to me, manipulates an appliance in such a way that I am awakened by Stevie Wonder. On such occasions I announce that if I wished to be awakened by Stevie Wonder I would sleep with Stevie Wonder.

Fran Lebowitz, *Metropolitan Life* (Dutton 1978)

This is what actually does come next:

> I do not, however, wish to be awakened by Stevie Wonder and that is
> why God invented alarm clocks. Sometimes the other realizes that I
> am right, sometimes the other does not. And that is why God invented
> many others.

With appropriate passages, ESL students can predict and explain
their predictions just as you would have done.

A related exercise in prediction is one applied to close reading
of a short one- or two-page essay. Students are given the first
lines of paragraphs and predict how each one will be developed
and what the body of each paragraph might contain. Michael Donley suggests a technique that combines prediction and close analysis. He dictates a paragraph to a class one line at a time, with discussion after each line of what the subsequent sentence might be.
When the complete paragraph has been dictated in this way it is
analysed for its grammatical and lexical links (1976).

It is important for ESL students to look at prose as a woven
fabric rather than as strands of meaning. If they have been
through ESL classes, they have written their obligatory pattern
sentences, practising the sentence grammar that is necessary for
effective communication. But when they compose, they have to
control their sentence grammar, at the same time dealing with
links between sentences, with cohesion. Now if any grammar is to
be taught in a composition class, it should surely be the grammar
of cohesion. Halliday and Hasan in their book *Cohesion in English* show how the internal logic of the ideas is revealed in the
surface structure of the ordering of the sentences, in the stated or
implied relationships between sentences, and in the grammatical
and lexical system: in pronouns, articles, demonstratives, omis-
sions, substitutions, conjunctions, and vocabulary ties. Halliday
and Hasan categorize the types of cohesive devices, showing that
cohesion is 'part of the system of a language . . . expressed partly
in the grammar and partly through the vocabulary' (1976, p. 5).

ESL teachers usually love systems, and for composition this
one is especially relevant, for it deals with connected discourse
and textual movement. Teachers who feel it imperative to continue teaching grammar in an ESL composition course will find
that this grammar at least gets students looking at sentence links
and thus logic; it provides a framework for analysing a piece of
writing so that we see what Tolstoy is after in composing: 'the

ability to combine what follows with what precedes'. It gets students looking beyond the sentence.

Let me here just illustrate briefly what this grammar of cohesion entails, with lines from the *New York Times*:

> An upstate utility company spent several months and who knows how much money dunning a man who had moved from Greenwood Lake to Brooklyn. It finally succeeded in locating him and the man paid. He had owed the company one cent.
>
> *The New York Times*, December 15, 1978

In these four lines alone there are a great many different cohesive links:

reference: pronouns — *it, him, he*
                 articles   — *the* man, *the* company (previously *a* man, *a* company)

conjuncts: *finally*
verb tense indicating time sequence: *had moved, had owed*
lexical links: repetition of *man* and *company*
                association of *paid-owed, money-cent*

Students can go through such a passage, circling the links and connecting them to referents. In this case, this involves looking at pronouns, articles, conjuncts, tenses and vocabulary. That's a lot of grammar for any composition class.

Let me emphasize that study of this grammar of cohesion is not an end in itself; it is a tool for close examination of a text, of how writers get their words to work for them. And indeed this applies to all I have been saying here about giving topics, marking papers and choosing readings: that in an ESL composition course we have got to make sure that we emphasize composing and not just ESL. And when we do, much of the necessary work on grammar, sentence structure and rhetoric begins to take care of itself. Lucy proclaims that once you have trees, a lake, a log cabin, a waterfall, a deer and a sunset, that's art; textbooks similarly proclaim that once you have an introduction, a body, a conclusion and correct grammar and punctuation, that's a composition. We know our students need more than that placebo. Virginia Woolf prescribed £500 a year and a room of one's own to relieve a writer's anguish. That kind of relief we can't provide. But we can change our prescription. Our ESL students in composition classes are engaged in the complex linguistic exercise of making meaning without which no language can truly be said to be learned. One remedy for the anguish of composing is to concentrate on that making of meaning, to concentrate on the act of composing instead of on peripherals. When we deal with ESL composition, when we give assignments, mark papers and provide readings, we are dealing not just with ESL on the one hand and with composition on the other. We are dealing with TSL: Thinking in a Second Language. If we can get our students to do just that, we have surely taught them something.

Bibliography

Abrams, M.H. (1953). *The Mirror and the Lamp*, New York: Oxford University Press.

Adams, A. (1981). 'Assessing, Monitoring and Response in the Teaching of English', in Pringle and Freedman (eds.), *Teaching, Writing, Learning*, Toronto, Ontario: Canadian Council of Teachers of English, 109–116.

Ames, L.B. (1966). 'Children's Stories', *Genetic Psychology Monographs*, **73**, 337–396.

Barnes, D. (1973). *Language in the Classroom*, London: Open University Press.

Barnes, D. (1976). *From Communication to Curriculum*, Harmondsworth: Penguin.

Barnes, D. and Shemilt, D. (1962). 'Transmission and Interpretation', *Educational Review*, **16/3**.

Barnes, D., Britton, J.N. and Rosen, H. (1969). *Language, the Learner and the Schools*, Harmondsworth: Penguin.

Barritt, L.S. and Kroll, B. (1978). 'Some Implications of Cognitive-Developmental Psychology for Research in Composing', in Charles R. Cooper and Lee Odell (eds.), *Research on Composing: Points of Departure*, Urbana, Illinois: National Council of Teachers of English (NCTE).

Bartlett Elsa J. (1981). *Learning to Write: Some Cognitive and Linguistic Components*. Washington, D.C.: Centre for Applied Linguistics.

Bartlett Elsa J. (1982). 'Development of Rhetorical Skills in Children's Narrative Writing'. Unpublished paper delivered at the 1982 annual meeting of the American Educational Research Association, New York, March 1982.

Beaugrande, R. de and Colby, B.N. (1979). 'Narrative models of action and interaction', *Cognitive Science*, **3**, 43–66.

Becker, A.L. (1966). 'A Tagmemic Approach to Paragraph Analysis', *The Sentence and the Paragraph*, Urbana, Illinois: NCTE.

Beginning Teacher Preparation Study, Report VII–1; Technical Report Series, Far West Regional Laboratory, 1979.

Bennett, Bruce *et al.* (1980). *An Investigation of the Process of Writing and the Development of Writing Abilities, 15–17*. Report to E.R.D.C., University of Western Australia.

Bereiter, C. (1980). 'Development in writing', in L.W. Gregg and E.R. Steinberg (eds.), *Cognitive Processes in writing*, Hillsdale, New Jersey: Lawrence Erlbaum.

Bereiter, C., Masterton, B. and Scardamalia, M. (1979). 'Revision of Text in Response to New Information'. Paper presented at the American Education Research Association, April 1979.

Bereiter, C. and Scardamalia, M. (1982). 'From Conversation to Composition: The Role of Instruction in a Developmental Process', in R. Glaser (ed.), *Advances in Instructional Psychology*, 2, Hillsdale, New Jersey: Lawrence Erlbaum.

Bereiter, C. and Scardamalia, M. 'Schooling and the Growth of Intentional Cognition: Helping Children Take Charge of Their Own Minds', in Z. Lamm (ed.), *New Directions in Education*, Tel Aviv: Yachdev (in press).

Bereiter, C., Scardamalia, M., Anderson, V. and Smart, D. 'An Experiment in Teaching Abstract Planning in Writing'. Paper presented at the annual meeting of the American Educational Research Association. Boston, Massachusetts, April 1980.

Berthoff, Ann (1978). 'Tolstoy, Vygotsky, and the Making of Meaning', *College Composition and Communication*, **29**, 249–255.

Bilsky, Manuel (1956). *Patterns of Argument*, New York: Holt, Rinehart and Winston.

Bloom, Benjamin (1976). *Human Characteristics and Learning*, New York: McGraw-Hill Book Company.

Bloom, B.S. *et al.* (1956). *Taxonomy of Educational Objectives*, London: Longman.

Bortz, D.R. (1969). 'The Written Language Patterns of Intermediate Grade Children When Writing Compositions in Three Forms: Descriptive, Expository, and Narrative'. Unpublished doctoral dissertation, Lehigh University.

Braddock, Richard, Lloyd-Jones, R. and Shoer, L. (1963). *Research in Written Composition*, Urbana, Illinois: NCTE.

Britton, James (1970). *Language and Learning*, Harmondsworth: Penguin.

Britton, James (1980). ' "Speak Hands for Me", or the Writer's Commitment'. Paper delivered at the Conference on College Composition and Communication, Washington, D.C.

Britton, James (1979). 'No, No, Jeanette: A Reply to Jeanette Williams' Critique of the Schools Council Writing Project' (with Myra Barrs and Tony Burgess), *Language for Learning*, **1/1**, 23–41.

Britton, J.L., Burgess, T., Martin, N., McLeod, A. and Rosen, H. (1975). *The Development of Writing Abilities (11–18)*, London: Macmillan Education.

Brumfit, C.J. and Johnson, K. (eds.) (1979). *The Communicative Approach to Language Teaching*, Oxford University Press.

Brumfit, C.J. (1979). ' "Communicative" Language Teaching: An Educational Perspective' in Brumfit and Johnson, (*op. cit*).

Bruner, J.S. (1975). 'The Ontogenesis of Speech Acts', *Journal of Child Language*, **2**, 1–19.

Bruner, J.S. (ed.) (1966). *Studies in Cognitive Growth*, New York: John Wiley.

Bull, N. (1969). *Moral Judgement From Childhood to Adolescence*, London: Routledge and Kegan Paul.

Burt, Marina K. (1975). 'Error Analysis in the Adult EFL Classroom', *TESOL Quarterly*, **9/1** 53–63.

Burt, Marina K. and Kiparsky, C. (1974). 'Global and Local Mistakes', in J. Schumann and N. Stenson (eds.), *New Frontiers in Second Language Learning*, Rowley, Massachusetts: Newbury House.

Burt, M. *et al.* (eds.) (1977). *Viewpoints on Aspects of ESL: In Honour of James E. Alatis*, New York: Regents.

Bussis, A.M., Chittenden, E.A. and Amarel, M.A. (1976). *Beyond Surface Curriculum: An Interview Study of Teachers' Understanding*, Boulder, Colorado: Westview Press.

Buxton, Amity P. (1981). 'Children's Journals: Further Dimensions of Assessing Language Development', in I. Pringle and A. Freedman (eds.), *Teaching, Writing, Learning*, Toronto, Ontario: Canadian Council of Teachers of English, 121–131.

Calkins, Lucy McCormick (1980). 'Children's Rewriting Strategies' *Research in the Teaching of English*, **14/4**, 331–341.

Calkins, Lucy McCormick 'Make it Messy to Make it Clear', *Copyright Teacher* (forthcoming).

Canale, Michael and Swain, Merrill (1980). 'Theoretical Bases of Communicative Approaches to Second Language Teaching and Testing', *Applied Linguistics*, **I**, 1–47.

Carroll, Brendan J. (1980). *Testing Communicative Performance*, Oxford: Pergamon Press.

Carroll, J.B. (1968). *Development of Native Language Skills Beyond the Early Years*, Princeton, New Jersey: E.T.S.

Carroll, Joyce (1980). 'Phenomenology and the Writing Process'. Paper presented at the College Composition and Communication Conference, Washington, D.C.

Cazden, Courtney B. (1972). 'The Development Process', in *Child Language and Education*, New York: Holt Rinehart and Winston.

Cazden, Courtney *et al.* (eds.) (1972). *Functions of Language in the Classroom*, New York: Teachers College Press.

Chall, Jeanne. (1977). *An Analysis of Textbooks in Relation to Declining S.A.T. Scores*, New York: College Entrance Examination Board.

Chomsky, Carol (1969). *The Acquisition of Syntax in Children from 5 to 10*. (Research Monograph No. 57). Cambridge, Massachusetts, and London: MIT Press.

Christensen, F. (1967). *Notes Toward a New Rhetoric*, New York: Harper and Row.

Christensen, F. and Munson, M.M. (1968). *The Christensen Rhetoric Program* (*The Student Workbook*), New York: Harper and Row.

Cole, P. and Morgan, J.L. (eds.) (1975). *Syntax and Semantics: Vol. 3 Speech Acts*, New York: Academic Press.

Combs, W.E. (1976). 'Further Effects of Sentence-Combining on Writing Ability', *Research in the Teaching of English*, **10**, 137–149.

Cooper, Charles and Odell, Lee (eds.) (1977). *Evaluating Writing: Describing, Measuring, Judging*, Urbana, Illinois: National Council of Teachers of English.

Cooper, Charles R. (1977). 'Holistic Evaluation of Writing', in Charles Cooper and Lee Odell (eds.), *Evaluating Writing*, Urbana, Illinois: NCTE, 3–31.

Corbett, E.P.J. (1965). *Classical Rhetoric for the Modern Student*, New York: Oxford University Press.

Corbett, Edward P.J. (1967). 'What is Being Revived?' *College Composition and Communication*, **18**, 166–172.

Corder, S. Pit (1974a). 'The Significance of Learner's Errors', in John H. Schumann and Nancy Stenson (eds.), *New Frontiers in Second-Language Learning*, Rowley, Massachusetts: Newbury House, 90–99. Reprinted from *IRAL*, **5/4**, 1967.

Corder, S. Pit (1974b). 'Idiosyncratic Dialects and Error Analysis', in John H. Schumann and Nancy Stenson (eds.), *New Frontiers in Second-Language Learning*, Rowley, Massachusetts: Newbury House, 100–113. Reprinted from *IRAL*, **9/2**, 1971.

Corder, S. Pit (1973). *Introducing Applied Linguistics*, Harmondsworth: Penguin.

Corder, S. Pit (1978). 'Language-Learner Language', in Jack C. Richards (ed.), *Understanding Second and Foreign Language Learning*, Rowley, Massachusetts: Newbury House, 71–93.

Coulthard, Malcolm (1977). *An Introduction to Discourse Analysis*, London: Longman.

Crowhurst, M. (1978). 'The Effect of Audience and Mode of Discourse on the Syntactic Complexity of the Writing of Sixth and Tenth Graders'. Unpublished doctoral dissertation, University of Minnesota.

Crowhurst, M. and Piché, G.L. (1979). 'Audience and Mode of Discourse Effects on Syntactic Complexity in Writing at Two Grade Levels', *Research in the Teaching of English*, **13**, 101–109.

Crystal, D. and Davy, D. (1969). *Investigating English Style*, London: Longman.

Currie, W.B. (1975). 'European Syllabuses in English as a Foreign Language', *Language Learning*, **25/2**.

Daiker, D., Kerek, A. and Morenberg, M. (1978). 'Sentence-Combining and Syntactic Maturity in Freshman English', *College Composition and Communication*, **29**, 36–41.

Daiker, D., Kerek, A. and Morenberg, M. (eds.) (1979a). *Sentence Combining and the Teaching of Writing*, Conway, Arkansas: L & S Books.

Daiker, D., Kerek, A. and Morenberg, M. (1979b). *The Writer's Options*, Oxford, Ohio: Miami University.

D'Angelo, Frank, J. (1975). *A Conceptual Theory of Rhetoric*, Cambridge, Massachusetts: Winthrop.

Diederich, Paul (1974). *Measuring Growth in English*, Champaign, Illinois: National Council of Teachers of English.

Dixon, John (1965). *Growth Through English*, Oxford University Press.

Donley, Michael (1976). 'The Paragraph in Advanced Composition: A Heuristic Approach', *English Language Teaching Journal*, **30**, 224–235.

Doughty, Peter *et al.* (1971). *Language in Use*, London: Edward Arnold.

Durkin, Delores 'What Classroom Observations Reveal About Reading

Comprehension Instruction', *Reading Research Quarterly*, **14/4**, (1978–1979), 481–533.

Elbow, Peter (1973). *Writing Without Teachers*, New York: Oxford University Press.

Emig, Janet (1971). *The Composing Process of Twelfth Graders*, NCTE Research Report No. 13, Urbana, Illinois: National Council of Teachers of English.

Emig, Janet (1980). 'The Tacit Tradition: The Inevitability of a Multi-Disciplinary Approach to Writing Research', in Aviva Freedman and Ian Pringle (eds.), *Reinventing the Rhetorical Tradition*, Conway, Arkansas: L & S Books.

Faigley, L. (1979a). 'Another Look at Sentences', *Freshman English News*, **I**, 18–21.

Faigley, L. (1979b). 'Generative Rhetoric as a Way of Increasing Syntactic Fluency', *College Composition and Communication*, **30**, 176–181.

Faigley L. (1979c). 'The Influence of Generative Rhetoric on the Syntactic Maturity and Writing Effectiveness of College Freshmen', *Research in the Teaching of English*, **13**, 197–206.

Finocchiaro, Mary (1974). *English as a Second Language: From Theory to Practice*, New York: Regents.

Flavell, John *et al.* (1968). *The Development of Role-Taking Ability and Communication Skills in Children*, New York: John Wiley.

Flavell, John *et al.* (1977). *Cognitive Development*, Englewood Cliffs, New Jersey: Prentice Hall.

Flower, L. and Hayes, J.R. (1980). 'The Cognition of Discovery: Defining a Rhetorical Problem', *College Composition and Communication*, **31/2**, 21–32.

Flower, L. and Hayes, J. R. 'Plans and the Cognitive Process of Writing', in C. Fredericksen, M. Whiteman and J. Dominic (eds.), *Writing: The Nature, Development, and Teaching of Written Composition* (forthcoming). .

Flower, L. and Hayes, J.R. (1977). 'Problem Solving Strategies and the Writing Process', *College English*, **39**, 449–461.

Freedman, Aviva and Pringle, Ian (eds.) (1980a). *Reinventing the Rhetorical Tradition*, Conway, Arkansas: L & S Books, for the Canadian Council of Teachers of English.

Freedman, Aviva and Pringle, Ian (1980b). 'Writing in the College Years: Some Indices of Growth', *College Composition and Communication*, **31/3**, 311–324.

Frogner, E. (1933). 'Problems of Sentence Structure in Pupils' Themes', *English Journal*, **22**, 742–749.

Gannaway, Howard (1976). 'Making Sense of School', in Stubbs and Delamont (eds.), *Explorations in Classroom Observation*.

Garfinkel, H. (1972). 'Studies of the Routine Grounds of Everyday Activities', in Sudnow (1972).

Gendlin, E. (1962). *Experiencing and the Creation of Meaning*, New York: Free Press.

Gibson, Rex (1978). 'A Slave to Limit: The Dogmatism of Educational Research', *Cambridge Journal of Education*, **8/1**, 22–31.

Glenn, C.G. (1978). 'The Role of Episodic Structure, and of Story Length in Children's Recall of Simple Stories', *Journal of Verbal Learning and Verbal Behavior*, **17**, 229–247.

Gombrich, Ernst, H.J. (1961). *Art and Illusion* (Bollingen Series, Vol. 35), Princeton, New Jersey: Princeton U.P.

Goswami, D. (1979). 'Teaching the Process of Revision'. Paper presented at Conference on College Composition and Communication.

Graves, Donald (1973). 'Children's Writing: Research Directions and Hypotheses Based Upon an Examination of the Writing Processes of Seven-Year-Old Children'. Unpublished doctoral dissertation, SYS, Buffalo, New York.

Graves, Donald (1975). 'We Won't Let Them Write', *Language Arts*, May, 635–640.

Graves, Donald (1975). 'An Examination of the Writing Processes of Seven-Year-Old Children', *Research in the Teaching of English*, **9/3**, 228–231.

Graves, Donald (1977). *Balance The Basics: Let Them Write*, New York: The Ford Foundation.

Graves, Donald (1979). 'What Children Show us About Revision', *Language Arts*, **56**, March.

Graves, Donald, *Writing: Teachers and Children at Work*, London: Heinemann (forthcoming).

Gray, Bennison (1977). *'The Grammatical Foundations of Rhetoric: Discourse Analysis*, The Hague: Mouton.

Gregory, Richard, L. (1977). *Eye and Brain*, London: Weidenfeld.

Grice, H.P. (1975). 'Logic and Conversation', in Cole and Morgan (1975).

Grierson, H.J.C. (1944). *Rhetoric and English Composition*, Edinburgh and London: Oliver and Boyd.

Gumperz, J.J. and Hymes, D. (eds.) (1970). *Directions in Sociolinguistics*, New York: Holt, Rinehart and Winston.

Halliday, M.A.K. (1970). 'Language Structure and Language Function', in Lyons (1970).

Halliday, M.A.K. and Hasan, R. (1976). *Cohesion in English*, London: Longman.

Hammarström, Göran (1976). *Linguistic Units and Items*, Berlin: Springer.

Harding, D.W. (1963). *Experience into Words*, London: Chatto and Windus.

Harpin, William (1976). *The Second 'R': Writing Development in the Junior School*, London: Allen and Unwin.

Harpin, William *et al.* (1973). *Social and Educational Influences on Children's Acquisition of Grammar*, School of Education, University of Nottingham, U.K.

Harrison, B. (1979). 'The Learner as Writer: Stages of Growth', *Language for Learning*, **1/2**, 93–109.

Hartog, P. and Rhodes, E.C. (1936). *An Examination of Examinations*, London: Macmillan.

Hayes, J.R. and Flower, L. (1980). 'Identifying the Organization of Writing Processes', in L.W. Gregg and E.R. Steinberg (eds.), *Cogni-*

tive Processes in Writing, Hillsdale, New Jersey: Lawrence Erlbaum.

Helmholtz, H.L.F. von (1903). 'Erinnerungen: Tischrede gehalten bei der Feier des 70. Geburtstages (Berlin, 1891)', *Vortrage und Reden* (3rd. ed.): Braunschweig.

Holbrook, D. (1961). *English for Maturity; English for the Secondary School*, Cambridge University Press.

Houghton, Diane (1980). 'Contrastive Rhetoric', *English Language Research Journal*, **1**, 74–91.

Hunt, Kellogg, W. (1964). *Differences in Grammatical Structures Written at Three Grade Levels, the Structures to be Analyzed by Transformational Methods*, Tallahassee, Florida: Florida State University. Cooperative Research Project No. 1998 ED 003 322.

Hunt, Kellogg W. (1965a). *Grammatical Structures Written at Three Grade Levels*. Research Report No. 3, Urbana, Illinois: NCTE.

Hunt, Kellogg, W. (1965b). *Sentence Structures Used by Superior Students in Grades Four and Twelve, and by Superior Adults*, Tallahassee, Florida: Florida State University. Cooperative Research Project, No. 5–0313. ED 010 047.

Hunt, Kellogg. W. (1970). *Syntactic Maturity in School Children and Adults*. Monographs of the Society for Research in Child Development, Serial No. 134, **35/1**, Chicago, Illinois: University of Chicago Press.

Hunt, Kellogg W. (1977). 'Early Blooming and Late Blooming Syntactic Structures', in Charles Cooper and Lee Odell (eds.), *Evaluating Writing*, Urbana, Illinois: NCTE, 91–104.

Hughes, Richard E. and Duhamel, P. Albert (1962). *Rhetoric: Principles and Usage*, Englewood Cliffs, New Jersey: Prentice-Hall.

Hymes, D. (1970). 'On Communicative Competence', in Gumperz and Hymes (1970).

Irmscher, W.F. (1976). *The Holt Guide to English: A Contemporary Handbook of Rhetoric, Language, and Literature*, (2nd. ed.), New York: Holt, Rinehart and Winston.

Jeffery, C. (1981). 'Teachers' and Students' Perceptions of the Writing Process', *Research in the Teaching of English*, **15**, 215–228.

Johnson, K. (1978). 'Adult Beginners: A Functional, or Just a Communicative Approach', mimeo, and in simplified form in *Modern English Teacher*, **6/2**.

Johnson, K. (1978). 'The Applications of Functional Syllabuses', in Johnson and Morrow (1978).

Johnson, K. and Morrow, K. (eds.) (1978). *Functional Materials and the Classroom Teacher*, Centre for Applied Language Studies, University of Reading.

Johnson, L.V. (1967). 'Children's Writing in Three Forms of Composition', *Elementary English*, **44**, 265–269.

Jones, R. (ed.) (1979). *Language Development Guidelines*, Somerset, U.K.: L.E.A.

Jones, C. Stanley (1980a). 'Collecting Data on the Writing Process of L2 Writers'. Paper presented at the Annual Meeting of Ontario TESL Association.

Jones, C. Stanley (1980b). 'The Composing Processes of an Advanced

ESL Writer'. Paper presented at the Annual Meeting of the Ottawa TESL Association.

Kameen, Patrick T. (1978). 'A Mechanical, Meaningful, and Communicative Framework for ESL Sentence Combining Exercises', *TESOL Quarterly*, **12**, 395–401.

Kaplan, Robert B. (1972). *The Anatomy of Rhetoric: Prolegomena to a Functional Theory of Rhetoric*, Philadelphia: The Centre for Curriculum Development.

Kaplan, Robert B. (1978). 'Contrastive Rhetoric: Some Hypotheses', *ITL*, **39–40**, 61–72.

Kaplan, Robert B. (1978). 'On the Notion of Topic in Written Discourse', *Australian Review of Applied Linguistics*, **2**, 1–10.

Kelly, L. (1972). *From Dialogue to Discourse: An Open Approach to Competence and Creativity*, Glenview, Illinois: Scott, Foresman.

Kincaid, G.L. (1953). 'Some Factors Affecting Variations in the Quality of Students' Writing'. Unpublished doctoral dissertation, Michigan State University.

Kinneavy, James L. (1971). *A Theory of Discourse*, Englewood Cliffs, New Jersey: Prentice-Hall.

Kinneavy, James L., Cope, J.Q. and Campbell, J.W. (1976a). *Aims and Audiences in Writing*, Dubuque, Iowa: Kendall/Hunt.

Kinneavy James L., Cope, J.Q. and Campbell, J.W. (1976b). *Writing — Basic Modes of Organization*, Dubuque, Iowa: Kendall/Hunt.

Kintsch, W. (1974). *The Representation of Meaning in Memory*, Hillsdale, New Jersey: Lawrence Erlbaum.

Kintsch, W. (1977). 'On Comprehending Stories', in M. Just and P. Carpenter (eds.), *Cognitive Processes in Comprehension*, Hillsdale, New Jersey: Lawrence Erlbaum.

Kintsch, W. and van Dijk, T.A. (1978). 'Toward a Model of Text Comprehension Production', *Psychological Review*, **85**, 363–394.

Klaus, Carl *et al.* (1979). *Composing Childhood Experiences: An Approach to Writing and Learning in the Elementary Grades*, St Louis: CEMREL.

Kohl, H. (1967). *Thirty-six Children*, New York: Signet Books.

Krashen, S.D. (1977). 'Second Language Acquisition', in M. Burt *et al.* (eds.), *Viewpoints on Aspects of ESL*, New York: Regents.

Krashen, S.D. (1978). 'On the Acquisition of Planned Discourse: Written English as a Second Dialect', *Proceedings of the Claremont Reading Conference*, Claremont, California.

Krashen, Stephen, D. (1981). *Second Language Acquisition and Second Language Learning*, London and New York: Pergamon Press.

Kroll, B.M. (1978). 'Cognitive Egocentrism and the Problem of Audience Awareness in Written Discourse', *Research in the Teaching of English*, **12/3**, 269–281.

Langer, Susanne, K. (1960). *Philosophy in a New Key*, (4th edition), Cambridge, Massachusetts: Harvard U.P.

Langer, Susanne K. (1967, 1972). *Mind: An Essay on Human Feeling*, Vols. I and II. Baltimore: John Hopkins Press.

Lapkin, Sharon, S. (1979). 'Writing Skills of French Immersion Students'. Paper presented at the 1979 CCTE Conference, Ottawa, Ontario.

Larkin, G. and Shook, R. (1978). 'Interlanguage, The Monitor, and Sentence Combining'. Unpublished Research Paper read at the Los Angeles Second Language Research Forum, 3.

Larson, Richard L. (1975). 'Discovery Through Questioning: A Plan for Teaching Rhetorical Invention', in W. Ross Winterowd (ed.), *Contemporary Rhetoric: A Conceptual Background with Readings*, New York: Harcourt Brace Jovanovich.

Lashley, K. (1961). 'The Problem of Serial Order in Behaviour', in S. Saporta (ed.), *Psycholinguistics: A Book of Readings*, New York: Holt Rinehart and Winston, 180–197.

LATE (London Association for the Teaching of English) (1965). *Assessing Composition*, London: Blackie.

Lauer, Janice M., Montague, Gene, Lunsford, Andrea and Emig, Janet (1981). *Four Worlds of Writing*, New York: Harper and Row.

Legge, D. (ed.) (1970). *Skills*, Harmondsworth: Penguin.

Levelt, W.J.M. (1975). 'Skill Theory and Language Teaching', in *Studies in Second Language Acquisition*, **1/1** Indiana: Linguistics Club.

Loban, Walter (1963). *The Language of Elementary School Children*. (Research Report, No. 1), Urbana, Illinois: National Council of Teachers of English.

Loban, Walter (1976). *Language Development: Kindergarten Through Grade Twelve*. NCTE Research Report No. 18. Urbana, Illinois: National Council of Teachers of English.

Lyons, J. (ed.) (1970). *New Horizons in Linguistics*, Harmondsworth: Penguin.

MacDonald, B. and Walker, R. (1977). 'Case Study and the Social Philosophy of Educational Research', in D. Hamilton *et al.*, *Beyond the Numbers Game*, London: Macmillan Education.

Macrorie, K. (1970). *Uptaught*, Rochelle Park, New Jersey: Hayden.

Mandel, Barrett, J. (1978). 'Losing One's Mind: Learning to Write and Edit', *College Composition and Communication*, **29**, 362–68.

Marckworth, M.L. and Bell, L.M. (1967). 'Sentence-Length Distribution in the Corpus', in H. Kučera and W.N. Francis (eds.), *Computational Analysis of Present-Day American English*, Providence, Rhode Island: Brown University Press.

Marland, M. (ed.) (1977). *Language Across the Curriculum*, London: Heinemann.

Martin, Nancy *et al.* (1976). *Understanding Children Talking*. Harmondsworth: Penguin.

Matsuhashi, Ann (1979). 'Planning During the First Draft: Implications from a Temporal Study of Composing'. Paper presented at the National Council of Teachers of English Annual Meeting, San Francisco.

McCarthy, D.A. (1954). 'Language Development in Children', in L. Carmichael, (ed.), *A Manual of Child Psychology*, New York: John Wiley, 492–630.

McNeill, David (1966). 'Developmental Psycholinguistics', in Frank Smith and George A. Miller (eds.), *The Genesis of Language: A*

Psycholinguistic Approach, Cambridge, Massachusetts: MIT Press, 15–84.

Mellon, J.C. (1967). *Transformational Sentence-Combining: A Method for Enhancing the Development of Syntactic Fluency in English Composition*, Cambridge, Massachusetts: Harvard University. Cooperative Research Project. No. 5–8418. ED 018 405.

Memering, W.D. and O'Hare, F. (1980). *The Writer's Work*, Englewood Cliffs, New Jersey: Prentice Hall.

Meyer, B. (1975). *The Organization of Prose and Its Effect on Memory*, Amsterdam: North-Holland.

Miller, G.A., Galanter, E. and Pribram, K. (1960). *Plans and the Structure of Behaviour*, New York: Holt, Rinehart and Winston.

Miller, James (1973). *Word, Self and Reality: The Rhetoric of the Imagination*, New York: Harper and Row.

Moffett, J. (1968). *Teaching the Universe of Discourse*, Boston, Massachusetts: Houghton Mifflin.

Moffett, J. and Wagner, B.J. (1976). *Student-Centered Language Arts and Reading, K-13* (2nd ed.), Boston: Houghton Mifflin.

Morenberg, M., Daiker, D. and Kerek, A. (1978). 'Sentence Combining at the College Level: An Experimental Study', *Research in the Teaching of English*, **12**, 245–256.

Morrissey, M.D. (1979). 'A Typology of Errors in Non-Finite Verb Complementation', *Linguistische Berichte*, **60**, 91–101.

Morrow, Keith (1979). 'Communicative Language Testing: Revolution or Evolution?' in C. Brumfit and K. Johnson, *The Communicative Approach to Language Teaching*, Oxford University Press, 143–158.

Mulder, J., Braun, C. and Holliday, W.G. (1978). 'Effects of Sentence-Combining Practice on Linguistic Maturity Level of Adult Students', *Adult Education*, **28**, 111–120.

Murray, Donald M. (1968). *A Writer Teaches Writing*, Boston: Houghton Mifflin.

Murray, Donald M. (1978). 'Internal Revision: A Process of Discovery', in Charles R. Cooper and Lee Odell (eds.), *Research on Composing: Points of Departure*, Urbana, Illinois: NCTE.

Murray, Donald M. (1980). 'The Feel of Writing and Teaching Writing', in A. Freedman and I. Pringle (eds.), *Reinventing the Rhetorical Tradition*, Conway, Arkansas: L & S Books.

National Assessment of Educational Progress (1977). *Write/Rewrite: An Assessment of Revision Skills*, Denver, Colorado: National Association of Educational Progress.

Newsham, Gwen (1975). 'Linguistic Aspects of Paragraph Unity'. Paper delivered at the Fourth AILA World Congress, Stuttgart, Federal Republic of Germany.

Odell, L. (1974). 'Measuring the Effect of Instruction in Prewriting', *Research in the Teaching of English*, **8**, 223–240.

Odell, L. (1977). 'Measuring Changes in Intellectual Processes as One Dimension of Growth in Writing', in Charles R. Cooper and Lee Odell (eds.), *Evaluating Writing: Describing, Measuring, Judging*, Urbana, Illinois: National Council of Teachers of English.

O'Donnell, R.C. (1976). 'A Critique of Some Indices of Syntactic

Maturity', *Research in the Teaching of English*, **10**, 31–38.

O'Donnell, R.C., Griffin, W.J. and Norris, R.C. (1967). *Syntax of Kindergarten and Elementary Schoolchildren: A Transformational Analysis*, NCTE Research Report No. 8. Urbana, Illinois: National Council of Teachers of English.

O'Hare, F. (1973). *Sentence Combining: Improving Student Writing Without Formal Grammar Instruction*, NCTE Research Report No. 15, Urbana, Illinois: National Council of Teachers of English.

Ohmann, R.M. (1962). *Shaw: The Style and the Man*, Middletown, Connecticut: Wesleyan University Press.

Parlett, M. and Hamilton, D. (1976). 'Evaluation as Illumination', *Curriculum Evaluation Today, Trends and Implications*, London: Macmillan Education.

Paulston, Christina and Bruder, Mary (1976). *Teaching English as a Second Language: Techniques and Procedures*. Cambridge, Massachusetts: Winthrop.

Peel, E.A. (1971). *The Nature of Adolescent Judgement*, London: Staple Press.

Perl, Sondra, (1977). 'The Composing Process of Unskilled Writers at the College Level'. Paper presented at Conference on College Composition and Communication.

Perl, Sondra (1979). 'The Composing Processes of Unskilled College Writers', *Research in the Teaching of English*, **13**, 317–336.

Perl, Sondra, and Egendorf, Arthur (1979). 'The Process of Creative Discovery: Theory, Research, and Implications for Teaching', in Donald McQuade (ed.), *Linguistics, Stylistics, and the Teaching of Composition*, University of Akron: L & S Books.

Perron, J.D. (1976a). *The Impact of Mode on Written Syntactic Complexity: Part I–Third Grade*, Studies in Language Education Report No. 24, Athens: Department of Language Education, University of Georgia.

Perron, J.D. (1976b). *The Impact of Mode on Written Syntactic Complexity: Part II–Fourth Grade*, Studies in Language Education Report No. 25, Athens: Department of Language Education, University of Georgia.

Perron, J.D. (1976c). *The Impact of Mode on Written Syntactic Complexity: Part III–Fifth Grade*, Studies in Language Education Report No. 27, Athens: Department of Language Education, University of Georgia.

Perron, J.D. (1977). 'Written Syntactic Complexity and the Modes of Discourse'. Paper presented during the annual meeting of the American Educational Research Association. New York: ERIC Document no. ED 139 009.

Perry, W.C. (1970). *Forms of Intellectual and Ethical Development in the College Years*, New York: Holt, Rinehart and Winston.

Piaget, J. (1932). *The Moral Judgement of the Child*. Translated from the French by Marjorie Gabain. London: Routledge and Kegan Paul.

Piaget. J. (1967). *Six Psychological Studies*. Translated from the French by Anita Tenger and David Elkind. New York: Random House.

Piaget, J. (1968). *Six Psychological Studies*, New York: Vintage Books.

Pianko, Sharon (1979). 'A Description of the Composing Processes of College Freshman Writers', *Research in the Teaching of English*, **13**, 5–22.

Pirsig, Robert (1975). *Zen and the Art of Motorcycle Maintenance*, New York: Bantam Books.

Polanyi, M. (1969). *Knowing and Being*, (M. Grene, ed.), Chicago: University of Chicago Press.

Popper, K. (1976). *Unended Quest*, London: Fontana/Collins.

Potter, Robert R. (1967). 'Sentence Structure and Prose Quality: An Exploratory Study', *Research in the Teaching of English*, **1/1**, 17–28.

Raimes, Ann (1978a). 'Problems and Teaching Strategies in ESL Composition', in *Language in Education Series*, Washington, D.C.: Center for Applied Linguistics.

Raimes, Ann (1978b). *Focus on Composition*, New York: Oxford University Press.

Richards, Jack C. (1971). 'A Noncontrastive Approach to Error Analysis', *English Language Teaching*, **25**, 204–219.

Richards, Jack C. (1973). 'Error Analysis and Second Language Strategies', in John W. Oller, Jr. and Jack C. Richards (eds.), *Focus on the Learner*, Rowley, Massachusetts: Newbury House.

Rivers, Wilga and Temperley, Mary (1978). *A Practical Guide to the Teaching of English*, New York: Oxford University Press.

San Jose, C. (1972). 'Grammatical Structures in Four Modes of Writing at the Fourth Grade Level'. Unpublished doctoral dissertation, Syracuse University.

Santana-Seda, Sr. Olga (1974). 'An Analysis and Contrast in the Organisation of Paragraphs Written by University Students'. Unpublished Ph.D. dissertation, Columbia University Teachers' College.

Santiago, Ramon (1968). 'A Contrastive Analysis of Some Rhetorical Aspects of Writing in Spanish and English of Spanish-Speaking College Students in Puerto Rico'. Unpublished Ph.D. dissertation, Columbia University Teachers College.

Scardamalia, M. (1980). 'How Children Cope with the Cognitive Demands of Writing', in C.H. Frederiksen, M.F. Whiteman and J.F. Dominic (eds.), *Writing: The Nature, Development and Teaching of Written Communication*, Hillsdale, New Jersey: Lawrence Erlbaum.

Schegloff, E.A. (1972). 'Notes on Conversational Practice: Formulating Place', in Sudnow D. (ed.), *Studies in Social Interaction*, New York: Free Press.

Schmeling, Herman Harold (1969). 'A Study of the Relationship Between Certain Syntactic Features and Overall Quality of College Freshman Writing'. Unpublished Ph.D dissertation, George Peabody College for Teachers.

Seegars, J.C. (1933). 'The Form of Discourse and Sentence Structure', *Elementary English*, **10**, 51–54.

Selinker, L. (1972). 'Interlanguage', in John C. Schumann and Nancy Stenson (eds.) (1974), *New Frontiers in Second-Language Learning*, Rowley, Massachusetts, Newbury House. Reprinted from *IRAL*, **10/3**.

Shaughnessy, Mina (1976). 'Diving in: An Introduction to Basic Writing', *College Composition and Communication*, **27**, 234–239.

Shaughnessy, Mina (1977). *Errors and Expectations: A Guide for the Teacher of Basic Writing*, New York: Oxford University Press.

Simon, H.A. (1972). 'On the Development of the Processor', in S. Farnham-Diggory (ed.), *Information Processing in Children*, New York: Academic Press.

Simon, J. (1973). *La langue écrite de l'enfant*, Paris: Presses Universitaires de France.

Smith, Frank (1977). 'The Uses of Language', *Language Arts*, **54/6**, 638–644.

Sodowsky, R.E. and Witte, S.P. (1978). 'Positive Measurement of the Writing of College Students'. Paper presented during the Ve Congrès International de Linguistique Appliquée, Montréal.

Sommers, Nancy (1978). 'Revision Strategies of Student Writers and Experienced Writers'. Paper presented at the Annual Meeting of the Modern Language Association.

Sowers, Susan (1979). 'A Six-Year-Old's Writing Process The First Half of First Grade', *Language Arts*, **56**, 829–835.

Squire, James R. and Applebee, Roger K. (1969). *Teaching English in the United Kingdom*, Urbana, Illinois: National Council of Teachers of English.

Stein, N.L. (1977). 'A Developmental Study of Children's Construction of Stories'. Paper presented at the Society for Research in Child Development Meeting.

Steiner, George, (1978). 'On Difficulty', *On Difficulty and Other Essays*, New York: Oxford University Press.

Stewart, M.F. (1978a). 'Syntactic Maturity from High School to University: A First Look', *Research in the Teaching of English*, **12**, 37–46.

Stewart, M.F. (1978b). 'Freshman Sentence Combining: A Canadian Project'. *Research in the Teaching of English*, **12**, 257–268.

Stibbs, A. (1979). *Assessing Children's Language*, London: Ward Lock.

Strei, Gerald, (1972). 'A Contrastive Study of the Structure of Rhetoric in English and Spanish Composition'. Unpublished M.A. Thesis, McGill University.

Strong, W. (1973). *Sentence Combining: A Composing Book*, New York: Random House.

Strong, W. (1980). *Sentence Combining, Paragraph Linking*, New York: Random House.

Stubbs, Michael and Delamont, Sara (eds.) (1976). *Explorations in Classroom Observation*, London: John Wiley.

Sudnow, D. (ed.) (1972). *Studies in Social Interaction*, New York: Free Press.

Thorndike, E.L. (1944). *Teacher's Word Book of 30,000 words*. New York: Bureau of Publications, Teachers' College, Columbia University.

Ts'ao Feng-fu (1977). 'A Functional Study of Topic in Chinese: The First Step Toward Discourse Analysis'. Unpublished Ph.D. Dissertation, University of Southern California.

Van Dijk, T.A. (1977). *Text and Context: Explorations in the Semantics and Pragmatics of Discourse*, London: Longman.

Veal, L. R. and Tillman, M. (1971). 'Mode of Discourse Variation in the Evaluation of Children's Writing', *Research in the Teaching of English*, **5**, 37–45.

Walker, Adrienne 'Changes in Writing', *English in Australia*, (in press).

Wallace, Karl R. (1975). '*Topoi* and the Problem of Invention', in W. Ross Winterowd (ed.), *Contemporary Rhetoric*, New York: Harcourt Brace Jovanovich.

Wallas, Graham (1926). *The Art of Thought*, New York: Harcourt Brace Jovanovich.

Weaver, Richard (1967). *Rhetoric and Composition: A Course in Writing and Reading*, (2nd. ed.), New York: Holt, Rinehart and Winston.

Welford, Alan, T. (1958). *Ageing and Human Skill*, London: Oxford University Press, for the Nuffield Foundation.

Welford, A.T. (1970). 'On the Nature of Skill', in Legge (1970).

Widdowson, H.G. 'Two Types of Communication Exercise', in Widdowson, (1973, 1979).

Widdowson, H.G. (1979). *Explorations in Applied Linguistics*, London: Oxford University Press.

Wilkinson, A.M. (1978). 'Criteria of Language Development', *Educational Review*, **30/1**, 23–33.

Wilkinson, A.M. and Wilkinson, M.E. (1978). 'The Development of Language in The Middle Years', in *English in Education*, **12/1**, 42–52.

Williams, Joseph M. (1979). 'Defining Complexity', *College English*, **40/6**, 603–605.

Williamson, Shirley (1978). 'English in Parallels: A Study of Arabic Style'. Unpublished paper read at the 1978 California Linguistics Association meeting.

Winterowd, W. Ross (1980). 'Developing a Composition Program', in A. Freedman and I. Pringle (eds.), *Reinventing the Rhetorical Tradition*, Conway, Arkansas: L & S Books.

Wiseman, S. (1949). 'The Marking of English Compositions in Grammar School Selection', *British Journal of Education Psychology*, **19**, 200–209.

Witte, S.P. and Davis, A.S. (1979). 'The Stability of T-Unit Length in the Written Discourse of College Freshmen: A Second Study'. Paper presented during the annual Conference of the Canadian Council of Teachers of English, Ottawa.

Witte, S.P. and Davis, A.S. (1980). 'The Stability of T-Unit Length: A Preliminary Investigation', *Research in the Teaching of English*, **14**, 73–81.

Witte, S.P. and Faigley, L. (1980). *A Comparison of Analytic and Synthetic Approaches to Teaching Freshman Composition*. An unpublished monograph.

Witte, S.P. and Sodowsky, R.E. (1978). 'Syntactic Maturity in the Writing of College Freshmen'. Paper read during the annual Meeting of the Conference on College Composition and Communication, Denver, ERIC Document no. ED 163 460.

Wittrock, Merlin, *et al.* (1975). 'The Generative Approach to Reading', *Journal of Educational Psychology*, **67**, 484–489.

Wolk, Anthony (1969). 'The Passive Mystique: We've Been Had', *English Journal*, **58**, 432–435.

Young, R.E., Becker, A.L. and Pike, K.L. (1970). *Rhetoric: Discovery and Change*, New York: Harcourt, Brace and World.

Young, R.E. and Koen, F.M. (1973). *Tagmemic Discovery Procedures: An Evaluation of its Uses in the Teaching of Rhetoric*. NEH Grant No. E0-4238-71-116. Ann Arbor, Michigan: University of Michigan.

Young, Richard (1980). 'Arts, Crafts, Gifts and Knacks: Some Disharmonies in the New Rhetoric', in A. Freedman and I. Pringle, (eds.), *Reinventing the Rhetorical Tradition*, Conway, Arkansas: L & S Books, 53–60.

Young, Richard (1978). 'Paradigms and Problems: Needed Research in Rhetorical Invention', in C.R. Cooper and L. Odell (eds.) *Research on Composing*, Urbana, Illinois: National Council of Teachers of English, 29–48.

Index